Self, Other, and Context in Early Modern Spain:
Studies in Honor of Howard Mancing

Juan de la Cuesta Hispanic Monographs

Series: *Homenajes,* 49

FOUNDING EDITOR
Tom Lathrop
University of Delaware

EDITOR
Michael J. McGrath
Georgia Southern University

EDITORIAL BOARD
Vincent Barletta
Stanford University

Annette Grant Cash
Georgia State University

David Castillo
State University of New York-Buffalo

Gwen Kirkpatrick
Georgetown University

Mark P. Del Mastro
College of Charleston

Juan F. Egea
University of Wisconsin-Madison

Sara L. Lehman
Fordham University

Mariselle Meléndez
University of Illinois at Urbana-Champaign

Eyda Merediz
University of Maryland

Dayle Seidenspinner-Núñez
University of Notre Dame

Elzbieta Sklodowska
Washington University in St. Louis

Noël Valis
Yale University

Self, Other, and Context in Early Modern Spain: Studies in Honor of Howard Mancing

Edited by

ISABEL JAÉN

CAROLYN A. NADEAU

JULIEN JACQUES SIMON

Juan de la Cuesta
Newark, Delaware

Copyright © 2017 LinguaText, LLC. All rights reserved.

Juan de la Cuesta Hispanic Monographs
An imprint of LinguaText, LLC.
103 Walker Way
Newark, Delaware 19711-6119 USA
(302) 453-8695

www.JuandelaCuesta.com

MANUFACTURED IN THE UNITED STATES OF AMERICA
ISBN: 978-1-58871-296-7 (HB)
ISBN: 978-1-58871-300-1 (PB)

Table of Contents

Introduction

    Howard Mancing's Autopoiesis: A Journey of Self-Creation and Adventure
    Isabel Jaén, Carolyn A. Nadeau, and Julien Jacques Simon 9

    Reflections on Howard's Life, Work, and Legacy
    Amy R. Williamsen 15

    The Publications of Howard Mancing 19

I. Cognitive Literary Studies

    The Case for Teaching Cognitive-Literary Studies: Approaches,
    Challenges, and Benefits
    Jennifer Marston William 29

    Psychologizing Literary Characters in Fernando de Rojas's *Celestina*:
    The Emergence of Mind in Early Modern Spanish Literature
    Julien Jacques Simon 43

    Cervantes's *El casamiento engañoso* and the Failure of Theory of Mind:
    The Machiavellian Abilities of Campuzano and Estefanía
    Steven Wagschal 57

    The Pleasures of Pretense: Quarantine and Cosplay in *Don Quixote*
    Barbara Simerka 75

    Inside Out: The Arts of Our Embodied Minds
    Catherine Connor-Swietlicki 91

II. The Human Body and the Mind

Skin and Touch: Flesh, Glass and *El licenciado Vidriera*
CHARLES VICTOR GANELIN...107

Hecho reloj: Human Clocks, Bodies and Sexuality in Early-Modern Spanish Humorous Literature
RACHEL SCHMIDT...121

De lo que se come se cría: Diet and Procreation in Early Modern Spain
ISABEL JAÉN..135

Se le secó el celebro: Food as an Empathetic Response in *Don Quixote*
CAROLYN A. NADEAU..149

Fear and Torture in La Mancha: The Embodied Memories of Sancho Panza
MASSIMILIANO ADELMO GIORGINI...165

III. Author and Protagonist: Inside the Mind of a Genius

The Unbearable Simulacrum of Being: Staging Ontology in Calderón de la Barca's *Great Stage of the World* and Charlie Kaufman's *Synecdoche, New York*
BRUCE R. BURNINGHAM..187

Banished from Parnassus: Cervantes in the Shadow of Success
FREDERICK A. DE ARMAS..201

The Mind's "I" in *Don Quijote*
EDWARD H. FRIEDMAN..215

Don Quixote and the Knight of the White Moon
JOHN JAY ALLEN...227

Chiaroscuro in Cervantes's *Persiles* (1617)
MARSHA S. COLLINS..247

ABOUT THE AUTHORS..261
TABULA GRATULATORIA..267

Howard Mancing[1]

[1] Photo courtesy of Steven Hutchinson.

Introduction:
Howard Mancing's Autopoiesis:
A Journey of Self-Creation and Adventure

It is with great affection that we present this volume of studies in honor of Howard Mancing. Those of us who have been fortunate to have him as mentor, colleague, and friend, know of his many qualities, both as a scholar and a human being. Among them we would like to highlight his thirst and energy for intellectual adventure, pioneering spirit, idealism, clarity, kindness, patience, enthusiasm, loyalty, sense of humor, ability to inspire and keep us inspired, academic rigor, and commitment to his work and to advancing our understanding of biology and culture as inseparable.

Howard's academic trajectory is far-reaching and impressive. Not only has he presided and spearheaded important organizations and projects (such as the Cervantes Society of America and at Purdue University the Center for Neurohumanities [formerly the Center for Cognitive Literary Studies]), produced groundbreaking and resourceful books and articles, and delivered dozens of presentations on themes as diverse as Cervantes, cognition and literature, the picaresque, Bakhtin, and Unamuno—to name a few—but he continues to be active in the profession with great fervor, the fervor of a scholar who knows there is still much to discover and say. He is currently at work on what will be undoubtedly a highly influential book in the field of cognitive literary studies as well as a book on the novel in Europe before 1700, another one of his life-long interests.

Among the extraordinary accomplishments of Howard's remarkable and fruitful career reigns his status as pioneer of cognitive approaches to literature. His landmark graduate seminar on Cognition and Literature, created in 1994 and in which some of us were lucky to participate, is one of the first cognitive literary studies courses ever taught in the United States and around the world. Howard may be considered, along with a few other critics including Norman Holland, one of the founding minds behind cognitive approaches to literature, a field that has flourished in the last two decades and that Howard has catalyzed with his teaching, his works, and academic endeavors, such as the organization of the first US conference on Theory of Mind and Literature at Purdue University in 2007.

This volume includes scholarship in some of the areas of research and themes that Howard has cultivated along his path of letters. It is intended to honor his autopoietic process of constant self-creation as a scholar and, also, to echo his voice, to make his work resonate with the strength of a polyphony sparked by admiration and friendship. We are very grateful to all the scholars who have contributed enthusiastically to this project and we are certain that, just as their essays are animated by Howard's ingenious research, they will in turn inspire the making of other original pieces, which will add to his legacy.

The first part of the book is dedicated to "Cognitive Literary Studies." This section opens with Jennifer Marston William's "The Case for Teaching Cognitive-Literary Studies: Approaches, Challenges, and Benefits," where she underscores the current need for a wider offer of cognitive literary studies courses and programs in academia. She argues for the importance of exposing our students to the cutting-edge interdisciplinary research that is being carried out at the crossroads of the humanities and the sciences within the cognitive literary studies interface. Pointing to the pioneering work of Howard Mancing, among others, William provides an overview of cognitive approaches to literature as practiced both in the US and abroad and finishes her piece by articulating some of the current challenges to the field and offering examples of how we may overcome them.

In "Psychologizing Literary Characters in Fernando de Rojas's *Celestina*: The Emergence of Mind in Early Modern Spanish Literature," Julien Jacques Simon exemplifies how modern-day cognitive notions of intentionality can enrich our understanding of the psychological development of characters. Entering in dialogue with the scholarly work of Howard Mancing, Isabel Jaén, and others on Theory of Mind and literature, Simon argues that *Celestina* is a fundamental piece in the evolution of literary discourse in the early modern period and shows us how modern-day cognitive notions of mind reading and intentionality can enrich Bakhtin's notion of dialogism to help us underscore the importance and innovation of Rojas's work.

In "Cervantes's *El casamiento engañoso* and the Failure of Theory of Mind: The Machiavellian Abilities of Campuzano and Estefanía," Steven Wagschal, also inspired by Mancing's work, analyzes Cervantes's exemplary novel in an effort to elucidate the multiple levels of mind misreading and deceit that we find in this story. He argues that Cervantes thematizes the potential failure of Theory of Mind (the ability to understand others' beliefs and desires) from an abstract/theoretical perspective (Theory-Theory) and a simulation/empathy one (Simulation Theory). Wagschal concludes that the Simulation Theory mechanism may be more effective at helping a character recognize deception than the more abstract Theory-Theory.

In the next essay, "The Pleasures of Pretense: Quarantine and Cosplay in *Don Quixote*," Barbara Simerka draws from the research of developmental psychologists who have explored childhood and adult forms of pretense and simulation and pointed to "quarantine" as the mechanism that enables us to delineate the boundaries between real world and imagined worlds. Using *Don Quixote* as the point of departure, Simerka explores the connections between early modern and contemporary forms of simulation and quarantine violation. While current psychological research most often treats the quarantine function as binary, Simerka postulates that Cervantes presents a more nuanced version of varying quarantine levels that is also seen in the cosplay (costume play) of psychologically healthy humans today. Might Cervantes have created *Don Quixote* as a satire not of readers who violate quarantine norms, but rather of excessive popular worries about how fiction might spur psychotic quarantine violations?

This section closes with the essay "*Inside Out*: The Arts of Our Embodied Minds," in which Catherine Connor-Swietlicki connects Cervantes's *Don Quixote* to the 2015 Peter Docter film *Inside Out* to explore how and why creativity is a bio-cultural necessity of both individual and social life systems. She examines the neurobiological-artistic strategies shared by both artists, focusing on how Docter uses two forms of animation and a series of visual metaphors to creatively portray the ways in which our minds and bodies continually self-organize. Connor divides her essay into three sections, where she discusses human emotions, memory systems, and neuro-biological societies of self respectively. Throughout the essay she returns to connections with Cervantes's masterpiece and shows how both artists depict similar neurobiological functions, although their artistic expressions are unique to their respective cultural and neurological personal experiences.

The second part of the volume, "The Human Body and the Mind," opens with a provocative essay by Charles Victor Ganelin. In "Skin and Touch: Flesh, Glass and *El licenciado Vidriera*," Ganelin explores what is considered the lowest sense in traditional Classical and Early Modern hierarchies: touch, which brings the most immediate contact between characters as well as between a character and the world. Drawing from contemporary theory on the senses, Ganelin posits that Cervantes pushes his reader to consider the importance of intimate contact as well as the dangers involved for human beings—like Tomás Rodaja—who refuse to engage with those around them and instead, live their lives through observation.

This section continues with a study of the phenomenological experience of time in the context of the shift to mechanized clocks in the early modern period. In "*Hecho reloj*: Human Clocks, Bodies and Sexuality in Early-Modern Spanish Humorous Literature," Rachel Schmidt examines ways in which the human body, mind, and relationships are gradually made to conform to the image of time. Considering works by Calderón, Cervantes, Quevedo, and others, Schmidt examines how authors made fun of embodied daily life, as bodily rhythms, social habits, and economic interactions began to be held to new standards brought about by regimented time.

In "*De lo que se come se cría*: Diet and Procreation in Early Modern Spain," Isabel Jaén explores Huarte de San Juan's recommendations for conceiving witty and wise (male) children, included in his *Examen de ingenios* [Examination of Men's Wits]. Jaén discusses both the medical-dietary and the philosophical-social ideas of Huarte's time, in order to demonstrate how Huarte's ideology of shaping the republic by shaping the wits that comprise it rests on a complex interrelation of physiological and moral beliefs, within a context that turns women into instruments of procreation. In this regard, Huarte's dietary advice is part of a project whose pragmatism transcends medical philosophy, becoming a tool for social regulation.

Continuing with the medical-dietary context of early modern Spain, Carolyn A. Nadeau's essay "*Se le secó el celebro*: Food as an Empathetic Response in *Don Quixote*," explores Cervantes's treatment of mental health and its relation to food, particularly in terms of restoring one's health. In *Don Quixote*, Cervantes takes a scientific approach to mental illness, dispelling the theologically-charged popular attitudes that mental illness was punishment for a moral defect. Her essay examines, specifically, the ways in which characters in the novel empathize (or not) with those who suffer a mental break and how certain characters emulate contemporary practices—as recorded by doctors and lawyers—to provide specific food and drink thought to help cure madness.

Turning to a different type of contact between the individual and society, "Fear and Torture in La Mancha: The Embodied Memories of Sancho Panza," by Massimiliano Adelmo Giorgini, investigates the affective signs of fear manifested by Sancho Panza during the episode of Clavileño in *Don Quixote, Part II*. Giorgini considers possible social, political, and religious triggers that may activate Sancho's affective state. He suggests that these triggers may point to a possible pain trauma event in the squire's past, and argues compellingly that it is connected to the practices of torture of the office of the Holy Inquisition.

The third and final part of this book, "Author and Protagonist: Inside the Mind of a Genius," focuses on the mind of the author and the relation between fiction and reality, with special attention to the work of Cervantes and Calderón. Bruce R. Burningham's "The Unbearable Simulacrum of Being: Staging Ontology in Calderón de la Barca's *Great Stage of the World* and Charlie Kaufman's *Synecdoche, New York*," invokes the metaphor of the world-as-stage in connection with his baroque defense of Catholicism in Counterreformation Spain. Nearly four centuries later, Charlie Kaufman revisits this world-as-stage metaphor in *Synecdoche, New York* as part of his own postmodern exploration of the intersection between life and art. Both texts are haunted by the specter of death, and both posit a kind of overlapping ontology. Through a comparison of these two texts, Burningham unpacks the philosophical conceit of the world-as-stage, highlighting the transformation of Calderón's notion of a "higher reality" into Kaufman's (almost Baudrillardian) sense of a "hyperreality."

In "Banished from Parnassus: Cervantes in the Shadow of Success," Frederick A. de Armas examines how Cervantes positions himself as author of *Don Quixote*. Using the prologue to *Don Quixote, Part I* (1605), de Armas explores Cervantes's need to defend his stance as outsider and both why and how he moves away from the realms of courtly literature and aristocratic concerns. De Armas argues that Cervantes, being in the shadow of those considered to be the great writers of his time, consciously crafts a new persona for himself as a solitary, Saturnine figure—not part of the great masses of poets—in an effort to overcome his perceived lack, thus becoming a critic of his own work, and even suggesting how the novel should be read.

Edward H. Friedman's essay, "The Mind's 'I' in *Don Quijote*," examines the artistic turns that Cervantes makes to privilege the act of writing and reading in the novel. Using the intercalated tale, *El curioso impertinente* [The Man Who Was Recklessly Curious], Friedman follows the thread of Howard Mancing's line of reasoning in his article "Camila's Story" (2005). Mancing maintained that narrative trumps abstract reasoning, that the women of the tale replace discourse with action, theory with praxis, and that Camila becomes the dominant agent of the novella. Friedman in turn evidences the inner workings of the artistic process demonstrating how throughout *Don Quixote* the narrative argument yields, to a great extent, to metanarrative. He argues that the accumulation of data, the organization of material, the dialectics of tradition and innovation, theory, criticism, and reception are ways that Cervantes, time and again, celebrates writing and reading.

In his essay, "Don Quixote and the Knight of the White Moon," John Jay Allen navigates through the transformative journey of knighthood. Focusing on the initial chapters of Part II of the novel, Allen follows Don Quixote's progress from his initial state of incredulity to that of skeptical irony. Allen shows how Cervantes presents a series of reversals in which the tricksters themselves end up tricked in the adventures of Part II. Using Sancho, Sansón, and Altisidora as examples, Allen demonstrates how the tables are turned on each of the characters one by one. He cogently argues that this process of re-orientation of the readers' perspective with respect to the encounters of Don Quixote in Part II is essential for the interpretation of the text.

The collection comes to a close with Marsha S. Collins's innovative reading of Cervantes's last novel, *Los trabajos de Persiles y Sigismunda* [The Trials of Persiles and Sigismunda]. In her essay, "Chiaroscuro in Cervantes's *Persiles* (1617)," Collins explores the role of the visual in Cervantes's final novel, specifically his use of chiaroscuro at multiple narrative levels. In doing so she shows how Cervantes merges episteme with techne and how this process reflects Cervantes's lifelong concern for matters of style and craft in creating fictional worlds. Collins teases out both the opening and closing scenes of the novel as studies in light and shade and shows how Cervantes mobilizes *chiaroscuro* throughout the text to advance a moralizing episteme and to exalt poetry, through its association with light and spiritual values.

It is our hope that this book will be as exciting to read as it has been for us to edit. Thank you once more to the scholars who have helped us celebrate Howard's outstanding career and thanks to you, our readers, for embarking with us on this knowledge adventure on this festive occasion.

Finally, we would like to express our gratitude to the School of Humanities and Social Sciences at Indiana University East for their financial support of this project and to Michael J. McGrath and Michael P. Bolan at Juan de la Cuesta for their professionalism, promptness and patience as we prepared this manuscript.

The editors

Reflections on Howard's Life, Work, and Legacy

Amy R. Williamsen
University of North Carolina, Greensboro

Precious few are the times in life when we have the opportunity to reflect upon the contributions of a mentor as beloved as Howard Mancing. Known throughout the world as both a luminary in Cervantes scholarship and a pioneer in cognitive literary studies, he remains devoted to his family. He cherishes his loving wife, treasures his delightfully individual daughters, and dotes upon his precious grandson. Equally as impressive is how he embraces his academic family, welcoming colleagues and students—past and present—as part of an extensive scholarly network that transcends geographic and ideological boundaries. Long before "mentor" became a fashionable term bandied about in administrative circles, he embodied the concept.

While pursuing his PhD at the University of Florida, he held his first faculty position as an Assistant Professor at Lycoming College, a small liberal arts school known for outstanding teaching. He completed his dissertation under the direction of John J. Allen, who at the time was finalizing his own influential study, *Don Quixote: Hero or Fool?* Fortunately for students in the Midwest, upon earning his doctorate, Howard accepted a tenure-track position at the University of Missouri-Columbia where he quickly stood out as a daring scholar and a stellar teacher.

In fact, the title of one of his earliest articles reveals both his admirable intellectual courage, evidenced by his risk-taking, and his irrepressible sense of fun, often expressed in his play with words. As an apparently fearless untenured assistant professor, he published his first article in *Hispanic Review* with the irreverent title "Dulcinea's Ass." Throughout his career spanning more than four decades, his lively spirit imbues his research which represents significant contributions to Cervantine studies and beyond. His publications on *Don Quixote* are without doubt the best known: *The Chivalric World of Don Quijote*, the *Cervantes Encyclopedia*, *Miguel de Cervantes' Don Quixote: A Reference Guide* and "Bakhtin, Spanish Literature and Cervantes," to name but a few. Nonetheless, his various articles on the picaresque, including *Lazarillo de Tormes* and *Guzmán de Alfarache*, and his study of Santa Teresa's "Noche oscura" are equally important. The monumental co-edited volume *Text, Theory and Performance: Golden Age Comedia Studies,* an impressive collection of essays, attests to his talents as an editor. Without question, his current work on cognitive science and literature heralds an exciting new field of intellectual inquiry that is proving to be especially fruitful for early modern Spanish studies.

Along with his notable literary and theoretical endeavors, he has also written several pieces that reflect his commitment to justice and fairness, particularly in academia. From his early co-authored article on Graduate Reading Lists to his essays entitled "Full Equal Partners" and "A Theory of Faculty Workload," he advocates for reasoned decision making. He placed these principles into practice, first during his tenure as chair at the University of Missouri and then during his headship at Purdue University. His influence extended beyond the department to encompass a daunting number of leadership positions, including his various roles editing *Purdue University Monographs in Romance Languages*. He also demonstrated his ability to master seemingly divergent realms, serving as a member and then as Chair of the Athletic Affairs Committee for several years. As he would later explain when asked how this related to his success as an administrator, he emphasized that we must engage in dialogue with those behind the decision making—or, to reduce his wisdom to a Sancho-like aphorism, "follow the money." His service to our profession, culminating in his presidency of the Cervantes Society of America, has helped shape our field by foregoing outdated practices in favor of more open policies. Despite these extensive obligations, he still found time to promote innovative projects including a live reading of the entire *Quixote* and various film projects in which he shared his passion for Cervantes.

In the classroom, Howard is equally bold and charismatic. As a rather naïve first-year undergraduate in the late 1970s, I found myself thrust into his Chivalric World, adrift amidst a talented group of advanced undergraduate and graduate students. To this moment, this class remains one of the most transformative learning experiences in my life. None of us wanted to disappoint him, so we worked hard. By the time we survived the semester many of us had actually read the entire two volumes—twice. We learned about great thinkers, from Aristotle to Bakhtin. We struggled with his tortuous final assignment: in an effort to wean us away from over-inflated empty rhetoric (or perhaps, in a cunning stroke of genius that spared him from reading hundreds of pages of poorly composed student prose full of "paja"), he required a one-page comparison between *Don Quixote* and another major literary work, complete with quotes and citations. (How he ever convinced me I could tackle Sterne's *Tristram Shandy* remains a mystery.) Each day, there was a sense of anticipation as we waited to see what our professor would do next. We never knew what to expect; yet, we never doubted that we would be challenged and engaged. Before cognitive literary studies would underscore the mind/body connection or illuminate the function of mirror neurons, he intuitively incorporated teaching techniques that anticipated how one might strategically employ these insights in a classroom setting. His striking appearance, striding across the front of the classroom proudly sporting a metal bowl on his head, became legendary. More important, however, is that every one of the students in the room would always remember our spirited discussion of the *baciyelmo* episode. In hindsight, his explications of hard vs. soft critics—of readers' readings of Cervantes over the years—encapsulated his analysis of their Theory of Mind. Laughter often filled the room; on memorable occasions, tears marked the moments in which he skillfully activated our empathy for the human suffering vividly captured in the text. On a weekly basis, he inspired us to read, to study, to question, to live, to love, to hope.

Although I did not have the chance to pursue graduate-level studies with Howard, he has been an unfailingly generous mentor to me as he has been for countless others. Whether we need encouraging words to help overcome the tyranny of tedious mundane tasks that threaten to numb our minds or a swift metaphorical kick to re-engage our intellectual rigor, he is there to help us find our way. Perhaps one of his greatest gifts is that he allows his students to flourish without imposing his vision; rather, he helps them discover their own voices.

Over the years at conferences and professional events, I have met others who have been blessed with the opportunity to study with Howard. Many have gone on to explore realms they first encountered in his classes, especially cognitive literary studies. No matter what our individual fields may be, we share a sense of kinship from having worked with him. This volume, a testament to his influence upon our scholarly community, brings together former students and colleagues to honor Howard. Indeed, it reflects our shared commitment to further his lasting legacy for, as his exemplary career demonstrates, *el todo es más que la suma de sus partes [The whole is more than the sum of its parts]*.

The Publications of Howard Mancing

BOOKS:

Leverage, Paula, Howard Mancing, Jennifer Marston William, and Richard Schweickert, eds. *Theory of Mind and Literature*. West Lafayette: Purdue UP, 2011.
Miguel de Cervantes' "Don Quixote": A Reference Guide. Westport: Greenwood P, 2006.
The Cervantes Encyclopedia. 2 vols. Westport: Greenwood P, 2004.
Ganelin, Charles, and Howard Mancing, eds. *Text, Theory, and Performance: Golden Age Comedia Studies*. West Lafayette: Purdue UP, 1994.
The Chivalric World of Don Quijote: *Style, Structure, and Narrative Technique*. Columbia: U of Missouri P, 1982.

ARTICLES AND ESSAYS:

Accepted:
"Narrative Imagination in *La dama duende.*" *Studies in Honor of Charles Ganelin*. Ed. Bonnie Gasior and Yolanda Gamboa. (in press)
"The Don Quixotes of Science Fiction." *Don Quixote: The Re-accentuation of the World's Greatest Literary Hero*. Ed. Stanislav Gratchev and Howard Mancing. (in preparation)
In print:
"Sancho Panza and the Ethical/Moral Norm in *Don Quixote.*" *Contextos* (Brazil) 29.1 (2016): 48-72.
"Embodied Cognition and Autopoiesis in *Don Quixote.*" *Cognitive Approaches to Early Modern Spanish Literature*. Ed. Isabel Jaén and Julien J. Simon. Oxford: Oxford UP, 2016. 37-52.
"The Deceptiveness of *Lazarillo de Tormes.*" *Lazarillo de Tormes*. Ed. Ilan Stavans. New York: Norton, 2016. 87-98. (Reprint of 1975 essay published in *PMLA*.)

"Nunca segundas partes … ." *El español en el mundo: Anuario del Instituto Cervantes, 2015*. Ed. Rebeca Gutiérrez Revilla. Madrid: Instituto Cervantes, 2015. 135-46.

"Spanish Fiction in the Seventeenth Century." *A History of the Spanish Novel*. Ed. J. A. Garrido Ardila. Oxford: Oxford UP, 2015. 142-72.

"*Guzmán de Alfarache* and After: The Spanish Picaresque Novel in the Seventeenth Century." *The Picaresque Novel in Western Literature: From the 16th Century to the Neopicaresque*. Ed. J. A. Garrido Ardila. Cambridge: Cambridge UP, 2015. 40-59.

"Applying Theory of Mind to *Don Quixote*." *Approaches to Teaching Cervantes's "Don Quixote."* 2nd ed. Ed. James A. Parr and Lisa Vollendorf. New York: Modern Language Association of America, 2015. 147-52.

"El *Quijote* y el autopoiesis." *Comentarios a Cervantes: Actas del VIII Congreso Internacional de la Asociación de Cervantistas; Oviedo, 11-15 de junio del 2012*. Ed. Emilio Martínez Mata and María Fernández Ferreiro. Asturias: Fundación María Cristina Masaveu Peterson, 2014. 460-67.

"*La Celestina*: A Novel." *Celestinesca* 38 (2014): 63-84.

"The Mind of a Pícaro: Lázaro de Tormes." *Cognition, Literature, and History*. Ed. Mark Bruhn and Donald Wehrs. New York: Routledge, 2013. 262-88.

"Embodied Cognitive Science and the Study of Literature." *Cognitive Cervantes*. Ed. Julien J. Simon, Barbara Simerka, and Howard Mancing. Spec. cluster of essays of *Cervantes: Bulletin of the Cervantes Society of America* 32.1 (2012): 25-69.

"La teoría de la mente de Sancho Panza." *Where is My Mind?: Cognición, literatura y cine*. Ed. Mike Wilson. Santiago de Chile: Editorial Cuarto Propio, 2011. 57-74.

"*Don Quijote de la Mancha* in Spanish American Literature and Culture." *World Literature in Spanish: An Encyclopedia*. Ed. Maureen Ihrie and Salvador Oropesa. Vol. 1. Westport: Greenwood P, 2011. 311-22. 3 vols.

"Sancho Panza's Theory of Mind." *Theory of Mind and Literature*. Ed. Paula Leverage, Howard Mancing, Richard Schweickert, and Jennifer Marston William. West Lafayette: Purdue UP, 2011. 123-32.

"Sancho Panza et la norme éthique." *Cervantes*. Ed. Jean-Raymond Fanlo. Spec. issue of *Europe* 979-80 (2010): 76-87.

"Reading 'Noche oscura' Twice." *Approaches to Teaching Teresa of Ávila and the Spanish Mystics*. Ed. Alison Weber. New York: Modern Language Association of America, 2009. 202-07.

"*Don Quijote*: The Texture of the Text." *Studies in Spanish Literature in Honor of Robert Fiore*. Ed. Chad M. Gasta and Julia Domínguez. Newark, DE: Juan de la Cuesta, 2009. 311-25.

"*Don Quixote* and Bakhtin's Two Stylistic Lines of the Novel." *Studies in Spanish Literature in Honor of Daniel Eisenberg*. Ed. Thomas Lathrop. Newark, DE: Juan de la Cuesta, 2009. 177-96.

"The Quixotic Novel in British Fiction of the Nineteenth and Twentieth Centuries." *The Cervantean Heritage: Reception and Influence of Cervantes in Britain*. Ed. John A. G. Ardila. Edinburgh: Legenda, 2008. 104-16.

"The Origin of 'The Impossible Dream.'" *"Aquí se imprimen libros:" Cervantine Studies in Honor of Tom Lathrop*. Ed. Mark Groundland. University, MS: Department of Modern Languages, U of Mississippi, 2008. 79-90.

"Coming to Grips with the Text of Mateo Alemán's *Guzmán de Alfarache*." *Approaches to Teaching "Lazarillo de Tormes" and the Picaresque Novel*. Ed. Anne J. Cruz. New York: Modern Language Association of America, 2008. 86-91.

"400 años de Dulcinea del Toboso." *Actas, I Congreso Internacional El Quijote en clave de mujer/es*. Ed. Fanny Rubio. Toledo: Sociedad Estatal de Conmemoraciones Culturales, 2007. 229-41. (Published in 2009)

"The Quixotic Novel in British and American Literature." *Cervantes and His Legacy in Contemporary Fiction*. Ed. A. Robert Lauer and Sonya S. Gupta. Spec. double issue of *CIEFL Bulletin* [New Series] 15.2-16.1 (2005-2006): 1-18.

"James Parr's Theory of Mind." *Critical Reflections: Essays on Golden Age Spanish Literature in Honor of James A. Parr*. Ed. Barbara Simerka and Amy R. Williamsen. Cranbury: Associated U Presses, 2006. 125-43.

"See the Play, Read the Book." *Cognition and Performance: Theatre Studies After the Cognitive Turn*. Ed. F. Elizabeth Hart and Bruce McConachie. London: Routledge, 2006. 189-206.

"Prólogo." *La mujer de Cervantes*. By María Luz Melcón. Madrid: Word & Image, 2006. 7-12.

"The Lessons of *San Manuel Bueno, mártir*." *MLN* 121.2 (2006): 343-66.

"Los embrujos del *Quijote*." *Estudios Públicos* 100 (2006): 153-68.

"Camila's Story." *Cervantes: Bulletin of the Cervantes Society of America* 25.1 (2005): 9-22.

"Response to 'On Narration and Theory.'" *Cervantes: Bulletin of the Cervantes Society of America* 24.2 (2005): 135-54.

"Pica Syndrome in Cervantes' *Curioso impertinente*." "*Corónente tus hazañas*": *Studies in Honor of John J. Allen*. Ed. Michael McGrath. Newark, DE: Juan de la Cuesta, 2005. 317-24.

"Don Quixote: Coming to America." *Cervantes y su mundo, III*. Ed. Kurt Reichenberger. Kassel: Reichenberger, 2005. 397-418.

"Dulcinea del Toboso—On the Occasion of Her 400th Birthday." *Hispania* 88.1 (2005): 53-63.

"Knighthood Compromised." *Miguel de Cervantes*. Ed. Harold Bloom. Philadelphia: Chelsea House, 2005. 7-35. (Reprint of Chapter 2 of *The Chivalric World of Don Quijote*.)

Entries on "Biological Foundations of Narrative," "Novel, The," "Picaresque Novel," and "Quixotic Novel." *The Routledge Encyclopedia of Narrative Theory*. Ed. David Herman, Manfred Jahn, and Marie-Laure Ryan. London: Routledge, 2005.

"Rastier Revisited: Paradigms in Conflict." *Semiotica* 145 (2003): 139-49.

"Cervantes as Narrator of *Don Quijote*." *Cervantes: Bulletin of the Cervantes Society of America* 23.1 (2003): 117-40.

"'Bendito sea Alá': A New Edition of *Belianís de Grecia*." *Cervantes: Bulletin of the Cervantes Society of America* 21.2 (2001): 111-15.

"Preface." *Engaños deste siglo y historia sucedida en nuestros tiempos, 1615*. By Francisco Loubayssin de Lamarca. Ed. Elisa Rosales Juega. Lewiston: Edwin Mellen P, 2001. vi-viii.

"Bakhtin, Spanish Literature, and Cervantes." *Cervantes for the 21st Century/ Cervantes para el siglo XXI: Studies in Honor of Edward Dudley*. Ed. Francisco La Rubia Prado. Newark, DE: Juan de la Cuesta, 2000. 141-62.

"Prototypes of Genre in Cervantes's *Novelas ejemplares*." *Cervantes: Bulletin of the Cervantes Society of America* 20.2 (2000): 127-50.

"Against Dualisms: A Response to Henry Sullivan." *Cervantes: Bulletin of the Cervantes Society of America* 19.1 (1999): 158-76.

"Embedded Narration in *Guzmán de Alfarache*." "*Ingeniosa Invención:*" *Essays on Golden Age Spanish Literature for Geoffrey L. Stagg in Honor of His Eightieth Birthday*. Ed. Ellen M. Anderson and Amy R. Williamsen. Newark, DE: Juan de la Cuesta, 1999. 69-99.

Don Quijote II, 29. Critical introduction, notes, text, bibliography for this chapter of the novel in the edition by Francisco Rico. 2 vols. Barcelona: Instituto Cervantes, 1998. I: 867-74; II: 162, 538-41, 777.

"The Protean Picaresque." *The Picaresque: Tradition and Displacement*. Ed. Giancarlo Maiorino. Minneapolis: U of Minnesota P, 1996. 273-91.

"A Theory of Faculty Workload." *Chairing the Foreign Language and Literature Department.* Spec. issue of *ADFL Bulletin* 25.3 (1994): 31-37.

"Cervantes." *Dictionary of the Literature of the Iberian Peninsula, Vol. I: A-K.* Ed. Germán Bleiberg, Maureen Ihrie, and Janet Pérez. Westport: Greenwood P, 1993. 383-95.

"Teaching, Research, Service: The Concept of Faculty Workload." *ADFL Bulletin* 22 (1991): 44-50.

"Full Equal Partners." *ADFL Bulletin* 21 (1990): 4-9.

"Jacinto María Delgado and Cide Hamete Benengeli: A Semi-Classic Recovered and a Bibliographical Labyrinth Explored." *Cervantes: Bulletin of the Cervantes Society of America* 7.1 (1987): 13-43.

"A Consensus Canon of Hispanic Poetry." *Hispania* 69 (1986): 53-81.

"Three Approaches to *Don Quixote.*" *Approaches to Teaching "Don Quixote."* Ed. Richard Bjornson. New York: Modern Language Association of America, 1984. 56-61.

"La retórica de Sancho Panza." *Actas del Séptimo Congreso de la Asociación Internacional de Hispanistas.* Ed. Giuseppe Bellini. Rome: Bulzoni Editore, 1982. 717-23.

"Cide Hamete Benengeli vs. Miguel de Cervantes: The Metafictional Dialectic of *Don Quijote.*" *Cervantes: Bulletin of the Cervantes Society of America* 1.1 (1981): 63-81.

"Alonso Quijano y sus amigos." *Cervantes: Su obra y su mundo. Actas del I Congreso Internacional sobre Cervantes.* Ed. Manuel Criado de Val. Madrid: Edi-6, 1981. 737-41.

"*El Diálogo del Capón* y la tradición picaresca." *Actas del Sexto Congreso Internacional de Hispanistas.* Ed. Alan M. Gordon and Evelyn Rugg. Toronto: Department of Spanish and Portuguese, U of Toronto, 1980. 494-97.

"The Picaresque Novel: A Protean Form." *College Literature* 6 (1979): 182-204.

"El pesimismo radical del *Lazarillo de Tormes.*" *La picaresca: Orígenes, textos y estructuras. Actas del I Congreso Internacional sobre la Picaresca.* Ed. Manuel Criado de Val. Madrid: Fundación Universitaria Española, 1979. 459-67.

"Cervantes y Saul Bellow." *Anales Cervantinos* 16 (1977): 125-37.

"The Art of Literary Allusion in Juan Rulfo." *Modern Fiction Studies* 23 (1977): 242-44.

"Fernando de Rojas, *La Celestina*, and *Lazarillo de Tormes.*" *Kentucky Romance Quarterly* 23 (1976): 47-61.

"A Note on the Formation of Character Image in the Classic Spanish Novel." *Philological Quarterly* 54 (1975): 528-30.

"The Deceptiveness of *Lazarillo de Tormes*." *PMLA* 90 (1975): 426-32.

"Cervantes and the Tradition of Chivalric Parody." *Forum for Modern Language Studies* 11 (1975): 177-91.

"The Comic Function of Chivalric Names in *Don Quijote*." *Names* 21 (1973): 220-35.

"A Study of Reading Lists for Graduate Degrees in Spanish." *Hispania* 56 (1973): 676-85. (co-authored with Vern G. Williamsen).

"Dulcinea's Ass: A Note on *Don Quijote*, Part II, Chapter 10." *Hispanic Review* 40 (1972): 73-77.

Book Reviews:

Davoine, Françoise. *Fighting Melancholia: Don Quixote's Teaching*. London: Karnac Books, 2016. *Cervantes: Bulletin of the Cervantes Society of America*. (Forthcoming)

Fine, Ruth. *Reescrituras bíblicas cervantinas*. Madrid, Frankfurt am Main: Iberoamericana, Vervuert, 2014. *Revista Canadiense de Estudios Hispánicos* 39.2 (2015): 519-21.

Byrne, Susan. *Law and History in Cervantes'* Don Quixote. Toronto: U of Toronto P, 2012. *Crítica Bibliográphica*. Academia Editorial del Hispanismo, 20 Dec. 2013. Web. 17 Nov. 2016.

Cavillac, Michel. "*Guzmán de Alfarache" y la novela moderna*. Madrid: Casa de Velázquez, 2011. *Hispanófila* 166 (2012): 147-49.

Scamuzzi, Iole. *Encantamiento y transfiguración: Don Quijote en el melodrama italiano entre los siglos XVII y XVIII*. Trans. Alicia Jiménez and Yolanda Lauroba. Vigo: Editorial Academia del Hispanismo, 2007. Biblioteca Miguel de Cervantes 6. *The Eighteenth-Century: A Current Bibliography* 33 (2007): 432-33.

Garcés, María Antonia. *Cervantes en Argel: Historia de un cautivo*. Madrid: Gredos, 2005. *Bulletin of Spanish Studies* 86.6 (2009): 842-43.

Cervantes, Miguel de. *Don Quijote de la Mancha*. Edición de Castilla-La Mancha. Al cuidado de Francisco Rico. Junta de Comunidades de Castilla-La Mancha. Empresa Pública Don Quijote de la Mancha, 2005; Francisco Rico. *El texto del "Quijote": Preliminares a una ecdótica del Siglo de Oro*. Valladolid: Centro para la Edición de los Clásicos Españoles, Universidad de Valladolid, 2005. *Cervantes: Bulletin of the Cervantes Society of America* 28.1 (2008): 199-201.

González Echevarría, Roberto, ed. *Cervantes' "Don Quixote": A Casebook.* Oxford: Oxford UP, 2005; Eric J. Kartchner. *Unhappily Ever After: Deceptive Idealism in Cervantes's Marriage Tales.* Newark, DE: Juan de la Cuesta, 2005. *Modern Language Review* 102.1 (2007): 252-53.

Gran Enciclopedia Cervantina. Volumen I: A buen bocado—Aubigné. Volumen II: Auden—Casa de los celos. Alcalá de Henares, Madrid: Centro de Estudios Cervantinos, Editorial Castalia, 2005, 2006. *Cervantes: Bulletin of the Cervantes Society of America* 27.2 (2007): 232-38.

Jurado Santos, Agapita. *Obras teatrales derivadas de novelas cervantinas (siglo XVII).* Kassel: Edition Reichenberger, 2005. *Bulletin of Spanish Studies* 84: 424-25.

Hart, Thomas. *Cervantes and Ariosto: Renewing Fiction.* Princeton: Princeton UP, 1989. *Hispanic Review* 61 (1993): 556-57.

Calderón, Héctor. *Conciencia y lenguaje en el "Quijote" y "El obsceno pájaro de la noche."* Madrid: Pliegos, 1987. *Hispanic Review* 61 (1993): 408-09.

Williamson, Edwin. *The Half-Way House of Fiction: "Don Quixote" and Arthurian Romance.* Oxford: Clarendon P, 1984. *Bulletin of Hispanic Studies* 64 (1987): 155.

Fiore, Robert. *Lazarillo de Tormes.* Boston: Twayne, 1984. Twayne's World Author Ser. 714. *Journal of Hispanic Philology* 10 (1986): 311-12.

Spires, Robert C. *Beyond the Metafictional Mode: Directions in the Modern Spanish Novel.* Lexington: UP of Kentucky, 1984. *Hispania* 68 (1985): 779-80.

Flores, R. M. *Sancho Panza Through Three Hundred Seventy-five Years of Continuations, Imitations and Criticism, 1605-1980.* Newark, DE: Juan de la Cuesta—Hispanic Monographs, 1982. *Cervantes: Bulletin of the Cervantes Society of America* 4.1 (1984): 84-86.

Alfaro, Gustavo. *La estructura de la novela picaresca.* Bogotá: Instituto Caro y Cuervo, 1977. *Journal of Hispanic Philology* 3 (1979): 311-12.

I. Cognitive Literary Studies

The Case for Teaching Cognitive-Literary Studies: Approaches, Challenges, and Benefits

JENNIFER MARSTON WILLIAM
Purdue University

DESPITE ITS CONTINUAL GROWTH as a discipline in recent years, coursework in cognitive-literary studies is still rare at the graduate level and almost non-existent at the undergraduate level in the United States.[1] However, given the recent increased push toward academic interdisciplinarity, the time is now for integrating cognitive-literary studies further into the university literature curriculum. As with any curricular paradigm shift, there are systemic and other challenges involved, and these must be met head on so that cognitive-literary studies can continue to flourish. In this essay, I first make the plea for increased curricular development in cognitive-literary studies so that current and future students are exposed to cutting-edge cognitive research that impacts how we understand literary production and reception. Second, I briefly survey the extent to which cognitive-literary studies is currently offered domestically and abroad. Third, I discuss multiple ways of incorporating cognitive-literary studies into existing

---

1   There are some notable exceptions, such as a number of undergraduate courses that have been taught consistently at Portland State University and the University of California, Santa Barbara in recent years. In addition, many scholars working in the field tend to include a cognitive-studies component even when that is not a main focus of the course. Lorna Martens of the University of Virginia notes, for example, that she makes an effort to mention conceptual metaphor in nearly all of her undergraduate literature courses (Message to the author). I do the same type of integration in my undergraduate classes on literature and film, particularly with the Theory of Mind concept.

curricula and outline some of the institutional challenges to this process that must be overcome in order for this field to thrive as it should.

The last few decades have brought steady developments in cognitive psychology, as well as the application of this new research to literature and film studies. Scientific studies on such cognitive aspects as memory, affect, Theory of Mind, and empathy have increasingly informed literary scholarship. This trend has led to numerous productive analyses of narrative, poetic, and dramatic works. Path-breaking books in cognitive studies such as George Lakoff and Mark Johnson's *Metaphors We Live By* (1980) and Gilles Fauconnier and Mark Turner's *The Way We Think* (2002) have shed light on everyday brain processes that enable and affect the reception and production of creative works. Since the turn of the century, well-reputed, peer-reviewed scholarly journals such as *Narrative*, *Poetics Today*, and *Style* have published articles that take a cognitive-theoretical approach to literature, and several anthologies in the field have appeared with prominent university presses within the past decade.[2]

Cognitive-literary scholars such as Howard Mancing at Purdue University, F. Elizabeth Hart at the University of Connecticut, and Lorna Martens at the University of Virginia have been among the pioneers in developing coursework in cognitive theory and its application to literature, and others have followed suit. However, given the relative lack of coursework in this area, it is clear that we need a concentrated effort from everyone working in this field in order to develop cog-lit curricula—and ideally, degree and minor/certificate programs in the subject—and to promote it vigorously. Part of the task at hand involves clarifying the nature of cog-lit studies to students and colleagues, and correcting the misconceptions that threaten to give the field an irreparably bad reputation. In the popular press, empirical approaches to literature have been placed in a relatively positive light in recent years, although literary Darwinism has been more an object of disparagement.[3] Meanwhile, theoretical approaches such as cognitive narratology and cogni-

---

2   See for example Aldama; Leverage et al.; Jaén and Simon, *Cognitive Approaches*; Jaén and Simon, *Cognitive Literary Studies*; Zunshine, *Introduction*; Zunshine, *The Oxford Handbook*.

3   For instance, the work of psychologists David Comer Kidd and Emanuele Castano suggesting that reading literary fiction improves empathy was quickly picked up by outlets such as *Scientific American* and *The New York Times* (see Chiaet; Belluck) shortly after its publication in *Science* in October 2013. For an example of negative criticism of literary Darwinism, see D. T. Max's well-known 2005 essay in the *New York Times Magazine*.

tive poetics have been largely neglected.[4] Literature scholar Frank Kelleter's 2007 essay, with its "worried reflections," did not help matters by grouping all scholars working on cognitive and scientific approaches to literature as "neo-naturalists," and consciously conflating cognitive and literary Darwinist approaches, "despite their obvious dissimilarities in scope and outlook" (155). Clearly, there is some difficult work to be done, not only to increase the visibility of cognitive approaches to literature, but also to further establish its credibility and clarify its aims. Isabel Jaén and Julien Simon's volume *Cognitive Literary Studies* (2012) addresses the ongoing nature of this endeavor and also highlights "both the continuity and the vitality of a field that is based on a dialogue among a variety of disciplines" (13). Combatting the misguided and rather widespread belief that cognitive studies presumes dangerous universals, Jaén and Simon (along with their volume's contributors) remind us of the important, indispensable role that cultural-historical context plays in cognitive literary analyses. This facet of humanistic cognitive studies, and particularly the extent to which context informs our research and our teaching, should be clarified explicitly and often.[5]

One means toward clearing up dangerous misconceptions is to address them directly with our students, some of whom will be inspired to carry the torch of productive cognitive-literary analyses with their dissertations and later scholarly work. In addition to integrating in all of our literature classes the principles of cognition as they apply to textual interpretation, we need to prioritize the development of permanent courses in cognitive-literary theory and applications at both the undergraduate and graduate levels, and to ensure that these are easily found in course catalogues and online searches. With

---

4   An exception to this neglect is Patricia Cohen's 2010 *The New York Times* article "Next Big Thing," which highlights the increased literary application of Theory of Mind and other cognitive principles in a mostly positive light. Cohen asserts that in a time of drastic university budget cuts, "the cross-pollination of English and psychology is providing a revitalizing lift." Still, one senses irony in Cohen's parenthetical warning, "Follow closely now; this is about the science of English," as she cites cog-lit scholar Lisa Zunshine's explanation of Theory of Mind via an example from popular culture.

5   Simon makes this point clearly in his 2016 essay on contextualizing cognitive approaches to early modern Spanish literature when he notes that, although cognitive studies emphasizes embodiment (i.e., the integrated body-mind), "this does not mean that the human subject is reduced to a set of universal cognitive principles. In fact, by stressing the key role of the environment, an embodied view of the brain safeguards the notion of cultural complexity and individuality, sacrosanct in the humanities" (15).

some notable exceptions as mentioned above, a Google search in 2016 reveals only spotty offerings in cognitive-literary studies both in the United States and abroad.[6] It is likely (and I am hopeful) that there is considerably more coursework in this field available than I found after fairly extensive searching. Because there is, to date, very little in the way of permanent, catalogued cog-lit coursework, many such courses are offered under "variable-title" numbers that I presume are readily available and known to students within a particular academic program who seek elective courses. However, it is worrisome, and does not bode well for the field, if this information remains relatively obscured from current and prospective students. Coursework should be well documented and maintain a web presence with detailed course descriptions and syllabi (when possible, and at the instructors' discretion).

Peter Stockwell, author of the valuable overview text *Cognitive Poetics: An Introduction*, has taught a free online course on the topic. Stockwell notes the following in his blog entry from 13 March 2014:

> I have felt that in a very short period, the main thing I can do is to say "Here is the most recent thinking in this area—what do you think?" This latest thinking has not yet become settled or paradigmatic enough to form the basis of a thing to be taught yet, so a short online course is much more like a conference presentation with a long space for discussion afterwards, or like a symposium in which everyone participates. (Stockwell, "Why Do We Get Angry")

Stockwell's efforts are commendable and a solid start toward increasing the visibility and broader understanding of cog-lit studies, although I believe that traditional classroom seminars can be even more effective as we, along with our students, continue to shape what the field looks like. As Professor Hart of the University of Connecticut has written as one of the objectives for her cog-lit seminar, "Our goal should be to develop as comprehensive an understanding as possible of the range, depth, and viability of cognitive theory for literary studies, creating for ourselves a blueprint of future studies in the field" (Course Syllabus). A full-length seminar provides an ideal forum for such explorations, and it empowers the students as agents in the process of defining and furthering a relatively nascent field of study. Along these lines, Fritz Breithaupt, a Professor of Germanic Studies at Indiana University, has offered an exemplary graduate course titled "Experimental Humanities and

---

6 In contrast, a search for coursework in the related but more established field of semiotics yields many more hits.

Narratology." Breithaupt acknowledges the developing nature of cognitive studies and its relation to "experimental humanities" in describing his course in the syllabus as one that will "lead students to expand our knowledge of narratives/narrative thinking by means of their own experiments." He also emphasizes the interdisciplinary nature of the field, stating that the course "is designed for students from literary studies and cognitive science. It is assumed that most students will have knowledge from only one of these two large fields and are willing to learn and listen to their peers" (Breithaupt).

Beyond individual faculty members offering courses related to cognitive-literary studies, some academic departments are coordinating efforts in this domain as well. The Department of English at UC-Santa Barbara, for instance, hosts a site called "Literature and the Mind: A Global Resource for Psychoanalytic, Philosophical, and Neuroscientific Approaches to Literary Study." In addition to news of co-curricular activities such as lectures and reading group meetings, the site boasts some exciting curricular developments as well. They offer an undergraduate specialization in "Literature and the Mind," as well as a graduate program that can be tailored to the topic: "Graduate students interested in the pursuit of psychoanalytic, philosophical, and neuroscientific approaches to literary study may take one segment of the First Qualifying Exam in 'Literature and the Mind,' in addition to courses on related topics." A list of related graduate seminars is also available on the website. While not a designated program in cognitive-literary studies per se, this track enables interested students to pursue a research concentration in this area and thus serves as a wonderful model for literature programs everywhere. It is also most encouraging that in 2015, the department advertised a position for a "tenure-track Assistant Professor in cognitive literary studies and/or neuroaesthetics who specializes in any period of British or American literatures" ("Tenure-track Assistant Professor"). This specialization request for new faculty is still rare, but should become more common over time.

Some faculty in my own academic unit, the School of Languages and Cultures at Purdue University, have provided a number of cognitive-literary graduate offerings in the past ten years, from Mancing's Theory of Mind seminars, to Paula Leverage's directed reading course on applied cognitive theory, to my course on cognitive approaches to women's writing. With the Center for Neurohumanities (formerly the Center for Cognitive Literary Studies) that is housed at Purdue, we are poised to make great strides and work toward creating a viable cognitive studies curriculum, and eventually certificate or degree programs. However, funding is a real obstacle. While our reading group meets regularly to discuss cutting-edge cognitive research, the Center does not currently have the means to invite prominent speakers or host larger events such as conferences, as we have in the past. We also are not in a position to hire replacements to teach our "usual" courses for our respective undergraduate and graduate programs when we offer the cross-departmental (and elective rather than required) cog-lit seminars. Thus, our opportunities to do so are quite limited, unless we take them on as an unpaid overload. For these practical and financial reasons, the visibility of cognitive-literary studies is suffering at a local level, and it is difficult to sustain student participation over the long term. In talking to colleagues in similar situations at other universities, it seems that we at Purdue are not alone in these challenges.

What can be done to remedy these and other practical problems so that cognitive studies can thrive within the humanities? As a first step, tighter connections and communication between seemingly disparate departments that deal with the various aspects encompassed by cognitive studies will be key in gaining eventual institutional support for introducing new curriculum, and perhaps even whole programs, dedicated to cognitive-*literary* studies. Related courses across campus should be sought out for students pursuing this track, and degree programs shaped and modified accordingly. Whether or not cognitive-literary analysis is a covered topic in a more general course on cognitive studies or even cognitive science, a degree program or minor / concentration program in cog-lit could allow students to count such a course toward the requirements. Particularly when specific cog-lit courses cannot be offered on a regular basis due to the practical concerns mentioned above, this kind of curricular flexibility is a must for enabling such programs to develop, and for furthering this field of study. Toward this end, instructors offering cognitive-studies overview courses in humanities units other than literature also should be encouraged to include cognitive approaches to literature in their course plans; a good model for this is a philosophy course offered by Paul Thagard at the University of Waterloo entitled "Seminar in Cognitive Science: Mind and Society," which devotes one week of class to discussion of literature, addressing such questions as "What are the brain processes that make possible emotional reading and empathy?" and "Can cognitive theory be used to evaluate literary works?" (Thagard). Ideally, scholars within an institution who are working on cognitive topics across departments are in frequent dialogue and can advise their students to attend related courses taught by colleagues across campus. Team-taught seminars, although certainly not without their logistical challenges, are also desirable in presenting subject matter of such a wide range. As Jaén indicates, team teaching creates the type of cooperative environment that reflects the collaborative nature of the field

("Teaching Cervantes's *Don Quixote*" 114). The administrative and bureaucratic hurdles involved can usually be overcome with enough concentrated pushing, and the ultimate benefits to the students make these struggles well worth the effort.

In the United States—and in many other countries even more so—universities today advocate and actively promote interdisciplinary endeavors. Grants and fellowships are increasingly available to, and even prioritized for, researchers who are collaborating across disciplines. At the curricular level, however, movements toward true interdisciplinarity have been quite slow or even stalled in recent years. The systemic challenges for cog-lit studies in particular include administrators who may have the totally wrong impression of the nature of the field.[7] Further, while interdisciplinarity has been an academic buzzword for some time, it is by no means a self-explanatory concept, and it means something very specific in the context of cognitive-literary studies.[8] Line Brandt clarifies the particular interdisciplinary nature of the field as follows:

> The *interdisciplinarity* in cognitive poetics is not a novelty in and of itself; what is novel is rather the consistent orientation toward shared patterns of thought and emotional responses, and the commitment to continually invite reassessment of one's claims, in the light of what is known about cognition, whether this knowledge, or the tools used to gain knowledge, stems from the literary part of the humanities or from some other branch of science. (31; emphasis in original)

As Brandt also points out, the inherent interdisciplinarity of cognitive-literary studies necessitates some careful thought regarding methodology and the boundaries of disciplinary identity. While it is wise to be informed by relevant empirical and scientific findings from fields outside of literary studies, textual analysis needs to remain at the heart of it all: "For cognitive lit-

---

[7] Bruce Michelson stresses that those of us in the field need to clearly communicate what our interdisciplinary undertaking entails, or else we will suffer the consequences: "In rough times all over for American academe, with campus administrators hunting for units and operations to trim back or sacrifice, there is no advantage to bolstering impressions that programs in the crosshairs have no clear or consequential subject, no coalesced methodology, or a penchant for promulgating nonsense" (218).

[8] Indeed, the nature of the interdisciplinary dimensions of cognitive-literary studies have been debated for years; see Mark Bruhn's essay for a comprehensive overview of this discourse.

erary studies to appeal to literary scholars, the subject will have to remain literature" (Brandt 15).[9] As a start, cognitive-literary studies must be taught as a unit in introductory literary theory courses (though importantly, not as a single "theory" unto itself). A designated degree program is not necessary for offering courses in the field, although this might be the ultimate goal. In the meantime, promoting cognitive-literary studies not as a method in itself but as "a call for inclusiveness and cooperation, an interdisciplinary approach to knowledge" can help integrate related coursework into various degree programs (Jaén and Simon, *Cognitive Literary Studies* 4).

Of course, introducing interdisciplinary curriculum (and really, *any* new course of study) is often easier said than done. In her 2014 article on teaching *Don Quixote* from a cognitive historicist perspective, Jaén considers how, due to institutional processes surrounding curriculum revisions, introducing cognitive perspectives into the literature classroom may be even more challenging than having these topics accepted into mainstream publication venues (111). Unfortunately, Marion Brady's remarks over a quarter century ago about the educational system in the US still largely apply today:

> Incredible as it may seem, American education, this vast institution which consumes so much of our wealth, time, and energy, offers the student not a coherent intellectual structure but a random heap fashioned by ancient concerns and assumptions, political expedience, accident, intellectual fads, hysteria, special interests, and myriad superficial views of the ends of education. (8)

---

9   Other scholars have expressed similar sentiments: e.g., Marie-Laure Ryan, who is skeptical about the use of brain imaging to understand how readers process narrative, asserting that "cognitive narratology is most productive when it proceeds bottom-up, getting its insights from the texts themselves" (489). I particularly enjoy the way Bruhn demonstrates the importance of this approach in his introduction to a set of articles in a special double issue of *Poetics Today* that

> clearly answer the demand for literary-critical, literary-historical, and/or literary-theoretical 'value added' in consequence of the interdisciplinary approach. Yet a large, indeed the preponderant measure of their value derives from the specifically disciplinary underpinnings of this interdisciplinarity, including above all an informed appreciation of the *differentia specifica* of literature. Nowhere here is the literary object flattened or otherwise distorted to fit the cognitive model; on the contrary, in every instance the cognitive model is required to adapt—for its own disciplinary good—to the literary example. (454; emphasis in original)

Brady lists various problems of American K-12 and post-secondary curriculum, some of which are particularly relevant to cognitive-literary studies with its inherently interdisciplinary nature. For instance, she observes that "[o]ur best minds tell us that all knowledge is related, yet our curriculum is fragmented and the fragments are moving farther apart;" and that "[t]he learning process requires that new information become part of a coherent conceptual structure, yet no systematic attempt is being made to create a curriculum which reflects that requirement" (9). In other words, students are lacking an integrated curriculum with an underlying conceptual structure that would result in the most effective learning. In this respect, we can consider our mission of enhancing cog-lit curriculum as not simply a bullet point on our own agenda, but also as a contribution to the development of more meaningful, more integrated, and more effective ways of learning. Cognitive studies can serve as a logical bridge between so many facets of the undergraduate general education curriculum. With proper coordination, it can connect a remarkably wide variety of departments and programs—including but not limited to English, (other) languages and cultures, linguistics, cognitive and social/behavioral psychology, philosophy, biology, film and media studies, and anthropology.

Once one gets beyond the institutional roadblocks and is indeed free to offer a cog-lit course, different (and much more welcome) challenges emerge. Students who enroll in such a course are likely to come into it with widely varied academic backgrounds. Some will have no knowledge of cognitive studies, while others do. They may not all be literature scholars, and even if they are, they will bring with them differing levels of experience with textual analysis. As Professor Martens of the University of Virginia notes, it can be difficult for the students in such a course to come up with an original final project on their own, especially if resources are not available for empirical studies (for example, ones that could measure cognitive-emotional responses to reading particular passages). Thus, the students are compelled to remain on the theoretical level with their pursuits, and as such may not get a sense of the full potential of cognitive studies for enhancing our understanding of literary production and reception (Martens, Message to the author). At the same time, such realities allow the students to experience firsthand the practical constraints on the field in many university settings.

To their great credit, cog-lit instructors tend to consider not only such logistical limitations, but also broader conceptual ones. For example, Martens assigns her students Ryan's critical article "Narrative and Cognitive Science: A Problematic Relation" (Course Syllabus), and Hart includes among her course objectives that participants will consider "cognitive theory's limits, i.e., the scope of its usefulness as a literary-critical instrument" (Course Syllabus). Professor Chantelle Warner of the University of Arizona discusses with her students the problem of the monolingualism that characterizes much cognitive studies research, which often "assumes one language read by a native-like reader" and thus is not always relevant to those of us teaching literature written in other languages to students who are not native speakers of that language (Message to the author). In any case, the nature of an ever-developing field requires a realistic presentation of what has been (and is being) done, what else could be done, and the probable outlook for the future. I have found that my students are eager to engage in exploring the exciting possibilities for cog-lit studies, while retaining a sharp critical perspective on its limitations as well. Scholars working in this field should, on the one hand, refrain from tentativeness about the need for introducing more cog-lit material into the standard curriculum, while on the other hand, retain this characteristic modesty and flexibility as the field continues to evolve.

In this essay, I have mainly considered overview courses in cognitive-literary studies that serve as introductions to the many principles underlying it. The hope for these courses is to spark a keen interest in the students, many of whom are being introduced to these concepts for the first time and who may pursue them further on their own. But if the eventual goal is dedicated degree programs and/or concentrations, a full complement of more specific courses needs to be offered too. Jaén offers an excellent model for applying cognitive approaches to a graduate seminar in her article on teaching *Don Quixote* with modules on psychiatry, differential psychology, and human development from contemporary and historical perspectives ("Teaching Cervantes's *Don Quixote*"). With some modifications, we can make use of such methods to cover cognitive-related concepts in the context of an advanced undergraduate literature course as well. Further, Jaén developed a prototype also based on a *Don Quixote* course with different modules that could be adapted to either the graduate or the undergraduate level ("Afterword"). Those of us working in the field can easily imagine (and some of us may have even taught already) an entire undergraduate course devoted to empathic responses to narrative,[10] for instance, or a graduate seminar on conceptual

---

10   See Ann Rider's excellent article "The Perils of Empathy" (2013), which "suggests that Holocaust literatures employing narrative techniques that disrupt empathic responses are pedagogically fruitful" (44). In outlining various typologies of empathy and relating them to issues of civic responsibility and prosocial action, Rider provides a guide for teaching students to critically engage with Holocaust texts and the different empathy-inducing or empathy-disrupting techniques they employ. See also Barbara

blending and its application to literature. But first things first: let's start by looking around us and surveying what is already happening. Many educators are already teaching material with extreme relevance to cognitive studies without labeling it as such. For example, memory is a common topic for graduate seminars in humanities (not only for literature classes, but also history, philosophy, women's studies, and others), and such courses necessarily rely on recent developments in cognitive psychology. Making this integrative connection more explicit to students up front, including it in the description and perhaps even the title of the course, is a start in the right direction.

In the absence of a permanent cognitive-literary curriculum—a state of affairs that we will hope to change in the near future—we can meaningfully expose our students in the meantime to cog-lit concepts in our current coursework across the curriculum. Hart's thoughts on this issue touch on this very point:

> I teach from a cognitive perspective in all my courses, even if I'm not explicitly teaching a 'cognitive' course. What I mean by that is that the cognitive perspective pervades all my understanding of literature and the uses of history in literature. Cognitive poetics informs all my understanding of the techniques of close-textual reading, especially when I teach poetry. So I have reached the point where the cognitive really isn't even a 'topic' anymore; it's an integrated methodology, fully useful. (Message to the author)

The ultimate goal may be to integrate cognitive studies into literary studies so fully that it becomes a natural part of all solid textual analysis, no longer cordoned off as something separate.[11] At this point, however, we have some concrete steps yet to take in pursuit of that ideal. By identifying the cross-departmental intersections of cognitive-related research at our institutions, as well as doing all we can to overcome the systemic obstacles that often stem

---

Simerka's thought-provoking essay on incorporating empathy studies into the teaching of Las Casas's *Brevísima relación de la destrucción de las Indias*. Simerka argues for an approach to the text that does not dismiss students' emotional responses and that promotes prejudice reduction. She contends that "literary teaching strategies that elicit student empathy and help them to conceptualize the relations among text, emotion, and (re)action can form the basis for a powerful new pedagogy" (215).

11   See Jaén and Simon's discussions on consilience (e.g., *Cognitive Literary Studies* 3; *Cognitive Approaches* 2), and also Zunshine on the "fuzziness of boundaries" as characterizing the project of cognitive cultural studies ("Introduction" 3).

from traditional disciplinary thinking, we can ensure that many more students receive exposure to the various interrelated facets of cognitive studies. The collaborative approach between colleagues and programs in multiple disciplines will demonstrate the clearly reciprocal relationship between cognitive studies in the sciences and in the humanities.[12] As such, cognitive-literary studies will become a model for an integrated curriculum that inspires students and future scholars to build new connections between knowledge bases. In the process, we will enhance our understanding of the brain processes that allow for the creation and enjoyment of narrative and poetic texts, and the effects that texts have, in turn, on the biology of the brain.

Works Cited

Aldama, Frederick Luis, ed. *Toward a Cognitive Theory of Narrative Acts*. Austin: U of Texas P, 2010. Print.

Belluck, Pam. "For Better Social Skills, Scientists Recommend a Little Chekhov." *The New York Times* 3 October 2013. Web. 26 June 2015.

Brady, Marion. *What's Worth Teaching? Selecting, Organizing, and Integrating Knowledge*. Albany: SUNY Press, 1989. Print.

Brandt, Line. "Literary Studies in the Age of Cognitive Science." *Cognitive Semiotics* 2 (2008): 6-40. Print.

Breithaupt, Fritz. Course Syllabus for "Experimental Humanities and Narratology." Indiana University, Spring 2015. PDF.

Bruhn, Mark J. "Introduction: Exchange Values: Poetics and Cognitive Science." *Poetics Today* 32.3 (2011): 403-60. Print.

Chiaet, Julianne. "Novel Finding: Reading Literary Fiction Improves Empathy." *Scientific American* 4 Oct. 2013. Web. 26 June 2015.

Cohen, Patricia. "Next Big Thing in English: Knowing They Know That You Know." *The New York Times* 31 March 2010. Web. 23 June 2015.

Fauconnier, Gilles, and Mark Turner. *The Way We Think: Conceptual Blending and the Mind's Hidden Complexities*. New York: Basic Books, 2002. Print.

Gerrig, Richard J. "Why Literature Is Necessary, and Not Just Nice." *Cognitive Literary Studies: Current Themes and New Directions*. Ed. Isabel Jaén and Julien Jacques Simon. Austin: U of Texas P, 2012. 35-52. Print.

---

12   On the relevance of literary studies and the humanities for scientific research, see Gerrig; Mishara; Oatley et al.

Hart, F. Elizabeth. Course Syllabus for "Seminar on Cognitive Approaches to Literature." University of Connecticut, Spring 2006. PDF.

———. Message to the author. 18 June 2015. E-mail.

Jaén, Isabel. "Afterword: Teaching Early Modern Spanish Literature with a Cognitive Approach." *Cognitive Approaches to Early Modern Spanish Literature*. Ed. Isabel Jaén and Julien Jacques Simon. New York: Oxford UP, 2016. 219-32. Print.

———. "Teaching Cervantes's *Don Quixote* from a Cognitive Historicist Perspective." *Cognition in the Classroom*. Guest ed. Nancy Easterlin. Spec. issue of *Interdisciplinary Literary Studies* 16.1 (2014): 110-26. Print.

Jaén, Isabel, and Julien Jacques Simon, eds. *Cognitive Approaches to Early Modern Spanish Literature*. New York: Oxford UP, 2016. Print.

———, eds. *Cognitive Literary Studies: Current Themes and New Directions*. Austin: U of Texas P, 2012. Print.

Kelleter, Frank. "A Tale of Two Natures: Worried Reflections on the Study of Literature and Culture in an Age of Neuroscience and Neo-Darwinism." *Journal of Literary Theory* 1.1 (2007): 153-89. Print.

Kidd, David Comer, and Emanuele Castano. "Reading Literary Fiction Improves Theory of Mind." *Science* 3 October 2013. Web. 26 June 2015.

Lakoff, George, and Mark Johnson. *Metaphors We Live By*. Chicago: U of Chicago P, 1980.

Leverage, Paula, Howard Mancing, Richard Schweickert, and Jennifer Marston William, eds. *Theory of Mind and Literature*. West Lafayette: Purdue UP, 2011. Print.

"Literature and the Mind: A Global Resource for Psychoanalytic, Philosophical, and Neuroscientific Approaches to Literary Study." *Literature and the Mind*. University of California-Santa Barbara, Department of English. Web. 12 May 2016.

Martens, Lorna. Course Syllabus for "Cognitive Approaches to Literary Study." University of Virginia, Spring 2014. PDF.

———. Message to the author. 14 June 2015. E-mail.

Max, D. T. "The Literary Darwinists." *New York Times Magazine* 6 Nov. 2005: 74-79.

Michelson, Bruce. "The Mind-Sciences in a Literature Classroom." *The Neuroscientific Turn: Transdisciplinarity in the Age of the Brain*. Ed. Melissa M. Littlefield and Jenell M. Johnson. Ann Arbor: U of Michigan P, 2012. 216-32. Print.

Mishara, Aaron L. "The Literary Neuroscience of Kafka's Hypnagogic Hallucinations: How Literature Informs the Neuroscientific Study of Self and Its Disorders." *Cognitive Literary Studies: Current Themes and New Directions*. Ed. Isabel Jaén and Julien Jacques Simon. Austin: U of Texas P, 2012. 105-23. Print.

Oatley, Keith, Raymond A. Mar, and Maja Djikic. "The Psychology of Fiction: Present and Future." *Cognitive Literary Studies: Current Themes and New Directions*. Ed. Isabel Jaén and Julien Jacques Simon. Austin: U of Texas P, 2012. 235-49. Print.

Rider, N. Ann. "The Perils of Empathy: Holocaust Narratives, Cognitive Studies and the Politics of Sentiment." *Holocaust Studies: A Journal of Culture and History* 19.3 (2013): 43-72. Print.

Ryan, Marie-Laure. "Narrative and Cognitive Science: A Problematic Relation." *Style* 44.4 (2010): 469-95. Print.

Simerka, Barbara. "The Role of Empathy in Reading, Interpreting, and Teaching Las Casas' *Brevísima relación de la destrucción de las Indias*." *Cognitive Approaches to Early Modern Spanish Literature*. Ed. Isabel Jaén and Julien Jacques Simon. New York: Oxford UP, 2016. 202-18. Print.

Simon, Julien J. "Contextualizing Cognitive Approaches to Early Modern Spanish Literature." *Cognitive Approaches to Early Modern Spanish Literature*. Ed. Isabel Jaén and Julien Jacques Simon. New York: Oxford UP, 2016. 13-33. Print.

Stockwell, Peter. *Cognitive Poetics: An Introduction*. London: Routledge, 2002. Print.

———. "Why Do We Get Angry, Moved, Annoyed or Sentimental about Fictional Characters in Imagined Worlds?" *Future Learn*. The University of Nottingham. 13 Mar. 2014. Web. 12 May 2016.

"Tenure-track Assistant Professor of Cognitive Literary Studies." *Academic Personnel Recruit*. University of California-Santa Barbara. Web. 17 May 2016.

Thagard, Paul. "Seminar in Cognitive Psychology (Course Syllabus)." *Computational Epistemological Laboratory*. University of Waterloo. Web. 12 May 2016.

Warner, Chantelle. Message to the author. 2 July 2015. E-mail.

Zunshine, Lisa, ed. *Introduction to Cognitive Cultural Studies*. Baltimore: Johns Hopkins UP, 2010. Print.

———. "Introduction: What is Cognitive Cultural Studies?" *Introduction to Cognitive Cultural Studies*. Ed. Lisa Zunshine. Baltimore: Johns Hopkins UP, 2010. 1-33. Print.

———, ed. *The Oxford Handbook of Cognitive Literary Studies*. Oxford: Oxford UP, 2015. Print.

Psychologizing Literary Characters in Fernando de Rojas's *Celestina*: The Emergence of Mind in Early Modern Spanish Literature[1]

JULIEN JACQUES SIMON
Indiana University East

IN THE SPAIN OF the unification of Queen Isabella's Kingdom of Castile and King Ferdinand's Kingdom of Aragon, in 1499, right before the turn of the century, the *Comedia de Calisto y Melibea* [Comedy of Calisto and Melibea] (its original name) was published. It would later become the *Tragicomedia de Calisto y Melibea* [Tragicomedy of Calisto and Melibea] to better reflect all the vicissitudes of its characters. This text tells the story of a low nobleman, Calisto, who falls madly in love with a beautiful lady named Melibea, only daughter of Alisa and Pleberio, a noble and particularly affluent family of Salamanca, Spain. In order to see Melibea and eventually to consummate his love, Calisto will, with the help of his servants, contract the services of a go-between named Celestina; modern editions of the *Comedia/Tragicomedia* now bear her name. The gusto for the adventures of the two lovers and the mastery of the go-between was such that the work was reprinted many times. An extended version, which included a development of the story towards the end was published in 1502. The work crossed the Pyrenees and soon the tale of Calisto and Melibea's love affair mediated by Celestina surfaced in Italian

---

[1] The title is an echo to David Herman's 2011 anthology *The Emergence of Mind: Representations of Consciousness in Narrative Discourse in English*. One of my goals in this essay is to focus on the emergence of mind in the Spanish literary tradition, showing that Fernando de Rojas's *Celestina*, constitutes a steppingstone. Although more narrow in scope than Herman's book, it will hopefully complement it by delving into the literature of a different region, Spain.

(1506), German (1520, 1534), French (1527, 1578, 1633), English (ca. 1530, 1598, 1631), Dutch (1550) and Latin (1624) (Botta). A decade or so after the first *Celestina*, writers took up the challenge of emulating it in various ways. The first one to do so was Pedro Manuel Ximénez de Urrea, who, in 1513, wrote an eclogue based on the first act of Rojas's work. Soon after, many continuations, imitations and adaptations mushroomed.[2] In sum, the infatuation of both writers and readers (and most likely listeners too) was such that it became a landmark of sixteenth-century literature in Spain as well as in Western Europe (the numerous translations attest to the latter).

The roots of the book's success are multifaceted and it may be in part due to its range of interpretations. Indeed, *Celestina* has been viewed by some as a moralizing and didactic fiction (see Bataillon), showing in a rather crude way the tragic consequences of a love affair carried out in an un-Christian manner,[3] while others have viewed it as a self-indulgent piece of fiction, risqué at times, in which lovers disregard proprieties in matters of courtship and instead flimsily restrain their hearts. Additionally, it has also been interpreted as a work of a Jewish *converso* [convert] expressing his deep criticism of the society of his time (Castro), as a social critique (Maravall), or as a parody of courtly love, *el amor cortés*, and its novelistic expression, the sentimental novel in fashion in Spain at the end of the XV century.[4] The origin of *Celestina*'s success may also stem from its realism, akin to the picaresque world of the anonymous *Lazarillo de Tormes*.[5] Rojas's fiction is indeed inhabited by lecherous wenches, Areúsa and Elicia, treacherous and greedy servants, Sempronio and Pármeno, and by an impecunious and covetous bawd who also engages in witchcraft, Celestina. About *Celestina*'s atmosphere and characters Joseph Snow states that:

> In its surrendering pride of protagonism to Celestina and her rag-tag confederation of avaricious servants and lusty wenches, in its revealing of the decay of urbanized moral order by penetrating its poorly-veiled hypocrisy and corrupt value system, and in investing all of its characters,

---

2   I am following here Joseph Snow and Ivy Corfis's definition of these terms: "Continuations" are works that directly use Rojas's characters, "Imitations" are works which borrow *Celestina*'s structure, and "Adaptations" are works whose connections to *Celestina*, while clear, are looser and more free-form (xiv).
3   A sort of *reprobatio amoris* (see Green 505).
4   See Severin, "La parodia;" Severin, *Tragicomedy*; Lacarra.
5   Several scholars (see Fothergill-Payne and especially Castells), using Bakhtin's concept of Grotesque Realism, underscored this trait.

regardless of social-level, with fully-rounded personalities that must be judged without the intervention of any controlling narrative voice, [*Celestina*] clearly was striking out on its own path, illuminating a darker side of the Renaissance. (2-3)

This last quote also hints at another potential source of *Celestina*'s longevity and success, namely the portrayal of characters. Their voices are recognizably human and are the vehicle of evolving fictional minds as Dorothy Severin notes in the introduction to her book, *Tragicomedy and Novelistic Discourse in* Celestina: "The voices of *Celestina* are human beings in metamorphosis, as Lazarillo will be nearly half a century later. Even the cardboard Calisto emerges as the hero of imagination" (4). The human-like quality of characters is really what put *Celestina* on a different path. They exhibit a well-developed literary consciousness, in the way they respond to each other and read each other's intentions. In *Celestina*, the characters' voices are no longer controlled by the author. They are independent voices. They speak freely and their story does not constitute an exemplar to insinuate certain moral values. They have emotions and emotional reactions that the readers can identify with. They have wants and beliefs we can relate to. In sum, they have a "theory of mind," in the psychological sense of the expression.[6]

Theory of Mind, which can be broadly defined as the ability to attribute beliefs, intentions, and desires to others, is a concept from the cognitive sciences useful to look into the mechanics of the literary minds at play, of the interactions between literary characters. Many scholars have shown how this cognitive ability constitutes a core aspect of how we experience and enjoy fictional narratives.[7] In *Celestina*, Rojas "psychologized" his characters, who exhibit in

---

    6   In a recent article, Mancing argued forcefully for the inclusion of the *Celestina* in the novelistic tradition (Mancing, "*Celestina*"). For the most part, the discussion revolved around its format, literary history, and the fact that how it was perceived by Rojas's contemporaries should not determine how we view it today. But he also discussed the rhetorical quality of the work. In doing so he highlighted that *Celestina* should be considered a novel rather than a play, in view of the fact that Theory of Mind and Machiavellian intelligence are "hallmarks of prose fiction" and of the modern novel (see p. 77). The close reading analysis I am doing in this essay is aimed at enriching this discussion by further developing ideas I had proposed in an earlier publication, Simon, "Celestina."

    7   The concept of Theory of Mind comes from Premack and Woodruff's 1978 seminal essay "Does the Chimpanzee Have a Theory of Mind?" in which the authors pondered whether chimpanzees could recognize the intentions of a human being. It is related to mindreading, intentionality, intersubjectivity, and the umbrella term

the dialogues an emergent Theory of Mind (not observed in prior literature), a certain degree of literary consciousness, as well as intentions, desires, and beliefs. In sum, their psychology suddenly becomes transparent. Most Celestina scholars agree that the dialogue is the locus and source of the characters' humanness and many have examined Rojas's art of dialogue (the most prominent among them may be Stephen Gilman[8]). However, the psychological concept of Theory of Mind opens a new dimension in this line of inquiry by going beyond the dialogic level and delving into the characters' mind.

In the second part of this essay, I will be showing how the study of the literary consciousness of characters from a Theory of Mind perspective can complement Mikhail Bakhtin's theory on the rise of the novelistic discourse. In doing so, I argue that: 1) *Celestina* should be included in his genesis of the genre and 2) the psychologizing of literary characters, as it is apparent in *Celestina*, constitutes another line of development of the modern discourse in addition to the two identified by Bakhtin in his essay "Discourse in the Novel." First, let me offer a representative example of how Theory of Mind is at work in *Celestina*.

Literary Characters' Intentionality in *Celestina*

At the beginning of the story (in Act I), Calisto meets by chance Melibea. He falls madly in love with her and afterwards shares his feelings with his servants, Pármeno and Sempronio. The latter tells his master about a procuress, Celestina, which can perhaps help him. Calisto agrees to hire her. To carry out this *empresa* [undertaking], Celestina goes to Melibea's house. There she sees Lucrecia, Melibea's maid, whom she knows from before. On the pretext of selling some yarn, she enters the house and manages to speak to Melibea. They talk about youth and old age and after some time Melibea politely dis-

---

folk psychology, as well as the concepts of social intelligence (see Humphrey) and Machiavellian intelligence (see Byrne and Whiten). In the field of cognitive literary studies, the human ability to "read" mental states, understand the thoughts, beliefs, feelings, desires, and intentions of others, and to engage socially with them has also been discussed in terms of sociocognitive complexity (Zunshine, "Sociocognitive"), nested mental states (Zunshine, "Approaching"), deep intersubjectivity (Butte), and intermental thought (Palmer), among others. For further discussion of the notion of Theory of Mind in relation to literature, see Leverage et al., Introduction; Mancing, "James." In relation to Spanish literature, see Barroso Castro; Jaén; Mancing, "Celestina;" Mancing, "The Mind;" Mancing, "Sancho;" Reed; Simon, "Celestina;" Simon, "Contextualizing."

8   See *The Art of* La Celestina.

misses Celestina and hands out the money for the yarn. From this point forward, in the ensuing conversation, Celestina's mastery in reading Melibea's intentions and adapting to her mental states will be evident.

Upon Melibea's polite dismissal, Celestina admits that she had come to speak to her on behalf of a 'Christian in pain.' The thought of a person in pain, furthermore a Christian, could have only been meant to provoke in Melibea some sort of empathetic response. In all this conversation, to mentally prepare Melibea, Celestina mixes 1) the appeal to her compassion (via the Christian in pain rhetoric), 2) the use of praises and compliments by punctuating her discourse with emphatic expressions, such as: "¡O angélica ymagen!" ["O my angelic girl!"] (160; 65)], "¡O perla preciosa!" ["O precious pearl!"] (160; 65), or "¡Donzella graciosa y de alto linaje!" ["Gracious maiden, of such fine breeding!"] (161; 66),[9] and 3) the inclusion of a potpourri of recommendations and advice, such as "Assí, que donde no ay varón todo bien fallesce" ["Where there is no man, nothing goes well"] (161; 65). Melibea seems to be receptive to what Celestina tells her and Celestina then indicates that she only needs a word from her to cure him (the 'Christian in pain').[10] Melibea is ambivalent however. She does not know what to think. On one hand, her Christian upbringing naturally leads her to want to help the mysterious Christian in pain, but she needs to maintain the necessary appearance of an honest young lady. Plus, the insidious allusions, like the one mentioned above, make her feel uneasy and are leading her to think that Celestina is hiding something. Melibea can no longer wait to know who is this person in need and presses Celestina to reveal his name. When she does, Melibea's response seems unequivocal. She appears to be deeply offended:

> ¡Ya, ya, ya! Buena vieja, no me digas más, no pases adelante. ¿Ésse es el doliente por quien as fecho tantas premissas en tu demanda, por quien has venido a buscar la muerte para ti, por quien has dado tan dañosos passos, desvergonçada barvuda? (163)

---

9   All citations from *Celestina* are from the edition by Piñero and the translations are from Peden.

10 "... con sola una palabra de tu noble boca salida que le lleve metida en mi seno, tiene por fe que sanará, según la mucha devoción [que] tiene en tu gentileza" ["... with only one word from your noble lips, which I will carry to him buried deep in my bosom, he will be healed, owing to the deep devotion he feels for your kindness"] (161; 66).

Enough, enough! Good woman, say no more; go no further. This then is the sufferer for whom you have presented such a preamble in your plea, for whom you have come to seek for yourself, for whom you have taken such perilous steps, you shameless, bearded old crone? (67)

In the same speech, she adds: "Quemada seas alcahueta falsa, hechizera, enemiga de onestidad, causadora de secretos yerros! ¡Jesú, Jesú! ¡Quítamela, Lucrecia, de delante, que me fino, que no me ha dexado gota de sangre en el cuerpo!" ["May you burn at the stake, you deceitful procuress, you vile convent-trotter, you witch, you enemy of decency, you cause of secret sins! Jesú, Jesú! Lucrecia! Take her from my sight. I am through; she has left no drop of blood in my body!"] (163; 67), and it continues on.

Her anger clearly makes her come out of her shell. She let her emotions loose and each time she speaks it's a monologue. She is no longer that even-tempered young lady à la courtly love she was at the beginning. Suddenly, for no particular reason (Celestina did not prompt her to do it), Melibea decides to provide some background information regarding the circumstances of her encounter with Calisto and says, still enraged:

Éste es el que el otro día me vido y començó a desvariar comigo en razones, haziendo mucho el galán. Dirásle, buena vieja, que, si pensó que ya era todo suyo y quedaba por él el campo, porque holgué más de consentir sus necedades, que castigar su yerro, quise más dexarle por loco, que publicar su [grande] atrevimiento. (164)

This then is the man who saw me the other day and began to rant and rave and act the gallant. Tell him, my good woman, that if he thought everything already won and the field his, I listened because I thought it better to listen than to publicize his flaws; I wanted more to treat him as a madman than to spread word of his outrageous boldness. (68-69)

In this speech, she appears to be trying to justify herself, to justify what she did or did not do the day they met, although she didn't have to. It is perhaps this fact that puts a flea in Celestina's ear and leads her to regain confidence.[11] The longer Melibea talks, the more confident Celestina becomes, and the more she realizes that Melibea's reaction more likely meant that she is in-

---

11   In another aside, she says: "¡Más fuerte estaba Troya, y aun otra[s] más bravas he yo amansado! Ninguna tempestad mucho dura" ["Stronger was Troy, but I have tamed even wilder maidens. No storm lasts forever"] (164; 69).

terested in Calisto. The final turning point in this exchange is when, in the midst of Melibea's diatribes, Celestina requests:

> [u]na oración, señora, que le dixeron que sabías de sancta Polonia para el dolor de muelas; assí mismo tu cordón, que es fama que ha tocado [todas] las reliquias que ay en Roma y Jerusalem. Aquel cavallero que dixe pena y muere dellas. (165)

> a prayer, Daughter, one he was told you know. One prayed by Saint Apollonia for toothache. And also the girdle you wear clasped around your waist, for it is widely known that it has touched all the relics in Rome and Jerusalem. The caballero I told you of is suffering, longing for that blessing. (69)

Melibea is trapped, all along she assumed that the pain the Christian (i.e., Calisto) was feeling was a sentimental pain (that he was in love with her), hence her anger when Celestina mentioned his name earlier on, and Celestina just tricked her by claiming that Calisto is suffering from a toothache. Melibea's first response upon hearing about Calisto's alleged toothache is: "Si esso querías, ¿por qué no me lo espresaste? ¿Por qué me lo dixiste por tales palabras?" ["If it is the girdle you wanted, why did you not tell me that in a few words?"] (165; 70). With this ruse Celestina not only forces Melibea to shed her façade of honest young lady, but also to realize that she made a fool of herself. This consequently gives Celestina the upper hand and will lead Melibea to eventually surrender her girdle, to cure Calisto.

The success of Celestina's mission is complete. She managed to enter Melibea's house and to talk to her. Celestina's strategy at first did not work out but she read between the lines of Melibea's reaction and did in the end obtain what she wanted: that is, the girdle which represents the proof that she talked to Melibea and that Melibea is agreeing to not put a stop to his courtship. What stands out in this exchange is Celestina's capacity to read the intentions of her counterparts and to respond to them in a 'human-like' fashion. In this scene, which serves as a case study of her mindreading abilities, Rojas's mastery is patent. He not only creates a character but also, an individualized mind.

Bakhtin and the Rise of the Modern Discourse

The interest in the human being, in the individual, is at the core of the birth of the Renaissance era and infiltrates the mentality of the Renaissance people. The human organism becomes the center of attention for scholars and scientists in search of medical and philosophical explanations. This interest is apparent in the development of the artistic and scientific endeavors of the epoch and also surfaces in literature, gradually making its way into Renaissance literary manifestations. As we saw earlier, characters begin to cut the strings that attach them to the narrator; they start walking on their own and their voice, not yet fully developed, becomes more independent and authentic. They are no longer worthless pawns pushed around and at the mercy of the omniscient author. Their vicissitudes at times constitute the fabric of the narrative, thereby shifting away from the idealism that formerly prevailed. The realistic discourse of witches, thugs, and pages entrenches the dialogues and serves as a counterpoint to the highly stylized language of courtly lovers, pastoral poets, or chivalric heroes.

This process of individualization of fictional characters' discourse, this questioning of prevailing aesthetic and ideological values, this rapprochement with the real or 'natural' world has perhaps been best illustrated by Bakhtin in his essay "Discourse in the Novel." In said work, he argues for the distinction, though not clear-cut,[12] of two lines in the development of the novel:

> In the further history of the European novel we will continue to notice the same two fundamental lines of development. The Second Line, to which belong the greatest representatives of the novel as a genre (its greatest subgenres as well as the greatest individual examples), incorporates heteroglossia[13] into a novel's composition, exploiting it to orchestrate its own meaning and frequently resisting altogether any unmediated and pure authorial discourse. The First Line, which most strongly exhibits the influence of the Sophistic novel, leaves heteroglossia outside

---

12   "It is very difficult to speak of a clear-cut genetic distinction between the two lines, especially in the early stages of their development" (Bakhtin 400).

13   Heteroglossia is a key concept in Bakhtin's theory of the novel. According to the editor of *The Dialogic Imagination*, it is defined as follows: "The base condition governing the operation of meaning in any utterance. It is that which insures the primacy of context over text. At any given time, in any given place, there will be a set of conditions—social, historical, meteorological, physiological—that will insure that a word uttered in that place and at that time will have a meaning different than it would have under any other conditions; all utterances are heteroglot in that they are functions of a matrix of forces practically impossible to recoup, and therefore impossible to resolve. Heteroglossia is as close a conceptualization as is possible of that locus where centripetal and centrifugal forces collide; as such, it is that which a systematic linguistics must always suppress" (Holquist 428).

itself, that is, outside the language of the novel; such language is stylized in a special way, a novelized way. (375)

Later, Bakhtin further differentiates these two lines by adding that:

Novels of the First Stylistic Line approach heteroglossia from above, it is as if they descend onto it (the Sentimental novel occupies a special position here, somewhere between heteroglossia and the high genres). Novels of the Second Line, on the contrary, approach heteroglossia from below: out of heteroglot depths they rise to the highest spheres of literary language and overwhelm them. (400)

For Bakhtin the greatest exemplar of this Second Line is *Don Quixote*. In this novel, as well as those that paved the way for Cervantes's masterpiece to come about, the language is authentic, free from the heavy pathos and all moribund and false accents. Down the genealogical tree of the Second Line could be found the picaresque novel, which for Bakhtin prepares the ground for the 'orchestration,' the culmination of the discursive innovations comprising the novel (Bakhtin 408-09). Bakhtin traces the abovementioned two lines of development as evolving along two planes: one "socio-linguistic" linked to the concept of heteroglossia and one "ideological" in which the author 'displaces' the belief-system and artistic conventions of the epoch.

Indeed, one of the elements of heteroglossia is the stratification of the 'languages' of the novel. A language for Bakhtin is not the tongue spoken within the border of a country—which would be a 'national language' in his theory—but rather a variant of that language which can only be 'uttered' in a specific place, at a particular time and within a given social group (age, professional, etc.). It means that the characters' speech will represent the age/social group they belong to, the professional milieu in which they evolve as well as the time period and historical context during which the story is being told. Heteroglossia along with the plurality of voices rendered in the work (polyglossia), the play with the artistic expression, or the stylistic (accentuation),[14]

---

14 Holquist's definition of the terms and concept 'Accentuation, Accentuating system, and Reaccentuation' is: "An accent, stress or emphasis. Every language or discourse system accents—highlights and evaluates—its material in its own way, and this changes through time. The parallel with a language's stress system is not accidental, but it might be noted that as a rule Russian words have only one stress per word, and this is highly marked, so changes in stress can substantially alter the sound of a word in context" (423).

the creation of a 'character zone'[15] all constitute coordinates of the socio-linguistic plane of Bakhtin's theory.

As for the ideological plane, its coordinates are parody and grotesque realism. For Bakhtin these concepts both participate in the displacement of the sociological and artistic conventions as well as of the 'ideology,'[16] or belief system, of the time and place in which a work is written. *Don Quixote* is a perfect example (cited in Bakhtin's essay) of how the parodying plume of the author can revisit or 'decenter' the conventions of a genre, the Chivalric Romance, and of fictional writing.

Fernando de Rojas, when composing *Celestina*, certainly was inspired by the Sentimental Novel, the literature of courtly love (a very popular genre at the turn of the XV century), and used it as a model. His rendering, however, would become a 'decentered' sentimental novel.[17] In *Celestina*, the idealistic world of the *amor cortés* between Calisto and Melibea is put in direct opposition to the realistic (under)world of the Madam (Celestina), her protégés (Areúsa and Elicia), and Calisto's servants (Sempronio and Pármeno), among others. Dorothy Severin and María Eugenia Lacarra have both shown how Rojas parodied the sentimental novel and in particular San Pedro's *Cárcel de amor* [Prison of Love]. Additionally, the (excessive) use of classical references (an essential attribute of the original genre) produces a subtle comic effect and leaves the audience wondering what the real intentions of the author were, especially when this highly stylistic and educated discourse is placed in the mouth of lay characters. This realistic facet of *Celestina*'s discourse struck a new path that would pave the way for the picaresque world of *Lazarillo de Tormes* half a century later.[18]

In sum, my argument here is that besides the two planes outlined above, there is another one, a psychological plane, whose coordinates are the development of a literary consciousness of characters, of their ability to understand and manipulate the minds of their literary counterparts. The passage

---

15   "Zones are both a territory and a sphere of influence. Intentions must pass through 'zones' dominated by other characters, and are therefore refracted. A character's zone need not begin with his directly quoted speech but can begin far back in the text" (Holquist 434).

16   "This is not to be confused with its politically oriented English cognate. 'Ideology' in Russian is simply an idea-system" (Holquist 429).

17   The closest predecessor to *Celestina* is Diego de San Pedro's sentimental novel *Cárcel de amor* [Prison of Love], which was published in 1492.

18   *Lazarillo de Tormes* is a work highlighted in Bakhtin's essay that belongs in his opinion to the second line of development of the novel.

analyzed earlier illustrates Celestina's ability to create a cognitive model of Melibea's psychology, to adapt to her responses and to manipulate her mind, all of this in a very human-like fashion which modern readers can appreciate and perceive as natural.

Theory of Mind is an intrinsically human ability that was noticed by psychologists and cognitive scientists about thirty years ago and is part of our development both as individuals and as a species. Likewise, the psychologization of literary characters is a feature of the literary discourse that we, modern readers, take for granted and that has developed over time. In the Spanish tradition (and in the Western tradition), *Celestina* constitutes a steppingstone in the evolution of this psychologization process, which soon begins to transpire in the literary works of Rojas's time and which will become an important piece in the puzzle of the rise of the early modern discourse; a piece that both Bakhtin's essay and Theory of Mind can help us interpret in the context of early modern expressions of mind development.

Looking at early literary texts with a synchronic perspective, Theory of Mind can also reveal the intricacies of the interplay of the characters' psychologies, an aspect which has not been fully analyzed previously; it can be the magnifying lens of this analysis of the mindreading abilities of fictional characters. Looking at the literature from a diachronic perspective, these two theories (i.e., Bakhtin's and Theory of Mind) complement each other in that they help shed light on the inner workings and the evolution of the discursive phenomenon as related to human psychology.

Bakhtin recognized the importance of *Lazarillo de Tormes* and *Don Quixote* in the development of the novelistic discourse. This essay argues for the inclusion of *Celestina* in the Bakhtinian genesis of the novel and, on the other hand, for the acknowledgement that the literary consciousness of characters, as evident in the dialogues' density of intentionality, constitute a 'psychological' plane along which modern discourse evolved and which complements Bakhtin's two other planes identified in his essay "Discourse in the Novel:" the 'sociological' and the 'ideological' planes.

Works Cited

Bakhtin, Mikhail. *The Dialogic Imagination: Four Essays by M. M. Bakhtin*. Ed. Michael Holquist. Trans. Caryl Emerson and Michael Holquist. Austin: U of Texas P, 1996. Print.

Barroso Castro, José. "Theory of Mind and the Conscience of *El casamiento engañoso*." *Theory of Mind and Literature*. Ed. Paula Leverage, Howard Mancing, Richard Schweickert, and Jennifer Marston William. West Lafayette: Purdue UP, 2011. 289-303. Print.

Bataillon, Marcel. La Célestine *selon Fernando de Rojas*. Paris: Marcel Didier, 1961. Print.

Botta, Patrizia. "La Celestina / Patrizia Botta." Alicante: Biblioteca Virtual Miguel de Cervantes, 2005. Web. 14 Nov. 2016.

Butte, George. *I Know that You Know that I Know: Narrating Subjects from Moll Flanders to Marnie*. Columbus: Ohio State UP, 2004. Print.

Byrne, Richard W., and Andrew Whiten, ed. *Machiavellian Intelligence: Social Expertise and the Evolution of Intellect in Monkeys, Apes, and Humans*. Oxford: Clarendon P, 1988. Print.

Castells, Ricardo. "Bakhtin's Grotesque Realism and the Thematic Unity of *Celestina*, Act I." *Hispanófila* 106 (1992): 9-20. Print.

Castro, Américo. La Celestina *como contienda literaria (castas y casticismos)*. Madrid: Revista de Oriente, 1965. Print.

Fothergill-Payne, Louise. "*Celestina* 'As a Funny Book': A Bakhtinian Reading." *Celestinesca* 17.2 (1993): 29-51. Print.

Gilman, Stephen. *The Art of* La Celestina. Madison: U of Wisconsin P, 1956. Print.

Green, Otis H. "Amor cortés y moral cristiana en la trama de *La Celestina*." *Edad Media*. Ed. Alan Deyermond. Barcelona: Editorial Crítica, 1980. 504-08. Print. Vol. 1 of *Historia y crítica de la literatura española*. Francisco Rico, gen. ed. 9 vols.

Herman, David, ed. *The Emergence of Mind: Representations of Consciousness in Narrative Discourse in English*. Lincoln: U of Nebraska P, 2011. Print.

Holquist, Michael, ed. *The Dialogic Imagination: Four Essays by M. M. Bakhtin*. By Mikhail Bakhtin. Trans. Caryl Emerson and Michael Holquist. Austin: U of Texas P, 1996. Print.

Humphrey, Nicholas K. "The Social Function of Intellect." *Growing Points in Ethology*. Ed. Patrick P. G. Bateson and Robert A. Hinde. Cambridge: Cambridge UP, 1976. 303-17. Print.

Jaén (Jaén-Portillo), Isabel. "Literary Consciousness: Fictional Minds, *Real* Implications." *Selected Papers from the 22nd International Literature and Psychology Conference*, June 29-July 4, 2005. Ed. Norman Holland. IPSA. Web. 1 July 2016.

Lacarra, María Eugenia. "La parodia de la ficción sentimental en la *Celestina*." *Celestinesca* 13.1 (1989): 11-29. Print.

Leverage, Paula, Howard Mancing, Richard Schweickert, and Jennifer Marston William. Introduction. *Theory of Mind and Literature*. Ed. Paula Leverage, Howard Mancing, Richard Schweickert, and Jennifer Marston William. West Lafayette: Purdue UP, 2011. 1-11. Print.

Mancing, Howard. "*La Celestina*: A Novel." *Celestinesca* 38 (2014): 63-84. Print.

———. "James Parr's Theory of Mind." *Critical Reflections on Golden Age Spanish Literature in Honor of James A. Parr*. Ed. Barbara Simerka and Amy R. Williamsen. Lewisburg: Bucknell UP, 2006. 125-43. Print.

———. "The Mind of a Pícaro: Lázaro de Tormes." *Cognition, Literature, and History*. Ed. Mark J. Bruhn and Donald R. Wehrs. New York: Routledge, 2014. 174-89. Print.

———. "Sancho Panza's Theory of Mind." *Theory of Mind and Literature*. Ed. Paula Leverage, Howard Mancing, Richard Schweickert, and Jennifer Marston William. West Lafayette: Purdue UP, 2011. 123-32. Print.

Maravall, José Antonio. *El mundo social de* La Celestina. Madrid: Editorial Gredos, 1964. Print.

Palmer, Alan. *Fictional Minds*. Lincoln: U of Nebraska P, 2004. Print.

Premack, David, and Guy Woodruff. "Does the Chimpanzee Have a Theory of Mind?" *Behavioral and Brain Sciences* 1.4 (1978): 515-26. Print.

Reed, Cory. "'¿Qué rumor es ése?': Embodied Agency and Representational Hunger in *Don Quijote* I.20." *Cognitive Cervantes*. Ed. Julien Simon, Barbara Simerka, and Howard Mancing. Spec. cluster of essays *of Cervantes: Bulletin of the Cervantes Society of America* 32.1 (2012): 99-124. Print.

Rojas, Fernando de. *Celestina*. Ed. Pedro M. Piñero. Madrid: Espasa Calpe, 2007. Print.

———. *Celestina*. Trans. Margaret Sayers Peden. Ed. and intro. Roberto González Echevarría. New Haven: Yale UP, 2009. Print.

Severin, Dorothy (Sherman). "La parodia del amor cortés en *La Celestina*." *Edad de oro* 3 (1984): 275-80. Print.

———. *Tragicomedy and Novelistic Discourse in* Celestina. Cambridge: Cambridge UP, 1989. Print.

Simon, Julien J. "Celestina, Heteroglossia, and Theory of Mind: The Rise of the Early-Modern Discourse." *Proceedings of the 2008 International Conference in Literature and Psychology*. Lisbon: Instituto Superior de Psicologia Aplicada, 2009. 119-26. Print.

———. "Contextualizing Cognitive Approaches to Early Modern Spanish Literature." *Cognitive Approaches to Early Modern Spanish Literature*.

Ed. Isabel Jaén and Julien J. Simon. New York: Oxford UP, 2016. 13-33. Print.

Snow, Joseph T. "Celestina (1499-1999) Medieval and Modern: Survival & Renewal of a Spanish Classic." *Medieval Perspectives* 15 (2000): 1-11. Print.

Snow, Joseph T., and Ivy A. Corfis. Introduction. "*Celestina* and Celestinas: Nearing the Fifth Centenary." *Fernando de Rojas and* Celestina: *Approaching the Fifth Centenary*. Ed. Ivy A. Corfis and Joseph T. Snow. Madison: The Hispanic Seminary of Medieval Studies, 1993. xi-xx. Print.

Zunshine, Lisa. "Approaching Cao Xueqin's *The Story of the Stone* (Honglou meng) from a Cognitive Perspective." *The Oxford Handbook of Cognitive Literary Studies*. Ed. Lisa Zunshine. Oxford: Oxford UP, 2015. 176-96. Print.

Zunshine, Lisa. "Sociocognitive Complexity." *NOVEL: A Forum on Fiction* 45.1 (2012): 13-18. Print.

Cervantes's *El casamiento engañoso* and the Failure of Theory of Mind: The Machiavellian Abilities of Campuzano and Estefanía

Steven Wagschal
Indiana University, Bloomington

In a seminal essay on Theory of Mind and early modern literature, "Sancho Panza's Theory of Mind" (2011), Howard Mancing examines cases of Sancho tricking Don Quixote based on the squire's knowledge of how Don Quixote's mind works, that is, through mindreading. One of Mancing's conclusions is that Sancho is "the greatest mind reader of a world full of expert mind readers [and] should be considered one of the best examples ever of a Theory of Mind at work" (126). In this essay, inspired by Mancing's, I compare two other Cervantine characters who battle against each other with Theory of Mind and ultimately both lose, in what amounts to what I claim is a more complicated dynamic of recursive states than Sancho's.

Throughout *El casamiento engañoso* [The Deceitful Marriage], multiple characters as well as the reader are subjected to various levels of deceit. For every mindreader who engages in successful trickery, there is at least one other character who is duped, exemplifying clearly that the misreading of other people's minds is an important part of mindreading. An analysis of the cases of Campuzano and Estefanía demonstrate that their abilities at mind-reading, while not entirely successful, are even more complex examples of Theory of Mind at work. Their failure to make accurate predictions about others in all cases is not a deficit of Theory of Mind but instead shows more subtly how human minds interact than would a case of pure mind-reading success. Also, as Lisa Zunshine has pointed out, failures in mindreading are a great part of the fabric of literature as "plots often depend on those failures" (134). I elucidate what precisely is going on in the characters' minds at key moments as informed by cognitive studies, comparing and evaluating the efficacy of two theoretical models, Theory-Theory and Simulation Theory, making a case for how literary examples can provide insights into such efficacy.

Theory of Mind (also known as Mindreading) refers to the cognitive capacity of attributing mental states such as believing, desiring, knowing and intending, to oneself and to others (Goldman 403). It is useful in describing the functioning of second- and higher-order beliefs about other mental states (also known as recursive sequences of intentionality). Cognitive scientist Celia Heyes explains in less technical terms:

> I assume that individuals have a theory of mind if they have mental state concepts such as "believe," "know," "want," and "see," and that individuals with such concepts use them to predict and explain behavior. Thus, an animal with a theory of mind believes that mental states play a causal role in generating behavior and infers the presence of mental states in others by observing their appearance and behavior under various circumstances. (101-2)

Theory of Mind was discussed scientifically only beginning in the 1970s, when psychologists working with people with autism noted that they had limited ability to hold second- and higher-order beliefs about others' mental states. Literary authors, of course, had brought to light this mental capacity hundreds or even thousands of years before that.[1]

As a branch of modern science, cognitive science must attempt to explain not only what Theory of Mind is and how it works, but also how this mental capacity is realized in the brain and ultimately how this biological function can be accounted for in evolutionary terms.[2] These investigations have led to competing hypotheses. Philosopher Alvin Goldman reviews various explanations of the capacity which he qualifies as "awash with competing theories and rival bodies of evidence" (420) noting that Theory-Theory and Simulation Theory are the two main explanations, either in isolation or conjoined. In her recent book on early modern Spanish literature analyzed from a cognitive perspective, Barbara Simerka has reviewed both of these

---

1   *Engaño* always relies on second- or higher-order beliefs and is a staple of literature from the earliest times, for instance, in Odysseus's famous blinding trick, which relies, in Homer's epic, on the Greek warrior's knowing in advance how the other cyclops will interpret Polyphemus's cries to them for help.

2   For more on the basic principles of cognitive science, written for scholars in the humanities, see Hogan 29-58.

explanations.[3] According to Theory-Theory, children and then adults act like little scientists positing theories about predictable patterns of behavior, based on certain cues and situations, in which the other's mental states become an abstract theoretical postulate (Simerka 7). The competing Simulation Theory (sometimes called "Empathy Theory") involves predicting behavior *not* based on an abstract postulate, but on answering the question to oneself, "What would I do if I were in that person's shoes?" (Simerka 7).[4] Based on research of Stephen Stich and Shaun Nichols, Simerka has argued that a combinatory approach to these two mechanisms is a salutary one, because there is no reason to believe that the brain would use only one "parsimonious" or unitary mechanism. As Stich and Nichols write, "mindreading depends on a motley array of mechanisms" (212), that is, it probably does not depend on just one solitary function of the brain. I very much agree with this combinatory approach, and yet, as a literary researcher, I find it of interest to point out the specific problems associated with characters potentially using one or the other mechanism (as I will elaborate further along).

For the sake of this discussion, one last cognitive mechanism—dubbed "Machiavellian Intelligence" by cognitive scientists—should be of particular interest to early modern literary scholars because of the period's obsession with literary *engaño* [deceit]. First described by R. W. Byrne and Andrew Whiten in the late 1980s, the mechanism of Machiavellian Intelligence is, in Simerka's words, conceived of as an "advanced cognitive system for understanding rivals' mental processes in order to better deceive another for material and/or social advantage" (11).[5] As a mechanism that relies on Theory of Mind, Machiavellian Intelligence may rely on Theory-Theory or Simulation Theory, or on a combination of the two. Since it deals with how people go about deceiving others, it is particularly apt for vast swaths of early modern

---

   3   Other important scholarly studies engaging Theory of Mind and the Hispanic literary tradition include Barroso Castro; Jaén; Reed; Simon, "Celestina;" Simon, "Contextualizing." José Barroso Castro treats this same novella by Cervantes and what he calls "Scholastic Theory of Mind" (294) analyzing the faculties of Campuzano's "soul" in a historicized manner.

   4   In the case of the authors and literature that concern us here, we might ask, what if I were in that person's *calzado*?

   5   In dubbing the term, Byrne and Whiten have clearly relied on a convenient and popular, that is, non-scholarly and unproblematized understanding of what Machiavellian thinking is, from the 1980s. This should not detract from their discovery since they make no historical argument about the cognitive mechanism nor its specific relationship to the Italian political philosopher.

Spanish literature, replete as it is with cases of *engaño* and *desengaño* [disillusionment], as Simerka has rightly noted.

Returning to Mancing's "Sancho Panza's Theory of Mind" (2011), the analysis centers on how the squire uses Machiavellian Intelligence to convince Don Quixote that Dulcinea is indeed enchanted, based on his deep knowledge of how Don Quixote thinks and how he would likely react. That is, Sancho makes predictions about Don Quixote's beliefs and behavior based on higher-order recursive mental states.[6] Mancing analyzes Sancho's six recursive levels of Theory of Mind in the following manner: "Sancho knows [1] that Don Quixote believes [2] that evil enchanters want [3] to foil his desire [4] to gain fame as a knight errant; therefore, he (Sancho) is sure [5] that he can make Don Quixote believe [6] that a peasant woman is Dulcinea" (126). While Mancing does not say so explicitly, his analysis of Sancho's Machiavellian Intelligence shows that the mechanism which the squire uses is more in line with the isolated theorizing of Theory-Theory rather than Simulation Theory or a combination of the two. Indeed, Sancho does not place himself in the master's shoes. Instead of relying on empathic understanding, he uses reasoning about his master's higher-order beliefs, constructing a theoretical model for tricking him.

In the same essay, Mancing also analyzes the grape-eating episode of Tratado 1 of *Lazarillo de Tormes* (1554) where the blind man uses Machiavellian Intelligence to outwit the young *pícaro*. In contrast to Sancho's reasonings, and while Mancing does not explicitly make this distinction in the essay, it would seem that Simulation Theory (rather than Theory-Theory) is the specific mechanism at play here, helping the blind man correctly divine exactly the kind of trickery that Lazarillo is engaged in, putting himself in the boy's shoes (only figuratively speaking, since Lazarillo will not own his first pair of

---

6   Mancing also rebuts the claim of English Professor George Butte who asserts that, only in the nineteenth century, Jane Austen developed what Butte calls "deep intersubjectivity" and what Mancing and fellow cognitive scholar Zunshine liken to "Theory of Mind." Mancing bases his critique in part on claims by evolutionary biologists that changes in human evolution would dictate that any trait that our species currently expresses widely would be at least 50,000 years old, making it somewhat ludicrous to imagine that Austen deployed it first. Clearly, as Mancing demonstrates with examples from the Renaissance onward, Spanish writers were already depicting Theory of Mind in complex ways; for Mancing, these texts are prototypical of the modern novel in large respect because the characters demonstrate a level of psychological complexity unprecedented in prior narrative, and certainly before Austen, and specifically of the kind that is privileged in definitions of the modern.

shoes until Tratado 4). As the blind man explains—making explicit his own understanding of his own and of Lazarillo's higher-order mental states—he has been eating two grapes instead of one, even after they had both agreed to eat the grapes one by one. Since the *ciego* [blind man] knows that he himself is eating two grapes and he knows that Lazarillo can *see* this fact and yet does not complain, the *ciego* correctly predicts that Lazarillo must be doing something even worse. After all, that is what he would do, if he were Lazarillo!

It is interesting that the blind man is able to *see* how his own mind works and, from this knowledge, to extrapolate empathically to Lazarillo's, in a way that is in line with how cognitive scientists view Theory of Mind. According to Goldman, the transparency of one's own thoughts to oneself are often taken for granted by lay people. But most cognitive theorists, including Goldman, believe that individuals need to apply Theory of Mind to their own minds to tease out their second-order or higher-order beliefs, and, indeed, that is, in effect, the kind of thought process involving simulation in which our blind man engages. Being socialized by the *ciego*, Lazarillo develops Theory of Mind as a child would, learning from the old trickster. By the end of Tratado 1, in fact, Lazarillo has developed his own astuteness and in an episode that generates significant literary irony, he switches places with the *ciego*, utilizing a similar psychic mechanism to dupe his master.

Putting himself in the blind man's shoes, so to speak, Lazarillo imagines what a blind man would want to know about the environment that he cannot see, while also knowing that he would want to think that Lazarillo is looking out for him. Knowing all of this, in the heavy rains, Lazarillo can be certain that the blind man would not want to get his shoes soaked, so Lazarillo instructs him to jump over what he claims, deceitfully, is the narrowest part of the water flow through the inundated streets:

"Tío, el arroyo va muy ancho; mas si queréis, yo veo por donde travesemos más aína sin nos mojar, porque se estrecha allí mucho, y saltando pasaremos a pie enjuto."
Parecióle buen consejo, y dijo:
"Discreto eres, por eso te quiero bien. Llévame a ese lugar donde el arroyo se ensangosta, que agora es invierno y sabe mal el agua, y más llevar los pies mojados." (1:17)

I told him, "Uncle, the stream is very wide. But if you'd like, I see where we can cross it faster without getting wet, because it gets pretty narrow right there, and if we jump over it we'll keep our feet dry."

This sounded like good advice to him, and he said, "You're sharp, that's why I like you so much. Take me there where the stream narrows down, because it's winter, and getting soaked stinks, and having wet feet is worse." (14)

This plot development leads of course to the violent and abrupt end of Lazarillo's relationship to his first master who smashes his head when he jumps into the stone pillar that was right in front of him. The *ciego* taught Lazarillo his methods, by cruel example, but ultimately was not ready for Lazarillo to become an adversary; in part, the blind man succumbs to the trick because he didn't have a sufficiently dynamic model of his charge, whom he continued to view as an innocent.

These examples of Machiavellian Intelligence from *Don Quijote* and from *Lazarillo de Tormes*, seem to rely on different Theory of Mind mechanisms. In the case of Sancho, Theory-Theory serves well as an explanation of how he tricks Don Quixote. But Simulation Theory seems to describe better what occurs in *Lazarillo de Tormes*, indeed, it proves to be a highly effective strategy for whichever character is trying to achieve his goals, both in the grape eating episode (the *ciego*) and in the case of the stone pillar trick (Lazarillo). It is important to note that success with this mechanism relies on a solid knowledge of what the other person's mind is actually like, and not understanding it well (for instance, the *ciego* not appreciating that Lazarillo has internalized that which he has been taught explicitly and implicitly by the *ciego*) has devastating effects.

An analysis of *El casamiento engañoso* vis-à-vis these two Theory of Mind mechanisms thematizes additional nuances than those that were seen in the analysis of the other narratives, with respect to complexity and success of Theory of Mind. The most salient difference of this novella's embodiment of Theory of Mind is that, while both Campuzano and Estefanía seem very adept at tricking others, they are not all that good at avoiding getting tricked. Indeed, these two Cervantine characters battle it out against each other with Theory of Mind and ultimately both lose, in what amounts, as I will demonstrate, to a less successful but more complicated level of recursive states than the blind man's or even Sancho's.[7] While excellent at deceiving with Machiavellian Intelligence, both Campuzano and Estefanía fail to detect that Machiavellian Intelligence is being used against them.

---

7   Robin Dunbar notes philosopher Daniel Dennett's claim that five or six orders of intentional propositions is about the maximum, for which Dunbar offers some empirical data (238-39).

Examining the episode of Sancho's duping of Don Quixote in a broader context of examples that includes *El casamiento engañoso*, it is clear that Sancho succeeds with Theory-Theory in part because he does not have to contend with an opponent who is equal or better than him at Machiavellian Intelligence; an illustration of Sancho's ability to successfully manipulate Don Quixote for his own ends can be found in chapter 10 of *Don Quijote*, Part II. However, in the case of *El casamiento engañoso*, the two protagonists use Machiavellian Intelligence on each other simultaneously, both facing a worthy opponent, with Theory-Theory and/or Simulation Theory. Miguel de Cervantes here thematizes the potential failure of Theory of Mind in an interesting way. While one might assume that the protagonists of the main plot of *El casamiento engañoso* would be better at anticipating trickery by another person—i.e., as was the blind man with Lazarillo's grape-eating—neither Estefanía nor Campuzano seem well equipped in this regard. Does their reliance on either Theory-Theory or Simulation Theory play a significant role in their success at trickery and their failure at not being tricked? Could it be that there are simply too many recursive levels to deal with when one is being simultaneously tricked? What other considerations are there to their mixed success and failure?

Early on in the novella, both Campuzano's intradiegetic listener, Peralta, as well as the notional reader, remain unaware of Campuzano's manipulation since he hides much of his deception from us and it is only revealed to us toward the end of the novella. In his first conversation with the woman whom we later learn is named Estefanía, she remains partially-veiled. The veil is a metonymy of how she discloses some clues about herself but not others, in her deliberate manipulation of him:

> [S]e sentó en una silla junto a mí, derribado el manto hasta la barba, sin dejar ver el rostro más de aquello que concedía la raridad del manto; y, aunque le supliqué que por cortesía me hiciese merced de descubrirse, no fue posible acabarlo con ella, cosa que me encendió más el deseo de verla. Y, para acrecentarle más, o ya fuese de industria [o] acaso, sacó la señora una muy blanca mano con muy buenas sortijas. (283)

The other sat down in a chair next to mine. Her veil had been lowered down to the level of her chin, leaving nothing of her face visible except what one could make out through the thinness of her veil. Though I begged her to do me the favor, out of courtesy, of uncovering her face, I could not prevail upon her to do so—a refusal that inflamed even more my desire to see what she looked like. And, as if to heighten my curiosity even more, the lady—whether by design or by accident—allowed me to see her hand, which was exceedingly white and sported expensive-looking rings. (435)[8]

Clearly, Estefanía has figured out what to do to increase a man's interest in her. Instead of revealing her face entirely, she has hidden her somewhat average looks behind a gauzy mantle that partially obscures her features, while displaying all of her white hands. Counterfactually, it seems that Campuzano would have desired her less were parts of her not so mysterious, as he explains that he felt "muerto por el rostro que deseaba ver" ["dying to see the lady's face"] (284; 435).[9] In case such physical attraction is not enough, she also knows that by wearing "muy buenas sortijas" ["expensive-looking rings"] (283; 435) she can make him think that she has significant wealth, thereby also appealing to a suitor's potential greed; these "buenas sortijas" are in fact fakes or borrowed because Estefanía is penniless. Campuzano is aware of his own mind's processes and discloses these to the reader, stating retrospectively that "me encendió más el deseo" ["inflamed even more my desire"] (283; 435). She knows that she can get him to act and tells him to have a page follow her to learn where she lives so that Campuzano can later visit her. She knows that he will do this to attempt to fulfill his desires, desires which she correctly reads.

Simultaneously, Campuzano holds higher-order beliefs about himself and about the effect that his own appearance has on women. Like Estefanía, he is consciously manipulating his good appearance. He is purposefully displaying (false) evidence of wealth in order to make people believe he is both attractive and wealthy:

> Estaba yo entonces bizarrísimo, con aquella gran cadena que vuesa merced debió de conocerme, el sombrero con plumas y cintillo, el vestido de colores, a fuer de soldado, y tan gallardo a los ojos de mi locura, que me daba a entender que las podía matar en el aire. (283-84)

---

8 All citations from *El casamiento engañoso* are from the edition by Harry Sieber and the translations from Michael Harney's edition and translation.

9 According to Laura Bass and Amanda Wunder, "a fine, almost transparent mantle could be draped over the face without impairing a woman's vision (and leaving her hands free)," noting specifically that Jorge García López glosses the word "raridad" in Cervantes's novella to indicate that the mantle was very sheer (108).

> In those days I cut a very dashing figure, with that long chain that your honor must surely remember me for, as well as that hat I used to wear, with its feathers and its hatband, and the many-colored suit of clothes—in short, every inch a soldier, and such a fashionable one, according to my own crazy perception of myself, that it seemed to me that I was a real lady-killer, able to shoot them down like birds in flight. (435)

Clearly, he believes that others will find him attractive and also wealthy enough to show off an ostentatious gold chain, attributes that he believes will make women desire him. He also makes a verbal promise to Estefanía, in particular, that he would give her "montes de oro" ["mountains of gold"] (284; 435), a promise that he knew that he could not fulfill, but which he knew that he appeared capable of making with his huge (counterfeit) gold chain.[10] Later, he shows Estefanía other apparently valuable objects, which he calls "otras joyuelas que tenía en casa" ["other jewels I had at home"] (286; 437) which are, unbeknownst to her, also counterfeit.

The counterfeit jewelry serves in the story as a counterbalance to the fake dowry that she claims to have. All told, Campuzano claims to have approximately 2,000 *ducados* [ducats], when his actual net worth is at best one fifth of that. Likewise, her dowry—she claimed—was worth approximately 2,500 *ducados*. As recompense for the time-investment conning the other, Estefanía ultimately absconds with practically everything that Campuzano owns. While he did not get to keep any part of her illusory dowry, he did get six of the best days of his life, benefiting from the use of the comfortable home, tasty cooking and plentiful sex, while she was catering to his every need and desire.

As the progression and dénouement of the novella show us, neither of the protagonists figure out—before it is too late—that the other is tricking her or him. In other words, while they are conscious of their own deceptive

---

10   Peralta confirms that many people are tricked by Campuzano's appearance of wealth: "Eso no es posible ... porque la que el señor Alférez traía al cuello mostraba pesar más de do[s]cientos ducados" (291). The Licenciado displaces the intentionality onto the chain itself, it "mostraba pesar" (291) which would be literally translated as "showed itself to weigh" although this literal quality is not kept in Harney's translation which is more idiomatic: "That's not possible ... because the chain your honor was wearing around his neck looked like it was worth more than two hundred ducats" (441). Of course, the intention to deceive is that of the person who is wearing the counterfeit object. Campuzano's displacement of agency is a subtle symptom here of his low morality.

cognitive processes, they are unwittingly duped because of an inattentiveness to the deceptive cognitive processes of another, despite the remarkable similarity between those processes and the workings of their own minds, and the fact that they trick each other in remarkably similar ways, namely with deceptive appearances. I would suggest that they are not sufficiently putting themselves in the others' shoes, but rather, are working more theoretically, with Theory-Theory.

The novella offers us the opportunity to compare the two protagonists' apparent lack of cognitive attentiveness to each other's Machiavellian Intelligence to the Theory of Mind of a minor character, *el capitán* Pedro de Herrera. The Captain appears only in one scene and might be thought of as Campuzano's wing man. About the Captain's thought processes, the reader has little information to go on, yet he provides a useful and much needed Theory of Mind mechanism, one that foresees *engaño*, as Campuzano and Estefanía do not. In his narration to Peralta, Campuzano relates what the Captain told him about his conversation with Estefanía's friend, which reveals his ability to foresee the friend's *engaño*: "Díjome el capitán que lo que la dama le quería era que le llevase unas cartas a Flandes a otro Capitán, *que decía ser su primo, aunque él sabía que no era sino su galán*" ["The captain told me that the lady he had been talking to wanted him to carry certain letters of hers to another captain who was in Flanders, *a man she said was a cousin of hers, although my friend knew that the man in question was in fact none other than her lover*"] (284; 435; emphasis added). The reader does not know what the Captain does with this knowledge of the woman's intentions, nor how he figured out that she was lying to him. We can only speculate about what alerted the Captain to her deception. However, the result is that he is essentially using what I will call Reverse Machiavellian Intelligence (RMI). Adapting Simerka's definition of Machiavellian Intelligence (MI), I define RMI as an "advanced cognitive system for understanding rivals' mental processes in order to better *avoid being deceived* and maintaining one's material goods and/or social advantages."

It is interesting to observe that a lying trickster such as Campuzano does not seem endowed with this ability or able to apply the same kind of reasoning to Estefanía, even after hearing from the Captain about Estefanía's friend's apparent lie. Instead, he continues thinking that he is the one tricking her. Again, as he continues, he is conscious of his deliberate attempts to manipulate her using Theory of Mind: "Pasé con ella luengos y amorosos coloquios. Blasoné, hendí, rajé, ofrecí, prometí y hice todas las demostraciones que me pareció ser necesarias para hacerme bienquisto con ella" ["Enjoying many long and amorous conversations with her, I bragged of soldierly exploits, slashing and hacking; I offered and promised her all manner of things, and, in short, demonstrated everything I thought needful in order to make myself as agreeable as possible to her"] (284; 435-36). Retrospectively, Campuzano does not blame his bad outcome on the lack of an appropriate Theory of Mind mechanism, but on a different modality of thinking altogether, as he says that she made him think not with his head, but with his feet: "tenía entonces el juicio, no en la cabeza, sino en los carcañares" ["{b}y this time my commonsense was located in my heels rather than in my head"] (285; 437) as he recalls to Peralta. The most intellectual of cognitive faculties, judgment, is not in the highest seat of reason, the head, but instead, in the lowest part of the body, where it fails to work properly.[11] It is most likely the embodied, multisensorial tact of her *engaño* that has overcome his resistance and use of reason. Not only does Estefanía use visual and verbal manipulation, including lies about her wealth (as she feigns that the house he visits and the borrowed things she wears are owned by her), but she is also a master of the other senses. For one, she speaks in sultry tones: "[T]enía un tono de habla tan suave que se entraba por los oídos en el alma" ["{F}or the tone of her voice was so soft that it seemed to go right through your ears and straight into your very soul"] (284; 435), as Cervantes modifies the Petrarchan *topos* of the eyes as windows of the soul, marking the beginning of this attraction as not quite as Platonically perfect as it would be were it to begin with vision. As Estefanía continues with the seduction, she promises to dazzle his taste buds with her cooking: "[N]o tiene príncipe cocinero más goloso ni que mejor sepa dar el punto a los guisados que le sé dar yo" ["For no prince ever had so delicious a cook, nor one more deft in making dishes just right and just for him"] (285; 436), fulfilling that promise during his lazy week of marriage:[12] "[A]lmorzaba en la cama, levantábame a las once, comía a las doce, y a las dos sesteaba en el estrado" ["I ate breakfast in bed, slept in every day until eleven in the morning, dined at noon, and napped at two o'clock in the parlor"] (286; 437). The narration is explicit about her higher-level

---

11   The *Diccionario de Autoridades* registers a similar phrase that was used at least as early as the sixteenth century: "Tener el sesso en los calcañares. Phrase vulgar, que se dice del sugéto que tiene poco assiento, y sus operaciones son sin reflexión y con poco juício" [Having one's mind in the heels of the feet: Common phrase, used to refer to someone who has little grounding, whose actions are carried out without reflection and with little judgment] (Entry for "Calcañar," 1:60; my translation).

12   I refer to this as "his" marriage, since all of the benefits he describes are egocentric and one-sided.

intentionality with the cooking, which was intended to awaken his taste and enliven his appetite: "El rato que doña Estefanía faltaba de mi lado, la habían de hallar en la cocina, toda solícita en ordenar guisados que *me despertasen el gusto y me avisasen el apetito*" ["The times that Doña Estefanía was not by my side, she could be found in the kitchen, carefully preparing dishes *that would arouse my taste buds and whet my appetite*"] (287; 437; emphasis added). She also provides olfactory pleasure, which he notes by describing his laundered clothes in hyperbolically grandiose terms, comparing them to the royal gardens at Aranjuez: "era un nuevo Aranjuez de flores, según olían, bañados en la agua de ángeles y de azahar que sobre ellos se derramaba" ["were as fragrant as the gardens of Aranjuez when in bloom, soaked as they were in sweet-scented water and sprinkled with essence of orange blossoms"] (287; 437-38). Finally, his sense of touch received pleasure: "Pisé ricas alfombras, ahajé sábanas de holanda" ["I trod on expensive carpets, I wrinkled sheets of Holland linen"] (286; 437).

While the reader may have suspicions earlier, it is only later in the novella that definitive evidence becomes available that they have both been duping each other, as well as other people, more broadly. At first it seems like Estefanía is the only one who misleads. The most complex moment in reference to her trickery occurs soon after the two are married and have taken up residence in the place that Estefanía has identified as her home, when the real owner, Doña Clementa, arrives unannounced. Estefanía then tells Campuzano a complicated story involving higher-order beliefs that is ultimately a fiction that he falls for, and for which he is fleeced of his (fake) jewelry and his (real) clothes. Despite the illogicality of this story,[13] he is unable to suss out her *engaño*, which relies on what Félix Lope de Vega would call "engañar con la verdad" [deceiving with the truth] (2: 65; my translation) since she states ironically that "sabed que todo lo que aquí pasare es fingido" ["But know this: everything that's happening here is a hoax"] (287; 438). It is about this same time that he (allegedly) started to feel remorse for conning her (according to what he later claims), letting Peralta know that his intentions had shifted, from his earlier ones which were "torcida y traidora" ["twisted and deceitful"] (286; 437) to what he now identifies as morally improved.[14]

---

13 Counterfactually, if the story that Estefanía told were true, why wouldn't she have told him about it in advance, warning him of the possibility that doña Clementa might arrive under the pretense of being the lady of the house?

14 "[I]ba mudando en buena la mala intención con que aquel negocio había comenzado" ["I was gradually changing my mind regarding the wicked intentions I had harbored as I had begun that business"] (287; 438).

Once more, Campuzano seems hyper-aware of his own hidden intentions, but not able to detect hers despite their similarity. If he were to put himself in her shoes, with his understanding of how one can trick another with false appearances and outright lies, he ought to be able to avoid being tricked, which is what leads me to surmise that Campuzano relies on Theory-Theory exclusively and not Simulation Theory.

As the story is focalized on Campuzano through his story-telling and emphasis on his suffering, Estefanía's perspective is not well represented, but whatever the reader may glean is important for the sake of assessing the success of her Machiavellian Intelligence. Considering how much time she invested in her scheme—weeks seducing him, several days in bed with him, several days cooking and waiting on him, all done apparently in the hopes of absconding with his alleged wealth[15]—ultimately she received little recompense, as she was forced to run out of town, with only his counterfeit jewelry and his clothes. While he seems to have lost more, including his good health, she also left the relationship at something of a loss. Indeed, despite her excellence at Machiavellian Intelligence and adeptness at higher-order beliefs about intentional states, she was incapable of sussing out his trick. But just like she did, he had switched one appearance with another, making her believe that he was significantly richer than he was. Toward the end of the novella, Doña Estefanía's friend illustrates the women's beliefs about Campuzano well. While she means to reveal the truth behind Estefanía's scheme to him explicitly, she inadvertently reveals that she too is under the same impression as Estefanía that Campuzano is quite the catch: "[L]a mentira es todo cuanto os ha dicho doña Estefanía; que ni ella tiene casa, ni hacienda, ni otro vestido del que trae puesto ... aunque, *bien mirado, no hay que culpar a la pobre señora*, pues ha sabido granjear a una tal persona como la del señor Alférez por marido" ["{E}verything Doña Estefanía has told you is a lie. For she has no house, nor any estate at all, nor any kind of wardrobe except for the clothes on her back ... . Although, *all things considered, you can hardly blame the poor lady,* seeing as how she has managed to get such a fine person as yourself, sir ensign, to be her husband"] (289; 440; emphasis added). The friend's opinion here, introduced with the phrase "bien mirado" [all things considered], involves strikingly a form of explicit empathic understanding, as she is putting herself in Estefanía's shoes. If she were *la pobre*

---

15   It is not entirely straightforward that Estefanía was going to leave him until she does. What would have happened if doña Clementa had not returned home as early as she did? What was Estefanía waiting for before abandoning him? Why did she not rob him sooner if that was her plan?

señora Estefanía, if she too had nothing except the dress that she was wearing to her name, perhaps she too would have tried to trick a man of the quality of the Alférez Campuzano into marrying her too. This putting oneself into another's shoes, the hallmark of Simulation Theory, seems to be something that both Estefanía and Campuzano fail to do. Rather they appear to employ abstract Theory-Theory rules and not empathic understanding in their high-level scheming. However, the recursive levels of Theory of Mind are much higher than Sancho's six, as exemplified by an analysis of Estefanía, who believes [1] that Campuzano wants [2] an attractive woman whom he can convince [3] to bring him pleasure and/or become his wife and take care of him; therefore she believes [4] that she can make him desire [5] her for her beauty and wealth and thereby make him desirous [6] of marriage by fulfilling his sensory needs in a domestic setting ultimately to con [7] him out of his money, and to accomplish this she thinks [8] she must lie and pretend to own a house, a lie which she believes [9] she must hide once she is caught in the lie when she tries to make him believe [10] that doña Clementa is the real liar who is [11] trying to trick another man into marrying her.

In resolving this literary situation ironically, with both con-artists reciprocally duping each other, Cervantes illustrates a popular old saying, well-known by Campuzano, which he cites toward the end of the novella: "Pensóse don Simueque que me engañaba con su hija la tuerta, y por el Dío, contrecho soy de un lado" ["Don Simueque thought to fool me with his one-eyed daughter, but God knows I put one over on him, for I'm deformed on one side"] (290; 441).[16] In the allegorical vignette, both Don Simueque as well as the unnamed first-person speaker veil physical defects and both receive less than what they thought they were being offered in the marriage (a healthy spouse), in a simple case of Machiavellian Intelligence in which the deceivers similarly failed to detect the scheming of the other party. In the novella, Peralta raises the discourse to a higher literary register, citing Petrarch from the *Triunfi* with a similar message: "Che chi prendre diletto di far frode; / No si de'lamentar s'altri l'inganna" [Whoever delights in committing fraud should not lament when another tricks him] (291; my translation). The irony of the mutual deceit is coupled with an ultimately ironic outcome for Campuzano, reminiscent perhaps even more than of Petrarch to the *contrapasso* of Dante's *Inferno*: In his bid to con Estefanía out of her alleged wealth, he is transformed into a double *pelón*: "Halléme verdaderamente hecho pelón,

---

16   Sieber, quoting González Amezúa, notes that it is similar to a Jewish saying (290). Julio Caro Baroja also observes that Cervantes appears to draw on Jewish lore here, highlighted by the dialectical use of "Dio" in lieu of "Dios" (100).

porque ni tenía barbas que peinar ni dineros que gastar" ["Finally I found myself literally and figuratively fleeced, because I had no hair to comb and no money to spend"] (292; 443). Figuratively broke (*pelón*), he literally suffers from alopecia (*pelón*) due to the syphilis he contracted from Estefanía.

Are the failures of these protagonists related to their using abstract thinking about the other rather than put-oneself-in-the-other's-shoes empathy? Would using Simulation Theory be superior to Theory-Theory as a mechanism in helping to avoid being tricked? From the examples explored above, including those within the novella of other minor characters, the Simulation Theory mechanism would seem better at helping a character predict deception than the more abstract Theory-Theory. The two protagonists' lack of empathy for each other is mirrored in their lack of Simulation Theory, and is brought to the fore by minor characters who express some empathic understanding and who do not end up being tricked—the Captain wisely avoids Estefanía's first friend and Estefanía's other friend at the end of the novella expresses empathy towards Estefanía, much greater empathy than Estefanía or Campuzano ever show. The sociopathy involved in the types of immoral deception committed by both Campuzano and Estefanía might demonstrate that a lack of emotional empathy ultimately becomes a deficit and a hindrance to flourishing. While we cannot expect that the neat irony of the novella should be fully in line with what would be predictable from an evolutionary hypothesis or functioning of Theory of Mind, it does seem appropriate that these two kinds of empathy would be linked.

Works Cited

Barroso Castro, José. "Theory of Mind and the Conscience in *El casamiento engañoso*." *Theory of Mind and Literature*. Ed. Paula Leverage, Howard Mancing, Richard Schweickert, and Jennifer Marston William. West Lafayette: Purdue UP, 2011. 289-303. Print.

Bass, Laura, and Amanda Wunder. "Veiled Ladies of the Early Modern Spanish World: Seduction and Scandal in Seville, Madrid and Lima." *Hispanic Review* 77.1 (2009): 97-146. Print.

Byrne R. W., and Andrew Whiten. *Machiavellian Intelligence*. Oxford: Oxford UP, 1988. Print.

Caro Baroja, Julio. *Los judíos en la España moderna y contemporánea*. 4th ed. Vol. 1. Madrid: Ediciones Istmo, 2000. Print.

Cervantes, Miguel de. *El casamiento engañoso.* Ed. Jorge García López. Barcelona: Crítica, 2001. Print.

———. *El casamiento engañoso.* In *Novelas ejemplares.* Ed. Harry Sieber. 2 vols. Vol. 2. Madrid: Cátedra, 1980. 279-95. Print.

———. *The Deceitful Marriage.* In *Exemplary novellas.* Ed., trans., and introd. by Michael Harney. Indianapolis: Hackett, 2016. 433-46. Print.

Diccionario de Autoridades. 3 vols. Madrid: Real Academia Española, 1726-39. Facsim. ed. Madrid: Gredos, 1990. Print.

Dunbar, Robin. "On the Origin of the Human Mind." *Evolution and the Human Mind: Modularity, Language and Meta-Cognition.* Ed. Peter Carruthers and Andrew Chamberlain. Cambridge: Cambridge UP, 2000. 238-53. Print.

Goldman, Alvin. *Oxford Handbook of the Philosophy of Cognitive Science.* New York and Oxford: Oxford UP, 2012. Print.

Heyes, Celia M. "Theory of Mind in Nonhuman Primates." *Behavioral and Brain Sciences* 21 (1998): 101-48. Print.

Hogan, Patrick Colm. *Cognitive Science, Literature and the Arts: A Guide for Humanists.* New York: Routledge, 2003.

Jaén (Jaén-Portillo), Isabel. "Literary Consciousness: Fictional Minds, *Real* Implications." *Selected Papers from the 22nd International Literature and Psychology Conference*, June 29-July 4, 2005. Ed. Norman Holland. IPSA. Web. 1 July 2016.

Lazarillo de Tormes. Ed. Everett W. Hesse and Harry F. Williams. Rev. Ed. Madison: U of Wisconsin P, 1976. Print.

Lazarillo de Tormes. In Lazarillo de Tormes *[Anonymous] and* The Grifter *[El Buscón, by Francisco de Quevedo]: Two Novels of the Low Life in Golden Age Spain.* Trans., ed., and introd. by David Frye. Indianapolis: Hackett, 2015. 1-50.

Lope de Vega, Félix. *Rimas.* Ed. Felipe B. Pedraza Jiménez. 2 Vols. Fuenlabrada, Madrid: Universidad de Castilla-La Mancha, 1994. Print.

Mancing, Howard. "Sancho Panza's Theory of Mind." *Theory of Mind and Literature.* Ed. Paula Leverage, Howard Mancing, Richard Schweickert, and Jennifer Marston William. West Lafayette: Purdue UP, 2011. 123-32. Print.

Reed, Cory A. "'¿Qué rumor es ése?:' Embodied Agency and Representational Hunger in *Don Quijote* I.20." *Cognitive Cervantes.* Ed. Julien J. Simon, Barbara Simerka, and Howard Mancing. Spec. cluster of essays of *Cervantes: Bulletin of the Cervantes Society of America* 32.1 (2012): 99-124. Print.

Sieber, Harry, ed. *El casamiento engañoso*. In *Novelas ejemplares*. 2 vols. Madrid: Cátedra, 1980. 279-95. Print.

Simerka, Barbara. *Knowing Subjects: Cognitive Cultural Studies and Early Modern Spanish*. West Lafayette: Purdue UP, 2013. Print.

Simon, Julien J. "Celestina, Heteroglossia, and Theory of Mind: The Rise of the Early-Modern Discourse." *Proceedings of the 2008 International Conference in Literature and Psychology*. Lisbon: Instituto Superior de Psicologia Aplicada, 2009. 119-26. Print.

———. "Contextualizing Cognitive Approaches to Early Modern Spanish Literature." *Cognitive Approaches to Early Modern Spanish Literature*. Ed. Isabel Jaén and Julien J. Simon. New York: Oxford UP, 2016. 164-80. Print.

Zunshine, Lisa. "Richardson's *Clarissa* and a Theory of Mind." *The Work of Fiction: Cognition, Culture, and Complexity*. Ed. Alan Richardson and Ellen Spolsky. Aldershot: Ashgate, 2004. 127-46. Print.

The Pleasures of Pretense: Quarantine and Cosplay in *Don Quixote*

BARBARA SIMERKA
Queens College

OVER THE PAST TWO DECADES, cognitive theorists have dedicated sustained attention to the topic of mental simulation and its role in a wide variety of fundamental human behaviors, including reading and pretense. In *The Storytelling Animal*, Jonathan Gottschall asserts that recounting and consuming narratives is what "makes us human;" in part because narrative spurs the mental simulations that allow humans to function and thrive in complex social worlds. Pretense is one of the most common forms of story-telling related simulation. Shaun Nichols and Stephen Stich propose a wide-ranging model of normative simulation and pretense in the essay "A Cognitive Theory of Pretense." In particular, they identify a "quarantine" mechanism which pretenders engage to establish the boundary between simulation and reality. Scholars have recently begun to study the phenomenon of cosplay at fan conventions as a form of simulation. In *Knowing Subjects* (2013) I devoted a chapter to cognitive theories of reading immersion; this essay will expand upon that work by exploring pretense and the quarantine function as underlying factors. I will delineate the unexplored connections among several newly conceptualized forms of cognitive simulation in order to shed new light on the role of fiction-based pretense in *Don Quixote*, on the part of the protagonist as well as supporting characters.

Nichols and Stich offer a highly detailed hypothesis concerning the cognitive mechanisms that support normative pretense activity. The most salient feature for the purposes of this study is their model of a "quarantine" function that brackets or marks pretend activities within a Possible World (PW) and sets them apart from the Real World (RW) (120). The quarantine function serves two purposes: first, "during the course of the pretense itself, what the pretender really believes is typically kept quite distinct from what she believes to be the case in the context of the pretense episode" (120). The quarantine function also serves to mark the conclusion of pretense, "When the episode is over, the pretender typically resumes her non-pretend activities, and the events that occurred in the context of the pretense have only a quite limited effect on the post-pretense cognitive state of the pretender" (120). In other words, the pretender employs a quarantine to identity events that are viable only in the PW and to separate them from the RW existence, while at the same time allowing for integration of those elements that do have relevance to the pretender's RW.

In order to evaluate cognitive deviations, scholars often begin by exploring developmental psychology to trace the stages of normative progression; Rebekah Richert and Erin Smith have delineated the development of quarantine norms in children. By age four, there is significant awareness of the need for a cognitive quarantine to distinguish impossible information and events provided within fantasy stories from reality. Development of the cognitive quarantine entails at least three stages: 1) learning to distinguish real from fantasy worlds to know when to engage a quarantine; 2) the quarantine is understood as a binary—*all* material encountered in a fantasy story is quarantined against use in real life situations; and 3) (which might have its own sub phases) children learn to distinguish which elements within a fantasy narrative or in pretend play are viable and can be integrated into the RW, and hence to engage quarantine ever more accurately (1114-17). Don Quixote's quarantine mechanism can be described as eccentric or defective because, in differing episodes, he fails at each of these tasks.

A team led by Kathleen Corriveau found that older children (ages 5-6) can engage the quarantine function in order to distinguish between historical and fantasy narratives with an 80% success rate: they recognize cues within the narrative that mark the ontological status and can explain the factors they consider (219). A smaller percentage of younger children (ages 3-4) can perform this task, but only if they are given factual information about the status of the characters (223). Younger children are not capable of recognizing textual cues. Corriveau and her colleagues explain that younger children analyze the status of narratives based on their rote learning about historical figures, while older children apply a more sophisticated understanding of what is or is not possible in the real world, to delineate the boundaries of fantasy and reality (214). Don Quixote's aberrant behavior is grounded in the breakdown of his quarantine function, which produces increasingly eccentric interpretations of the textual cues within the PWs in his preferred chivalric texts.

In order to integrate reading or pretend experience with real life, we must use quarantines correctly to determine the worth of various kinds of data contained within texts that we label as nonfiction, realistic fiction, and fantastic. As readers consume each genre, the quarantine must be engaged correctly to determine the validity of information, ethical and moral lessons, psychological insights, and practical life lessons encountered in the PW, to determine if they can be carried over and integrated into the RW. The studies of the quarantine function cited above take for granted that all cognitively stable adults can perform quarantine and integration acts perfectly and effortlessly. In Corriveau et al.'s essay, there seems to be a tacit assumption that normal developmental progress will eventually bring all children to complete competence. I could not find evidence of any study that examined quarantine skills to determine if there remains a small percentage of developmentally mature adults who commit errors when engaging the quarantine. I would like to propose the term "quarantine violation" for those moments when the characters in *Don Quixote* do not follow the cognitive norms described here as they engage in pretense behaviors: 1) when they do not distinguish adequately between what is possible in the PW and in the RW; 2) when they allow pretense to alter their post-pretense beliefs or actions; and 3) when they engage in pretense for extended rather than limited periods of time.

Don Quixote, as a character and a novel, has served as the point of departure for a wide variety of literary and philosophical studies concerning both the ontology of the real world and the epistemological processes used to determine the nature of reality, focusing on episodes in which the novel questions clear cut distinctions (Ihrie; Cascardi; Mancing 158-60). This essay does not seek to intervene in that discussion; but rather to explore episodes of role playing and pretense in which the narrative establishes clear boundaries between the PW and the RW that characters transgress though quarantine violations.

Don Quixote's indiscriminate vision of heroism, with no distinction among the people and characters found in historical sources, epic literature, and chivalric novels, makes clear that he does not engage the quarantine function in any sort of normative fashion as he evaluates the content of the narratives he consumes. In the narrator's very first description of his quarantine process, he points out that Alonso Quijano does notice a detail of a chivalric novel that should lead him to label it as nonrealistic fiction and its protagonist not only as imaginary but also fantastical and thus not a viable role model, "No estaba muy bien con las heridas que don Belianís daba y recebía, porque se imaginaba que, por grandes maestros que le hubiesen curado, no dejaría de tener el rostro y todo el cuerpo lleno de cicatrices" ["Our gentleman was not very happy with the wounds that Don Belianís gave and received, because he imagined that no matter how great the physicians and surgeons who cured him, he would still have his face and entire body covered with scars"] (1245; 20).[1] However, Alonso disregards the textual cue that should have induced him to quarantine such characters not only as fictional but also fantastic. The first chapter of each volume features conversations between Don Quixote and his friends in which he equates categorically ambiguous figures like El Cid or Aeneas, whose actual exploits have been greatly exaggerated, both with historical agents and with fictitious characters whose exploits veer into the supernatural, "Decía él que el Cid Ruy Díaz había sido muy buen caballero, pero que no tenía que ver con el Caballero de la Ardiente Espada ... . Diera él, por dar una mano de coces al traidor de Galalón, al ama que tenía y aun a su sobrina de añadidura" ["He would say that El Cid Ruy Díaz had been a very good knight but could not compare to Amadís, the Knight of the Blazing Sword ... . He would have traded his housekeeper, and even his niece, for the chance to strike a blow at the traitor Guenelon"] (1277; 21). The narrator explicitly links quarantine anomalies with lunacy; he follows up the first description of such a conversation with the conclusion, "rematado ya su juicio" ["his brains dried up"] (1279; 21). Don Quixote's failure to quarantine the fantastic events encountered in the chivalric PW from those possible in the RW is a crucial component of the mindset that allows him to imagine *himself* capable of heroic activity. These quarantine violations mark him as cognitively peculiar; scholarly disagreements about the exact nature of and degree of Don Quixote's insanity often involve differing evaluations of his quarantine function. The violations cited above are on par with those of the average three-to-four year-olds who cannot use textual cues to determine when to quarantine PW events and beings. However, Don Quixote commits quarantine violations despite several decades of education and reading that should enable him to distinguish the ontological status of key figures in his society's historical, theological and fictional pantheons. Furthermore, even when characters such as the canon reaffirm common quarantine practice by pointing out that Amadís and his ilk are fictional characters, and thus firmly in the realm of the PW, Don Quixote still judges the fantastic events depicted in chivalric tales as historically accurate and thus possible in his world.

---

[1] All citations from *Don Quixote* are from the Kindle edition by Florencio Sevilla Arroyo and the translations from Edith Grossman's edition.

And, unlike the sage five-year-olds who can identify relevant textual cues to quarantine a narrative as unrealistic or fantastic, Don Quixote employs an entirely irrelevant criterion for his quarantine purposes, insisting that chivalric texts approved with a royal license cannot be untruthful.

Don Quixote's quarantine function conflates not only the fictional and the factual but also the miraculous; Bible stories are quarantined according to the same "logic" as chivalric and historical texts. The quarantine status of the Bible—as factual or fictional—has piqued cognitive scholars' interest; several experiments have analyzed the ways in which a secular or spiritual upbringing impacts the way that children process the "impossible" events within religious narratives (Corriveau et al. 224). Corriveau's team notes the quandary that religious narrative features "miraculous deviations from ordinary causality" that are not presented to children as fictional (224). Nonetheless, by age five most children are capable of moving beyond the dichotomy of reality and fantasy; Corriveau et al. posit that religious parents who present Biblical stories to their children quarantine them as distinct from both fairy tales and historical narrative. In addition, she suggests that children who receive a religious upbringing learn that seemingly fantastic actions can be categorized as real if performed by God (224). Research by Jacqueline Woolley and Victoria Cox has confirmed that in families where the parents report a strong religious affiliation, children are far more likely to judge supernatural Biblical events as real (686). However, this very specific modification of the quarantine function does not impact a child's general level of categorization ability for other types of real and fantastic narratives (Woolley and Cox 686).

Where the quarantine blurring of religious children is self-contained, the minor quarantine errors that appear in Alonso Quijano's initial conversations with his neighbors are the harbinger of the more dramatic violations that lead to a new name and identity. He does concede that some miraculous episodes may not be entirely true, "—En esto de gigantes—respondió don Quijote—hay diferentes opiniones, si los ha habido o no en el mundo" ["'In the matter of giants,' responded Don Quixote, 'there are different opinions as to whether or not they ever existed in the world'"] (10720; 466). However, as in the case of Don Belianís's scars, he does not follow the standard practice of using textual cues to measure plausibility. Instead, he once again refers to a form of authority as the guarantor of factuality and for this reason does not engage his quarantine. Here, Don Quixote cites the infallibility of Scripture as the determinant factor, "la Santa Escritura, que no puede faltar un átomo en la verdad, nos muestra que los hubo, contándonos la historia de aquel filisteazo de Golías que tenía siete codos y medio de altura" ["Holy Scripture, which cannot deviate an iota from the truth, shows us that [giants] did [exist] by telling us the history of that huge Philistine Goliath, whose stature was seven and a half cubits"] (10725; 467). As these examples indicate, and as the innkeeper confirms in the discussion about how a modern knight errant should behave on his journey in regards to provisions and payments, Don Quixote's flawed quarantine process derives from granting extreme authority to narrators and censors as the ultimate arbiters of reality. He values these forms of authority over all other criteria, somewhat like the three-to-four-year-olds who depend upon the information that authoritative figures like teachers and parents have given them concerning historical people and fictional or mythic heroes. Aside from that passing reference to scars, he rarely employs the advanced level of quarantine practice that elementary school children display: paying attention to textual clues in order to mark off supernatural events within heroic and chivalric narrative worlds as part of a fantastical PW that should be quarantined from the RW.

One of the many innovative aspects of *Don Quixote* is that the novel dedicates extended attention to how a wide variety of humans engage their quarantine mechanism—examining not just the cognitively compromised protagonist but also the secondary characters. The way that characters respond to Don Quixote when they meet him indicates that the pretense involved in taking on roles from the chivalric fictional world is so pleasurable, that even "normal" people violate quarantine norms. The behaviors of the secondary characters suggest that the quarantine may function like a dimmer switch, with a range of positions, rather than as a binary operation akin to a simple on/off switch. Even in the novel's earliest conversation between Don Quixote and his neighbors, we see that the priest and the barber appear to derive pleasure from pretending to share Don Quixote's aberrant quarantine practices as they compare the relative merits of El Cid and chivalric heroes. Furthermore, it is his friends who initiate one of Don Quixote's most common quarantine violations, when they blame the library mishap on an enchanter. Moving from mere discussion to action, Dorotea is happy to postpone returning home with Fernando to begin her life as a respectably married noblewoman in order to enact the role of Princess Micomicona. She indicates that she needs no coaching from the curate, "No dejó de avisar el cura lo que había de hacer Dorotea; a lo que ella dijo que descuidasen, que todo se haría, sin faltar punto, como lo pedían y pintaban los libros de caballerías" ["she replied that there was no need to worry; everything would be done to the letter, exactly as demanded and depicted by the books of chivalry"] (6120; 243). Dorotea appears to enjoy the pretense for its own sake, while the barber struggles with controlling both his costume and his mirth at Don Quixote's gullibility. However, the narration makes clear that these characters are completely aware that they are engaging in pretense. The apparent quarantine violations are themselves a pretense that they perform for Don Quixote.

In the second volume, characters who read the first volume are presented with a unique challenge to quarantine protocols, because they are offered the opportunity to interact in "real life" with a character from a narrative that is termed historical but has many aspects which correlate more closely with fiction. This dichotomy can be seen in the initial observations of characters such as the Duchess, who are surprised by both the consistencies and the gaps between the characters in the first volume and the "people" they encounter. Across volume two we see that the quarantine violations spurred by encountering Don Quixote occur on a continuum: the Barcelona nobility can provide pretense interludes for Don Quixote for a few days, without evidence of quarantine difficulties; the adventures that they create are brief and self-contained and do not cause them to compromise their own identity or the fiction/reality boundary. But Sansón and the ducal couple invest their time, energy, and resources far more extensively. While none of these characters appear to actually forget about the RW as they enact characters from the chivalric PW, the duke and duchess dedicate the most prominent members of their household to an extended series of pretense scenarios that consume all of their leisure time and scarce funds. After Don Quixote leaves, they even send out servants to kidnap him and bring him back for one final adventure. Likewise, Sansón leaves his home and travels for a few weeks to track down and challenge the knight errant who defeated him. If Alonso Quijano violates quarantine norms in his 24-hour-a-day pretense of occupying a higher social rank and possessing extraordinary strength and valor, the aristocratic couple does so in pretense of possessing unlimited resources. Their behavior constitutes a moderate form of quarantine violation, as does Sansón's extended pursuit of a revenge that is rational only within the chivalric PW.

Sancho Panza presents a unique case study in literary-inspired forms of pretense and quarantine violation. Although he cannot read chivalric novels, he is nonetheless capable of learning the norms for this story world by listening to his master and observing his social interactions. Because he engages in quarantine violating activities only when there is a possibility for personal benefit, his form of pretense is mostly directed outward, to those who will allow him unusual economic or social benefits. In these cases, he consciously anticipates that those with whom he engages will enter into the pretense to a sufficient degree to permit these transgressions of class norms. Especially noteworthy is the episode with Dorotea/Micomicona. Despite the obvious fictionality of her tale of woe, Sancho appears unaware that he is engaged in someone else's scenario of pretense and quarantine violation when the damsel in distress offers a title in exchange for vanquishing her enemy. His total belief in this opportunity and his condemnation of his master's refusal to marry her and reap the rewards are intense and sincere,

> ¿cómo es posible que pone vuestra merced en duda el casarse con tan alta princesa como aquésta? ¿Piensa que le ha de ofrecer la fortuna, tras cada cantillo, semejante ventura como la que ahora se le ofrece? ... Cásese, cásese luego, encomiéndole yo a Satanás, y tome ese reino que se le viene a las manos de vobis, vobis y, en siendo rey, hágame marqués o adelantado. (6353)

> How can your grace have any doubts about marrying a princess as noble as this one? Does your grace think fate will offer you good fortune like this around every corner? Marry, marry right now, Satan take you, and take the kingdom that has dropped into your hands without you lifting a finger, and when you're king make me a marquis or a governor. (254)

Across the two volumes, Sancho alternates between skilled exercise of his quarantine function in situations that pose physical danger, and gleeful violation of the quarantine in order to take full advantage of opportunities that range from fine meals and the spoils of a "battle" to socializing with the aristocracy and even exercising a governorship. Other characters occupy a fairly stable and consistent position in terms of their level of quarantine normativity and violation, but Sancho adjusts his quarantine to fit the unpredictable situations in which he finds himself.

At the other end of the spectrum, the clergy in both volumes represents the reader who performs excessive quarantine by rejecting the viability of any information presented within an implausible narrative. After the conclusion of "El curioso impertinente" [The Man Who Was Recklessly Curious], the curate refuses to engage in discussion of the ethical aspects of the tale, because the basic premise that a husband would engage in such an endeavor seems so implausible to him,

—Bien—dijo el cura—me parece esta novela, pero no me puedo persuadir que esto sea verdad; y si es fingido, fingió mal el autor, porque no se puede imaginar que haya marido tan necio que quiera hacer tan costosa experiencia como Anselmo. Si este caso se pusiera entre un galán y una dama, pudiérase llevar, pero entre marido y mujer, algo tiene del imposible. (7551)

"This novel seems fine," said the priest, "but I cannot persuade myself that it is true; if it is invented, the author invented badly, because no one can imagine any husband foolish enough to conduct the costly experiment that Anselmo did. If this occurred between a lover and his lady, it might be plausible, but between a husband and his wife it seems impossible." (312-13)

Because the curate finds one detail of the novella to be fantastic, his quarantine function overreacts and leads him to place the entire narrative completely beyond the bounds of realism—and thus also outside of the realm of exemplary fiction from which readers might derive beneficial instruction.

The ecclesiastic who resides at the palace takes a similarly negative attitude to his patrons' engagement with the story world of their new guest. However, the harsh manner in which he chides the protagonist is nearly as excessive as the acts and narrative he condemns. Don Quixote once again refers to authority to decide an important issue; rather than address the specific accusations he turns to his hosts for validation, "Mis intenciones siempre las enderezo a buenos fines ... si el que desto trata merece ser llamado bobo, díganlo vuestras grandezas, duque y duquesa excelentes" ["I always direct my intentions to virtuous ends, which are to do good to all and evil to none; if the man who understands this, and acts on this, and desires this, deserves to be called a fool, then your highnesses, most excellent Duke and Duchess, should say so"] (14926-27; 666). It is conceivable that a reader who applies a scrupulous quarantine to the first volume of *Don Quixote* might, like these two demanding clerical readers, be unwilling to consider or discuss any of the relevant social, political, or philosophical issues that are raised. Such a reader might ask: "How could readers ever enjoy a book in which a character violates the quarantine as drastically as does Don Quixote?" And, "How could readers ever benefit from engaging with such an implausible tale?" The sequels and adaptations that range from Avellaneda's and Cervantes's early efforts to Terry Gilliam's decade-long effort to make a Quixotic film provide a clear answer: readers and viewers revel in exploring narratives of quarantine violation. In addition, like the Cervantine characters, modern readers also enjoy engaging in such violations.

Cervantes does not limit himself to quarantine violations related to the chivalric novel; one of the most prevalent subthemes is character engagement with the pastoral novel. The characters who take to the fields and inscribe Leandra's name on every available bit of tree bark, like those who recreate Arcadia, engage in temporary and partial interludes of quarantine violation as a form of leisure activity, as opposed to Don Quixote's long term, complete quarantine collapse. Marcela and Grisóstomo provide an interesting counterpoint to these characters and to Don Quixote. Marcela's adoption of the pastoral lifestyle entails performing the actual labor of sheep tending, in the company of real shepherdesses, and does not include courtship behavior. She violates the norms for her social class but is not engaged in pretense and thus does not interact in any way with the quarantine. On the other hand, Grisóstomo presents an even more extreme case than Don Quixote because he is willing to die in order to fulfill the norms of the role that he performs. His type of quarantine violation is similar to that of the martyr Ginés in *Lo fingido verdadero* (Simerka, "Acting").[2] As these characters and episodes demonstrate, Cervantes depicts the quarantine as a highly nuanced psychosocial function through his representation of a wide range of quarantine violations across the two volumes of the novel.

The specific social settings through which adults engage in narrative-based pretense are historically and culturally variable; at our current moment, cosplay is a preeminent format. Cosplay—costume play—is the type of extended pretense enacted at conventions dedicated to fictional worlds such as Star Trek, Harry Potter, or Steampunk. The most popular sites for cosplay include theme parks or Comic-Con gatherings dedicated to super heroes from American comics and Japanese Manga or Anime. In exploring the PWs enacted in *Don Quixote* and modern cosplay a significant homology is apparent: like the enhanced medieval world that chivalric fiction offers,

---

2   The exact cause of Alonso Quijano's death, and its relation to the end of his quarantine violation phase is unclear, like the pseudo-shepherd's demise (Friedman). These episodes are typical of those that have engaged philosophical readings over the centuries; they fail to provide the reader with a clear division between PW and RW. In each case the explanations of their abrupt deaths, as posited by narrators and companions, include at least two possible explanations. When we as readers seek to engage our quarantine, we are confronted with one explanation that belongs solely to the literary or PW realm, death as the result of a broken heart, juxtaposed with equally unsatisfactory explanations such as suicide or a sudden illness.

popular cosplay worlds also feature a large variety of heroic characters who operate within a magically enhanced quasi-feudal world. Matthew Thorn defines the conventions where cosplay occurs as "a liminal space and time, where participants could shed many of the restraints of mundane society" (175). Thorn emphasizes the desire to violate gender norms; many people who engage in cosplay cross dress for gender and "Even when one is cos-playing a character of the same sex, I believe one is very much 'playing gender' ... men can suddenly become icons of idealized masculinity" (176). Thorn's essay posits that cosplay can be inspired by dissatisfaction with the limitations a particular society places upon specific categories of identity and on the possibilities for social advancement. We can see this boundary crossing at work as Don Quixote and Sansón choose hyper masculine roles and Sancho gains license to exercise social power. Although the duke and duchess do not actually change clothing, it is reasonable to assert that there is nonetheless a form of cosplay at work as they enact the aristocracy of an earlier era when the upper nobility had far more social power and agency.

Nicolle Lamerichs notes, many cosplayers do not limit themselves to convention attendance. They dedicate sustained time and effort to creating elaborate costumes in order to enter competitions at the conventions, which may entail mere modeling or forming groups to rehearse and enact scenes (par. 1.2). They may also engage in role-play through online sites; write fan fiction; create fan art; or use the cosplay character as an avatar during chat sessions or games (par. 1.4, 1.7). Unlike the quarantine violations found in *Don Quixote*, cosplay does not involve entering into daily life while engaged in role play; it occurs either at a specific social site dedicated to the Possible World or as virtual role in a dedicated online site. The scholars who write about cosplay conceptualize this as an activity akin to Butler's model of performativity (Lamerichs; par. 5.4-5.7). I would like to offer cosplay as a modern example of a form of quarantine violation that is similar to that of the faux shepherds as well as Sansón and the duke and duchess. Thorn, Lamerichs and others depict this media subculture as an eccentric but rational form of entertainment. They also depict cosplay as offering personal affirmation and empowerment, "by stating that a narrative or character is related to me—that I can identify with this particular story or person—I make a statement about myself. There is transformative potential in this ability to express who we are through fiction" (Lamerichs; par. 5.4). Cosplay, like the feudal-oriented role play seen in *Don Quixote*, has arisen in response both to new genres of nostalgic fantasy narrative and also to shifting norms for social identity and mobility, as described in many recent analyses of *Don Quixote*, courtier manuals and the picaresque novel (Simerka, *Knowing*, chaps 3, 4, 7).

Lamerichs links cosplay to Butler's model of degrounding, "when we're standing in two different places at once; or we don't know exactly where we're standing; or when we've produced an aesthetic practice that shakes the ground" (qtd. in Segal and Osborne). She asserts that degrounding or indeterminacy are exactly what cosplay allows for participants. Degrounding is a very promising concept for the study of those moments in the second volume when a character stands in two or more places at once—as a real person who discovers himself to be inscribed as a fictional character, or who encounters a fictional character within his everyday existence. Despite repeated references in volume one to the sage historian who will inscribe his glorious deeds, Don Quixote nonetheless experiences a momentary flash of degrounding when he learns that the adventures from which he has barely recovered are already in print, "no se podía persuadir a que tal historia hubiese, pues aún no estaba enjuta en la cuchilla de su espada la sangre de los enemigos que había muerto" ["he could not persuade himself that such a history existed, for the blood of the enemies he had slain was not yet dry on the blade of his sword"] (10870; 473). However, he immediately takes cognitive refuge in his customary quarantine violation of explaining any unusual event in his life as the work of an enchanter, "imaginó que algún sabio, o ya amigo o enemigo, por arte de encantamento las habrá dado a la estampa" ["he imagined that some wise man, either a friend or an enemy, by the arts of enchantment had printed them"] (10871; 473). Don Quixote functions at the extreme end of quarantine violation: not only is his basic interpretation of reality grounded in the fundamental violation of admitting fantastic PW events into his RW on a regular basis, but also because he categorizes every questionable event as the work of an enchanter, a being who exists solely in the PW.

When Sansón Carrasco first encounters Sancho Panza and Don Quixote at the beginning of the second volume, he does not appear to experience degrounding or quarantine confusion. This may be because the bachelor was already acquainted with the two men; Sancho tells Don Quixote that he learned about the book when he went to welcome the young man home upon his return from college. Sansón initially treats the published work as historical in nature, so that the series of queries he launches about factual discrepancies are almost journalistic in nature. His questions do not address the episodes that current criticism focuses on as philosophically ambiguous, nor does he query the quarantine practices of his neighbors. However, the speed with which Sansón transforms himself into a crusader bent on revenge after

Don Quixote defeats him demonstrates the fragility of the quarantine function. Even though he does not truly believe himself to be a knight, his evaluation of his status matters less than the fact that he begins to behave more like the fictional characters that populate chivalric romance than like a prosaic country gentleman. The bachelor's engagement with cosplay is among the most extensive of any character save for the protagonist himself. Indeed, when Alonso Quijano announces that upon retiring the knight Quijote he now intends to become the shepherd Quijotiz, Sansón is quite eager to extend his quarantine violation to a new PW. Although the narrator assures us that the friends will participate in this new Arcadia for the sole purpose of keeping Don Quixote safe in his village, Sansón's enthusiasm seems to exceed that modest goal:

> yo soy celebérrimo poeta y a cada paso compondré versos pastoriles, o cortesanos, o como más me viniere a cuento, para que nos entretengamos por esos andurriales donde habemos de andar; y lo que más es menester, señores míos, es que cada uno escoja el nombre de la pastora que piensa celebrar en sus versos. (20271)

> I am a celebrated poet and shall constantly compose pastoral verses, or courtly ones, or whatever seems most appropriate, to entertain us as we wander those out-of-the-way places; and what is most necessary, Señores, is for each to choose the name of the shepherdess to be celebrated in his verses. (932)

The priest and barber declare their intent to engage in a very limited pretense, performing a minimal quarantine violation; perhaps for purely altruistic reasons, or for their own amusement. The bachelor's description of the activity he will perform in this new cosplay universe indicates that he intends to engage in a full-fledged revival of the Grisóstomo role, incarnating literary precepts with a fidelity that rivals that of Don Quixote and of the deceased student. This final example of well-planned pretense on the part of a group of friends dedicated to inhabiting a specific fictional universe is perhaps the best parallel to the highly enthusiastic participants at contemporary cosplay conventions, who prepare and perform scenes from their favorite fantasy narratives.

Rather than see the cognitive activity in such moments as a failure of quarantine, we might rethink them as an alternative type of playful, creative quarantine. A very recent example of the attractions of cosplay is Daniel

Radcliffe, who spent a decade playing one of the most iconic cosplay roles and appeared at a Comic-Con event last summer in the guise of the Spider Man.[3]

Current psychological research most often treats the quarantine function as binary—either a person is completely aware of pretense and is always accurate in engaging the quarantine—or completely loses track. As this essay demonstrates, Cervantes points to a more nuanced approach, like that of degrounding, that the current cosplay fad confirms: among psychologically healthy humans, there exists a substantial variation of quarantine states, including not only pathological disruptions, but more prevalent and harmless "recreational" violations. It is possible to link current accusations that link the type of quarantine violations spurred by violent virtual role-play games to mass shootings with early modern Spanish discourses that expressed exaggerated concerns about genre fiction. The characters in the novel who engage in mild quarantine violations could be seen as exonerating the relatively harmless forms of "early modern cosplay" that actually do occur in a fiction-obsessed society. The protagonist himself presents a Possible World character that readers would quarantine as implausible, and thus as a repudiation of alarmist social discourses concerning the dangers of leisure reading and quarantine ruptures. In my recent study *Knowing Subjects* (2013), I explore reader engagement with fictional worlds in *Don Quixote*, tracing a continuum of "participatory responses" ranging from mild absorption to complete immersion (204-09). I had envisioned this commentary as a Cervantine critique of the types of genre fiction that encourage immersive forms of reading, concluding "The final indictment of formulaic literary genres that incite excessive immersion—and of those readers that fall into addiction—is that for the most severely afflicted, life in the real world becomes unbearable" (210). However, as this essay indicates, I have come to believe that Cervantes mocks not only the immersed reader, but also the social discourses that exaggerate and pathologize the quarantine violations that lead to immersive reading behavior.[4]

---

3   Although space constraints do not allow me to pursue this, analysis of the connections between cosplay and pretense in *Don Quixote* can benefit from integration with Christopher Weimer's recent studies of real people who dress like super heroes in order to try to perform acts of heroism as crime fighters in the real world; this is another example of quarantine violation (110).

4   This essay seeks to contribute to the growing body of cognitive explorations of Cervantes, such as those found in *Cognitive Approaches to Early Modern Spanish Literature* (Jaén and Simon), *Cognitive Cervantes* (Simon, Simerka, and

Works Cited

Cascardi, Anthony. *The Bounds of Reason: Cervantes, Dostoevsky, Flaubert.* New York: Columbia UP, 1986. Print.

Cervantes y Saavedra, Miguel de. *Don Quijote.* Ed. Florencio Sevilla Arroyo. Madrid: Editorial Bolchiro SL, 2012. Kindle E-book.

———. *Don Quixote.* Trans. Edith Grossman. New York: Harper Collins, 2003. Print.

Connor, Catherine. "Why Autopoiesis and Memory Matter to Cervantes, *Don Quixote*, and the Humanities." *Cognitive Approaches to Early Modern Spanish Literature.* Ed. Isabel Jaén and Julien J. Simon. Oxford: Oxford UP, 2016. 53-73. Print.

Corriveau, Kathleen H., Angie L. Kim, Courtney E. Schwalen, and Paul L. Harris. "Abraham Lincoln and Harry Potter: Children's Differentiation between Historical and Fantasy Characters." *Cognition* 113 (2009): 213-25. Web. 6 Nov. 2016.

Friedman, Edward H. "*Executing the Will:* The End of the Road in *Don Quixote*." *Indiana Journal of Hispanic Literatures* 5 (1994): 105-25. Print.

Gallese, Victor. "Neoteny and Social Cognition: A Neuroscientific Perspective on Embodiment." *Embodiment, Enaction and Culture: Investigating the Constitution of the Shared World.* Ed. Christoph Durt, Thomas Fuchs, and Christian Tewes. Cambridge: MIT P, 2017. In press. *Academia.edu.* Web. 6 Nov. 2017.

Gottschall, Jonathan. *The Storytelling Animal: How Stories Make Us Human.* New York: Mariner, 2013. Print.

Ihrie, Maureen. *Skepticism in Cervantes.* London: Tamesis, 1982. Print.

Jaén, Isabel, and Julien J. Simon, eds. *Cognitive Approaches to Early Modern Spanish Literature.* Oxford: Oxford UP. 2016. Print.

Lamerichs, Nicolle. "*Stranger than Fiction*: Fan Identity in Cosplay." *Transformative Works and Cultures* 7 (2011): n. pag. Web. 6 Nov. 2016.

Mancing), and Catherine Connor's study of autopoiesis. The model of cognitive study proposed here is not at all deterministic. As Victor Gallese writes, "There cannot be any mental life without the brain. Thus, cognitive neuroscience is necessary to shed new light on the human mind and existence. Is this level of description also sufficient? Probably it isn't. Certainly, it isn't sufficient if we study the brain by isolating it from the body, from the world and from other individuals ... . In other words, cognitive neuroscience should resist the solipsistic 'brain-in-a-vat'-like attitude purported by classic cognitive science and study how situated brain-bodies map their mutual relations and their interactions with the physical world" (3).

Mancing, Howard. "Against Dualisms: A Response to Henry Sullivan." *Cervantes: Bulletin of the Cervantes Society of America* 19.1 (1999): 158-76. Print.

Nichols, Shaun, and Stephen Stich. "A Cognitive Theory of Pretense." *Cognition* 74 (2000): 115-47. Web. 6 Nov. 2016.

Richert, Rebekah A., and Erin I. Smith. "Preschoolers' Quarantining of Fantasy Stories." *Child Development* 82.4 (2011): 1106-19. Web. 6 Nov. 2016.

Segal, Lynne, and Peter Osborne. "Gender as Performance: An Interview with Judith Butler." *Radical Philosophy* 67 (Summer 1994): 32-39. Rpt. in *Theory.org.uk*. n.d. Web. 6 Nov. 2016.

Simerka, Barbara. "Acting and Believing: Mirror Neurons, Simulation, and Quarantine in *Lo fingido verdadero*." *Making Sense of the Senses in Comedia Studies: Essays in Honor of Charles Ganelin*. Ed. Bonnie Gasior and Yolanda Gamboa. Newark, DE: Juan de la Cuesta, Forthcoming. Print.

———. *Knowing Subjects: Cognitive Cultural Studies and Early Modern Spanish Literature*. West Lafayette: Purdue UP, 2013. Print.

Simon, Julien J., Barbara Simerka, and Howard Mancing, eds. *Cognitive Cervantes*. Spec. cluster of essays of *Cervantes: Bulletin of the Cervantes Society of America* 32.1 (2012). Print.

Thorn, Matthew. "Girls and Women Getting Out of Hand: The Pleasure and Politics of Japan's Amateur Comics Community." *Fanning the Flames: Fans and Consumer Culture in Contemporary Japan*. Ed. William W. Kelly. Albany: SUNY P, 2004. 169-88. Print.

Weimer, Christopher B. "Leaping New Media in a Single Bound: The Quixotic Would-Be Superhero in Contemporary Graphic Fiction and Film." *Don Quixote: A Multidisciplinary Study of a Modern Hero*. Ed. Matthew Warshawsky and James Parr. Newark, DE: Juan de la Cuesta, 2013. 85-106. Print.

Woolley, Jacqueline D., and Victoria Cox. "Development of Beliefs about Storybook Reality." *Developmental Science* 10.5 (2007): 681-93. Web. 6 Nov. 2016.

Inside Out: The Arts of Our Embodied Minds*

CATHERINE CONNOR-SWIETLICKI
University of Vermont

*For Howard, whose inside-out knowledge and experience continue to inspire my own embodied cognition and ever-changing mind maps.[1]

INSIDE OUT: AN ARTISTIC INTRODUCTION TO OUR LIVING SYSTEMS

PETE DOCTER'S MOST RECENT animated film *Inside Out* is not just for youngsters. The film entertains while it enlightens scholars, educators, parents and children over the age of six or seven. Rather than yet another tale of superheroes, princesses, transformers or scary and cute fanciful creatures, *Inside Out* proves to be clever, amusing and more effective in terms of stimulating spectators' self-awareness and personal development. In effect, Docter's film is about ourselves, metaphorically represented by animated characters whose life stories, identities and neurobiology continually self-organize as do our own bodies and minds. Docter thus helps us trace how our embodied minds change *inside* our brains and bodies in ways parallel to our *outside* and conscious notions of ourselves and others.

For the general public *Inside Out* may be the most convenient way of keeping pace with neuroscience-related discoveries now strongly influencing every aspect of our personal lives. With a combination of art and science, Docter's film illustrates how the humanities, social sciences and sciences are

---

[1] Recently, Howard Mancing has discussed how Cervantes and his readers develop their embodied cognition and self-realization (*autopoiesis*) as they engage with the *Quixote*. In the same volume, my essay further explores how each one's *autopoiesis* and embodied cognition are continuing processes of recreating memory ("Why Autopoiesis").

necessarily integrated in life and art. *Inside Out* thus offers non-experts a primer on the neurosciences and their reliance on the arts to explain how our embodied minds work. For artists, scholars of literature, all the humanities and social sciences, the film is an introduction to and a demonstration of how and why creativity is a bio-cultural necessity of our individual and social life-systems. For scholars of literature in particular, *Inside Out* can be a short-cut to learning more about the current appeal of neurobiological approaches to all the arts, humanities and social sciences.

This essay is an explanation and evaluation of the neurobiological underpinnings of all arts and sciences operating in *Inside Out* and in all of us. More than a separate organ, each person's brain is an organization of all her body's semi-independent cells.[2] Each cell is a little society of self, a microcosmic system working to self-organize before it can integrate within an individual's entire macrocosmic body-brain. The term *autopoiesis* summarizes all these processes of self-realization, embodied cognition and/or memory.[3] Like Maturana and Varela, I use the term "neurobiological" because it is more inclusive of all the bio-cultural-ecological circumstances of everyone's embodied minds and of how the film *Inside Out* was created. Like Riley Andersen, the film's human protagonist, each of us is constantly changing, creating and re-organizing through inside-out interactions and integration. Each one's bio-cultural self-realization takes place inside our bodies and brains as we adapt to social-cultural-eco developments outside our skin. In short, Docter's film is a good starting place for understanding that creativity, culture and social relations are biological imperatives.

The film's creator follows a long tradition of artists as leaders of the "humanistic sciences." Most easily identifiable is Leonardo da Vinci, but equally significant examples are the Spaniards Santiago Ramón y Cajal and Miguel de Cervantes. Because Ramón y Cajal was artistically inclined, his creative experience enabled him to perceive what other neurologists could not, and he is now recognized as the father of neuroscience (Kandel 61-67). Where other neurologists saw only mesh-like masses in brain tissues, the Spaniard

---

2 In his review of *Inside Out*, neuropsychologist Pavel Somov thus summarizes what the film, has in common with what highly influential neurobiologists Humberto Maturana and Francisco Varela demonstrate in their work. Our body-brains are self-realizing organizations, from a single cell to our entire embodied selves. *Autopoiesis* is their term to explain how even a single cell of a living being is self-organizing and self-realizing.

3 Maturana's and Varela's term *autopoiesis* was inspired by the *Quixote* and the humanities. See Mancing; Connor-Swietlicki,"Why Autopoiesis."

saw that such networks are in fact individual neurons learning to communicate and work together, connecting our insides-and-outsides all across our body-brain areas. *Scientific American* illustrator Amanda Montañez has recently discussed how Ramón y Cajal's perceptual-muscular-cognitive act of drawing stimulated his memory's imaginative processes. In observing and recreating what he saw, he necessarily interpreted and infused new meanings into the tissues under his microscope.

Similarly, creative humanists like Cervantes and Docter transform their observations of "insides" and "outsides" of life, infusing new meanings as they interpret and create. Both are examples of how artists and neurobiologists influence each other. Both drew on life experiences, especially traumatic ones, in expressing how cognitive-emotive processes are realized in their creative works. In Cervantes's case, experience with and knowledge of humanistic medicine and sciences are especially notable in the first chapter of the *Quixote*. There, with remarkable accuracy his narrator explains that Alonso Quijano's mental deterioration was caused by sleep deprivation—a grave body-brain affliction starting at the cellular level (Connor-Swietlicki, "Why Autopoiesis"). In global terms, however, Cervantes's most remarkable inside-out observations are realized throughout all the embodied-mind operations he creates for his characters in the novel.

Neurobiological Artistic Strategies

As with Cervantes and Ramón y Cajal, Docter's life experiences are detectable in his art. When interviewed, Docter has traced the initial autobiographical impetus for *Inside Out* to the drastic changes in his inner-outer life when, at age eleven, he moved with his family from Minnesota to Denmark (Gross; Robinson). Like his eleven-year-old protagonist Riley, Docter had a difficult time adjusting to the radical changes in his emotional and memory systems—and therefore in his sense of self—when discovering totally new relations of environment-language-culture-society and individuals! But while Cervantes had to depend on readers' experiences extracting memories from texts and detecting changes in his protagonists' embodied minds, Docter relies on his viewers' more immediate abilities to interpret two sets of visual, animated characters. In general, he depends on their abilities to make connections between inside and outside characters. More specifically, viewers need to cultivate their abilities to interpret the voices, facial-bodily expressions and perceptions of both types of animations. Like all visual and performance arts, his film works on us neuro-biologically, showing us how our self-realization is a constant process of reworking our own inner-outer relationships with everyone and everything in our environmental and sociocultural surroundings.

Docter's first type of animated characters are the "normal" humans we are accustomed to perceiving in everyday life and visual arts. In his film, these protagonists are the main character Riley Andersen, her parents, friends, hockey teammates, classmates, neighbors, fellow citizens and so forth. Docter shows that all such relationships are necessarily emotional, social and cognitive connections—like our own.

The second type of characters he draws is what makes Docter's work so innovative and so inside-out. These are animated and metaphorical representations of our major bio-cultural operations. Chief among them are our most familiar emotions: Joy, Sadness, Fear, Anger and Disgust. Each in our individual ways has experienced how these emotions feel inside, how we might express them outside and how others might detect them in our body movements, facial expressions, eye positioning, voice tones and more. In everyday life, as in films and other performance or visual arts, our capacity to interpret others' cognitive-emotive states depends on our practiced abilities to read faces and other exterior manifestations of their internal activity. This is why literature and the arts are such powerful instruments of learning and all human development.

As he structures the film, Docter relies on three major artistic strategies—all of which are patterned after the actual bio-cultural systems we humans develop as we self-realize over the course of our lives. Discussed in order, these are human emotions, memory systems and our individually complex, neuro-biological societies of self. Emotions are the first major component, not only in the film but for the vital role they always play in linking together our insides and outsides in every facet of life, from the most personal to the most social and intellectually complex. They are our initial and supposedly primitive responses to exterior or interior stimulation. But as Docter shows, without these emotional connections, our brain's centers of judgment and knowledge cannot "make up our mind." Without emotions inside-outside, we have no means of "working-together socially" with the rest of our body-brain, let alone with the external societies on which we rely from conception. Docter researched emotions with experts before writing his storyline and drawing his characters (Keltner and Ekman).[4]

---

4   In general, however, *Inside Out* shows the more profound neurobiological influence of our emotions as seen in Antonio Damasio's work.

Docter also consulted experts on *memory/learning systems*, the second major embodied-mind component of the film's artistry and of self.[5] As his protagonist Riley's inside characters illustrate, we all "learn and grow" *memories* inside at the microscopic, neurobiological level. When we make memories, our body-brain cells are learning and "memorizing" how to connect inside themselves and, more importantly, how to form a system or society of similar cells working together. Because memory and learning are really a series of practiced, organizing connections across the body and brain, Docter could not draw memory as a single anthropomorphized character. Instead, he imaginatively and realistically portrays his five emotional characters actively struggling to interconnect with other animated representations of our body-mind systems. Their inside efforts work interactively with Riley's outside struggle when her systems of self are shocked by her life in inner-city San Francisco.

The third strategy of Docter's artistry is his portrayal of how our complex emotional and memory systems must always function together as inside-out, neurobiological "systems" or "societies," to use very literal metaphors from biological life and art (Maturana and Varela). *Inside Out* depicts metaphorically represented brain processes trying to self-organize their connections and work together to recreate Riley's inside-out social and personal problems. Although they represent many types of brain cell functions, Docter has cleverly drawn them as ordinary workmen—some in hardhats, others dressed as security guards or train conductors. Part of the attraction that these "brain workers" hold for a popular audience is that they are not anatomically precise neuron-based drawings of the brain. Because Docter's anthropomorphized characters are more familiar forms, they more easily teach us that even a single brain cell is organized as a living society, as I illustrate in the following section.[6]

---

5   He cites the general consultation with Columbia University's Zuckerman Mind Brain Behavior Institute (Robb). Eric Kandel of Columbia received the Nobel Prize for his work on memory as learning. Kandel's work, along with that of Maturana and Varela, is essential to understanding our neurobiological organization of learning and memory.

6   These artistic lessons on neurobiology are a fitting response to neurologist Lisa Barrett and Daniel Barrett's failure to recognize that neurons and all brain functions are represented metaphorically throughout the film. The inside emotional metaphors she refers to as "blobs" were drawn in glowing, human-like shapes in order to convey how powerfully our emotions connect us inside-out. Docter's fluorescent

Our Emotional-Social Selves

Docter's major plotline for *Inside Out* was inspired, not only by his sad memories and inward turn at age eleven when his Minnesota family moved to Denmark. He was inspired also by his adult emotional-cognitive concerns for his eleven-year-old, prepubescent daughter. He and his wife realized they were acting as many parents do, wanting her to remain the joyful child she had always been in the face of accelerating changes in their lives (Gross; Robinson). All their memories, emotions and social-environmental relations were challenged to adapt as do those of Riley and her parents when they move her to San Francisco. Essentially Docter is portraying a neurobiological inside reality that is also an outside emotional-social and cognitive self-organization for a new environment and new human conditions. Hence he depicts Riley's difficulties simultaneously at the inside, microscopic and cellular level when her emotions try to interact to and with her outside macrosystems of culture, society and environment.

Of the five anthropomorphized emotions starring in the animated film—Joy, Sadness, Disgust, Fear and Anger—Riley's dominant inside-out tendency is definitely Joy. But as the narrative progresses, Riley's emotional-cognitive relationship with herself and her surroundings is forced along a bumpy road to maturity. This reorganization of her inner-outer self is portrayed chiefly in the shifting balance between Joy and Sadness and their sporadic interactions with Disgust, Fear and Anger. These are some of the best examples of how our reading literature and interpreting performance or visual arts offer us abundant opportunities for our individual self-realization. This is why attentive, interactive reading and viewing so enrich those who take the time to engage fully in the arts.

The inner and outer narratives Docter has drawn help adults as well as youngsters remember and understand how their own embodied minds necessarily develop slowly and at their own individual rates of self-organization. Above all, by engaging with the film's characters and other arts, we can learn more about our own emotional-social-cultural-cognitive-environmental conditions than science alone can teach us. For example, the power of observation, imitation and mind-reading seen in the film are in fact how we learn to become ourselves. The first example is when the newborn Riley's eyes first focused on the blurry faces of her parents smiling at her, calling her "Riley" and their "bundle of joy." It is her first exposure to visual mirror neurons: she

---

depictions of all five emotions operate like neurons in their vital, energetic contributions to our embodied minds.

smiles back at them, they beam back at her and they all take the first steps toward learning to mind read as they exchange and interpret facial manifestations of emotive-cognitive states.

Early memories of where and when emotions other than Joy shaped Riley are mainly from toddler years. Disgust and Anger show how Riley reacted to spoon-feedings of broccoli. Fear characterized her encounter with electrical outlets around her home, and Sadness only briefly flashed on her face when Riley fell in her first attempts to ice skate. But as a whole Joy reigns over all, even in what she and her family call "goof-ball" as in imitating monkeys.

Once the family bids farewell to their lovely middle-class home in suburban Minnesota, leaving behind Riley's beloved friends, backyard and hockey memories, Sadness moves toward center stage. Stranded between the past and her totally unfamiliar and insecure present and future, Riley's first day in her inner-city San Francisco neighborhood school is an emotional disaster. When greeted by her teacher and asked to tell the class about herself, Riley's warm recollections about Minnesota and hockey friends rapidly deteriorate. Sadness takes over, and Riley melts into tears about everything she now misses in San Francisco. Unable to summon her joyful, core memories from Minnesota times, Anger brings Riley to snap at her parents and to cut off her Skyping session with her best friend from back home.

When Docter has Joy and Sadness struggle over how to reorganize Joy's memories in terms of Riley's present, he sets up the pair for a wild ride into the most inner reaches of Riley's mind-brain. Their journey is metaphorically expressed from Joy's point of view as a search for and retention of the joyful core memories of Riley's childhood: good family times, friendship, hockey and goofball fun. However, in their encounters with some of Riley's earliest and now discarded memories, it is Sadness who wisely shows Joy how and why Riley needs Sadness to develop empathy for other parts of her inner and outer self, her family and the new friends and classmates she will eventually make in San Francisco. Thus, it is emotions like Sadness that help all humans rework their inner societies, reevaluating the past, readjusting Joy's naïveté and her narcissism while bringing Riley greater depth of purpose and values. Young spectators of the film can thus learn the value of quiet introspection and even melancholy in their lifelong processes of self-realization.

Learning/Re-Membering: Self-Realizing Inside-Out

With Joy's and Sadness's allegorical journey inside Riley's self, Docter shows that our embodied minds need memory-based operations for everything. At every minute of our existence, our insides are reworking memory. These continuing processes reorganize our cellular neurochemistry as they simultaneously recreate our outside relations with our social, cultural and natural surroundings. Neuroscientist reviewers of *Inside Out* have correctly objected that Docter depicts a "headquarters" for the brain, giving the illusion that one actually exists and, adding insult to injury, by depicting a supposed mind-control panel at headquarters. However, the poetic license Docter takes with neuroscience accomplishes far more in reaching a broader public than he could have with strict neuroanatomical correctness. By putting our emotions in a position of control, Docter's *Inside Out* creates a bio-neurologically correct impression of how powerfully our brains need our emotions to re-organize, to remember and to socialize our diverse inside-out systems as they weigh circumstances and arrive at decisions together.[7] In sum, Docter's metaphoric control panel and headquarters represent the hard social work of self-organization, not a single organ or center of control. Our embodied mind processes struggle among themselves in ways similar to how the film's anthropomorphized emotions debate and scuffle, trying to agree on how to feel and to act and what to learn from current circumstances.

Several newly discovered brain activities can be metaphorically interpreted among the additional animated figures Docter drew for the allegorical journey that Joy and Sadness take when connecting memories in Riley's brain. Among the neuroscientists commenting on *Inside Out*, few have recognized the aptness of these metaphors for brain functions, and as a whole their interpretations have been very brief and limited.[8] Most neuroscientists have either forgotten or are not aware of the inside-out origins of metaphors, synesthesia, narrative, drama, rhythm and rhyme in human physiology and neurology. Like Ramón y Cajal's contemporaries in neurology, most neuroscientists today are specialists and not the "specialist-generalists" whose work is better known to humanists. Experienced scholars are needed to identify and explain how artists and writers necessarily observe, imagine and re-create the inside-out.

---

7   Damasio's neurobiological explanations for the power of emotions can be detected in Docter's metaphorical portrayal of emotions and decision making.

8   Although none recognizes all the relevant neurological material offered in the film, several make significant observations. Steven Novella and Alice Robb acknowledge the metaphorical values of *Inside Out*. Meg Kirch offers the most comprehensive survey. Somov and Erica Warp focus on the valuable concepts youngsters and parents can learn from the film. Somov calls attention to the social neurobiology of selves as Buddhist principles.

A key example in need of informed scholarly comment is Docter's metaphoric creation of crystal balls to represent Riley's memories. Of course our memories are not round forms like crystal balls, but our memory systems do operate like the memory systems Docter depicts inside each crystal ball. As neurological studies of memory and learning affirm, memories are a series of complex connections across brain areas "wiring" together bio-cultural-environmental content—including emotional content (Kandel; Connor-Swietlicki, "Why Autopoiesis"). Complex organizational connections are, in fact, what Docter portrays in Riley's crystal ball memories. Inside each ball is a memory video of something Riley has lived and retained—from learning to skate with her parents on their backyard pond to inadvertently scoring her first goal in hockey. In these ways Docter's crystal ball memory videos are appropriate complex metaphors for how real anatomical memories organize connections across the brain!

Scholars of literature and all the arts should also recognize another recent discovery about memory in Docter's crystal ball imagery. A crystal ball is an especially apt representation of the recently encountered single-identity neurons. These have been called Jennifer Aniston neurons, grandmother neurons or Luke Skywalker neurons because they respond to single-identities of a person an individual might have met or learned of in our lifetimes. These were discovered when neurology patients reported recalling one individual, such as one's grandmother, in the very instant that their neurosurgeons inadvertently stimulated one of these specialized identity neurons during brain surgery (Quian Quiroga 159-79).[9]

Since most spectators probably have our own "grandmother" or other identity-specific neurons, it is bio-neurologically accurate, as well as entertaining, for viewers to interpret Docter's crystal ball imagery similarly. A good example in the film is when Joy encounters various crystal ball memories of identity-specific "princess dolls" among the stacks in Riley's brain labyrinth. At that very moment, the "hardhat workers" of Riley's brain are in the process of retiring each princess-doll memory ball to the pit of forgotten memories. When Joy struggles to recover them, viewers have an opportunity to remember their own resistance to letting go of the powerful emotional attachments we have to some past-lived experiences or individuals. This is a prime moment for recollection, personal self-realization and discussion among spectators as well as Riley's inside-out characters.

---

9   During brain surgery no anesthetics are needed because patients' brains do not feel pain. They can, however, note if memories are activated during surgery, as in the case of single-identity neurons.

At this point in the film, Docter's themes of inner-outer-emotional life and his narrative's goals turn toward the changes that Riley, and all of us at some point, must make in order for our embodied minds to adapt. Our dominant childhood emotions, like Joy's, must learn to accommodate Sadness and the benefits associated with her in our lives. Sadness helps Joy realize her society of self—i.e., her need for others and for the empathy that draws her to them and them to her. And Sadness, as scholars should recognize, is also a form of melancholy and even depression—so long identified with artists, a scholarly life, with inwardness and contemplation as well as the wisdom and peace that can become part of anyone's self-realization through life.

One of the memory processes most lauded by neuroscientists viewing *Inside Out* is how Docter depicts sleep and dreaming. Science can now document neurologically what artists, philosophers or writers like Cervantes have known for millennia: when we sleep, our body-brains rework memories, self-organizing them with what we have experienced during time awake. This is why students who sleep seven to eight hours after studying can learn more than those who stay up all night trying to cram. This also explains why Don Quixote can't begin mental recovery until he sleeps solidly and stops reinforcing his chivalric memories with his daytime exploits as a knight errant. In effect, sleep is highly significant to anyone's *autopoiesis* or self-realization. When sleeping and dreaming we recycle and consolidate memories, converting them into our present cognitive-emotive selves.

Docter cleverly incorporates this discovery about our body-brain self-organization into Joy's and Sadness's disagreement about how Riley should remember her first full day in San Francisco. They have witnessed Riley's disastrous day in her new school and her brooding, angry reactions at home with her parents and even her angry termination of a Skype session with her best friend back home. Joy and Sadness try to interrupt Riley's night-brain consolidation of these memories by getting involved in Riley's brain's dream and memory-making activities. Docter portrays these as a brain-based movie that Joy and Sadness interrupt intentionally. This enables them to cause nightmares and wake up Riley. He thus entertains us while explaining how and why we might feel stressed or frightened when waking up in the midst of our own nightmares!

TRAIN OF THOUGHT, IMAGINATION AND CREATIVITY INSIDE-OUT

Similar to the nightmares and night-time consolidation of memory as described above, other neurological structures that Docter recreates for *Inside*

Out will sound familiar to most spectators and scholar-teachers.[10] One of the most amusing and exemplary discoveries that Joy and Sadness encounter in Riley's allegorical brain is the "train of thought." Depicted as an actual train, Joy and Sadness use it for rapid transportation in their journey back to headquarters. In order to advance his plot and to reveal more about how our brains work, Docter has the train come to an eight-hour halt. The reason is that Riley has fallen asleep and, as the train's engineers explain, their train only runs on conscious, wakeful thought. Although this means that Joy's and Sadness's return gets derailed, the circumstances allow them to stumble into Imagination Land. There Docter represents the all-important relationships among imagination, creativity, consciousness, dreaming and day-dreaming. This enables him to illustrate several neurobiological realities that are highly significant to all of us—young and old, scientists and humanists.

In truth, neither humanists nor scientists know exactly what consciousness really is in any profound, definitive way. We do know, however, that conscious thought is less common than is our *default mode* of thought (Connor-Swietlicki, "Beyond Cognition" 254). This is the state of inside-focused thought that most frequently occupies our mind-brains. It turns out that our *default mode* is associated with reworking memory, daydreaming and even dreaming while asleep. We often see the *default mode* of memory, for example, in the *Quixote* when Don Quixote attends to inside brain activity. Inside, his chivalric memories make him inattentive to realities outside his embodied mind-brain that are easily perceived by others. Similar examples of *default mode* occur in *Inside Out*. When Riley is distracted, day-dreaming and dreaming, she is also most likely to be more individually creative and imaginative. Docter has Joy and Sadness accidentally stumble into Riley's Imagination Land where a sign above the entry portal warns "Danger!" He cleverly demonstrates how anyone's day-dreaming or *default-mode* processes are a double-edged sword. They can become a disastrous distraction if we are not paying attention when we should be. But they can turn imagination into productive creativity and personal growth.

Docter has cleverly planted a topic of concern for individuals that is highly appropriate for classroom discussion, literary-artistic analysis or fam-

---

10   Space limitations allow me only to mention other worthy examples of how *Inside Out* enlightens and entertains. One is a demonstration of "earworms," those tunes we just can't get out of our heads. These illustrate the formative power and long-livedness of music from infancy to old age, even for Alzheimer's patients (Levitin). Another example is how our brains' visual imagery might represent "abstractions" and "dimensions" quite literally.

ily chats. Anyone's *default mode* is closely related to that individual's imaginative and creative processes of reworking memory. That is, when an individual allows her mind to wander and imagine constructively, her *default mode* activates inner attention, enabling her to sustain concentration, recreate memory, reorganize and thus learn anew. This is how our own personal creativity at the neuro-biological level necessarily helps us self-organize inside-out. An individual's sustained, creative attention to her internal societies can, in turn, become recognized by others as creative and innovative if her creativity represents a beneficial change for other individuals in her surrounding social-cultural relations. In effect, this is how the outward, conventional sense of creativity necessarily begins when an individual's self-realizing creativity has exterior benefits. Such neurobiological processes had to occur inside great artist-inventors like Leonardo da Vinci or great writers like Cervantes for their creations to eventually become known to the world outside.

These are lessons for scholar-teachers, parents and students as they learn to interpret the imaginative yet realistic worlds of all the arts and humanities—not just for *Inside Out*. When we are attentively mind-wandering, we can create new inside-out connections for learning and remembering. This is why multitasking robs our brains of the sustained attention required for making the new neuronal connections constituting our self-realization. The shallow and inattentive levels of concentration used for multitasking are not sufficient to reorganize memory and create critical thinking (Carr). At the neurobiological level, the creative changes of neuronal self-realization are the same processes we rely on for all our embodied minds' learning, remembering and critical thinking. Such are the potential benefits of learning to analyze and interpret a film like *Inside Out*. Much more than trying to interest new generations in science-based careers or STEM fields, *Inside Out* is valuable for revealing the profoundly personal and social values of the humanities. That is, when artists, literary specialists and social scientists develop inside-out awareness of self, they are better prepared for the humanistic sciences of scholarship, teaching and parenting.

Finally, *Inside Out* suggests additional questions for future scholarly and classroom discussion on how neurobiological awareness is the starting point for greater socio-cultural and political-economic awareness. For example, why is Docter's protagonist Riley a sporty-girl with a non-gender-specific name and not a girly-girl? The neurobiology of culture points to the "natural" multiplicities of sexuality and gender. And why did Docter depict the blue-eyed and fair-complexioned Riley as a distinct minority among her ethnically diverse cohorts in her new San Francisco classroom? And why does

Docter show that other human characters in the film have inside-out "emotional" relationships? We see examples inside the heads of Riley's parents, her teacher and even a neighborhood dog! These questions are opportunities to learn to recognize empathy and culture operating neuro-biologically within us all. The film closes a year after Riley and her family have moved to San Francisco. Docter depicts each as having adapted inside-out. Each is newly self-realized within the new environment and society, but all are bracing for puberty.

Works Cited

Barrett, Lisa Feldman, and Daniel J. Barrett. "How Pixar's *Inside Out* Gets One Thing Deeply Wrong." WBUR, Boston. *Massachusetts General Hospital. Center for Law, Brain, and Behavior.* 5 July 2015. Web. 10 July 2015.

Carr, Nicholas. *The Shallows: What the Internet Is Doing to Our Brains.* New York: Norton: 2010. Print.

Connor (Connor-Swietlicki), Catherine. "Beyond Cognition: Don Quijote and Other Embodied Minds." *Cognitive Cervantes.* Ed. Julien J. Simon, Barbara Simerka, and Howard Mancing. Spec. cluster of essays of *Cervantes: Bulletin of the Cervantes Society of America* 32.1 (2012): 231-61. Print.

———. "Why Autopoiesis and Memory Matter to Cervantes, *Don Quixote*, and the Humanities." *Cognitive Approaches to Early Modern Spanish Literature.* Ed. Isabel Jaén and Julien J. Simon. Oxford: Oxford UP, 2016. 53-73. Print.

Damasio, Antonio. *The Feeling of What Happens: Body, Emotion and the Making of Consciousness.* London: Heinemann, 1999. Print.

Gross, Terry. "It's All in Your Head: Director Pete Docter Gets Emotional in *Inside Out*." *Fresh Air.* WHYY Philadelphia. 10 June 2015. Web. 11 June 2015.

Kandel, Eric. *In Search of Memory: The Emergence of a New Science of Mind.* New York: Norton. 2006. Print.

Keltner, Dacher, and Paul Ekman. "The Science of *Inside Out*." *Sunday Review. The New York Times.* 5 July 2015: 10. Print.

Kirch, Meg. "Turning the Brain *Inside Out*." *Neuwrite San Diego. 2 July 2015.* Web. *5 July 2015.*

Inside Out. Dir. Pete Docter. Co-dir. Ronnie del Carmen. Perf. Amy Poehler, Phyllis Smith, Richard Kind, Bill Hader, Lewis Black, Mindy Kaling, Kaitlyn Dias, Diane Lane, Kyle MacLachlan. Pixar, 2015. Film.

Levitin, Daniel. *This Is Your Brain on Music: The Science of a Human Obsession*. New York: Penguin, 2007. Print.

Mancing, Howard. "Embodied Cognition and Autopoiesis in *Don Quixote*." *Cognitive Approaches to Early Modern Spanish Literature*. Ed. Isabel Jaén and Julien J. Simon. Oxford: Oxford UP, 2016. 37-52. Print.

Maturana, Humberto, and Francisco Varela. *The Tree of Knowledge: The Biological Roots of Human Understanding*. Trans. Robert Paolucci. Rev. ed. Boston: Shambhala, 1998. Print.

Montañez, Amanda. "Ramón y Cajal and the Case for Drawing in Science." *Scientific American Visual*. 23 June 2015. Web. 1 July 2015.

Novella, Steven. "*Inside Out*: A Neuroscience Metaphor." *Neurologica Blog*. 22 June 2015. Web. 5 July 2015.

Quian Quiroga, Rodrigo. *Borges and Memory: Encounters with the Human Brain*. Trans. Juan Pablo Fernández. Cambridge: MIT P, 2012. Print.

Robb, Alice. "*Inside Out* Nails the Science of How Our Memories Function." *Vulture (Devouring Culture)*. 23 June 2015. Web. 5 July 2015.

Robinson, Tasha. "Pete Docter on the Goals and Milestones of *Inside Out*." *The Dissolve*. 23 June 2015. Web. *1 July 2015*.

Somov, Pavel. "*Inside Out* Movie—Buddhism of Modern Day Neuroscience." *360° of Mindfulness*. Psych Central. 21 June 2015. Web. 1 July 2015.

Warp, Erica. "Pixar's *Inside Out* Will Grow Your Mind." *Kizoom*. n.d. Web. *2 July 2015*.

II. The Human Body and the Mind

Skin and Touch: Flesh, Glass and *El licenciado Vidriera*

CHARLES VICTOR GANELIN
Miami University

T HE "SENSUAL TURN" IN humanistic study has brought with it an effort to understand the nature of embodied representation from perspectives not afforded by many approaches evolving out of the 1970's and 1980's "theory turn" in literary studies.[1] The place of the human sensorium in our understanding of culture helps us to track changing mores and the inevitable conflicts among individuals, societies, and nations. Of course language evolves to enable us to explore new realities by providing us with a distinct vocabulary germane to our queries, yet that language frequently is insufficient to the task of describing the human dimensions of literary texts. Social and political transformations bring with them alterations in sensorial experience reflective of shifts in ideology or the practices of everyday life. As anthropologist David Howes, the scholar perhaps most responsible for a shift toward renewed understanding of the sensorium, has written, "If [sensory values] are intrinsic to the immutable order of the universe, then to question the sensory model is to question the nature of reality"

---

1   I am indebted to my friend and colleague Howard Mancing for his groundbreaking work on cognition and literature and the resulting insights that have helped me focus on the senses. I dedicate this study to him. While I do not engage directly with the concept of Theory of Mind (for a fundamental bibliography on the topic, see Mancing, "Embodied") or Mancing's insightful idea of Theory of Body ("Embodied" 38ff.), to approach literary characters as if they were real will attract wide-ranging interest. Indeed, Mancing's "Embodied" essay provides specific applications to *Don Quixote* and incorporates the primary references to cognitive approaches to Cervantes.

(11). Counter-Reformation Spain, with its sensuous painting and sculpture, literature, and daily life, employed the traditional hierarchy of the five senses to attract the faithful to Church and to organize and control discourse in support of the monarchy;[2] clearly this discourse also informs much of the period's literary production. Those who would contest the ideologies employed rhetorical tactics drawn from the same well. Manifestations of the sensorium imbued in literary and other texts enable a fuller comprehension of seventeenth-century Spain, for example, than we might otherwise obtain. For present purposes Cervantes and his exemplary tale *El licenciado Vidriera* [The Glass Graduate] will provide a suitable object to explore how one aspect of the senses—touch and its immediate transmitter, skin—helps to enlighten the author's position respective of mind and body interaction and what it means to engage with a society.[3]

The power of human skin to sense carries broad implications as metaphor for clothing, houses, or any kind of external protection, a membrane—regardless of its porousness—between the self and the outer world.[4] Nina Jablonski has spoken to skin as an evolving tapestry that "tells the world about who we are or who we want to be" (3). As a primary locus for the sense of touch it offers a "vital dimension" of immediacy (Connor 34).[5] With contiguous contact/location between the body and its context—other people, the objects of daily life—skins stands as a transmitter of cultural values that we imbue within the individual as a testimony to the non-verbal power of touch. Skin is a trope of awareness, a signifier of a grammar of bodily continence. So the transformations of Tomás Rodaja to the Licenciado Vidriera

---

2 Enrique García Santo-Tomás remains the fundamental study on sensuous daily life in Spain and its manifestations in numerous cultural texts.

3 There are two complicating issues in any study of this sort, which I cannot address fully here: how to express the sensual, that is, felt experience, through language; and how to define and communicate sensual experiences from the past. For the first, see Majid and Levinson; for the second, see Corbin, especially Chapter 13, "A History and Anthropology of the Senses."

4 I refer the reader interested in this topic to Serre; Connor; Jablonski. Connor, particularly, summarizes contemporary philosophical writing on skin, and Jablonski provides a sociobiological perspective. In literary studies, Harvey remains indispensable.

5 The problems inherent in defining, locating, and "ranking" the sense of touch date to Aristotle; in *De anima* and *De sensu*, Aristotle lays out the problems associated with the sense of touch, its locus, and its definitions, and discussions of these topics appear throughout his writings. For a contemporary argument on touch as the overarching sense, see Heller-Roazen.

to Tomás Rueda come to represent cultural moments and movements across a continuum of bodily and political borders. When touch becomes blocked, as in this curious case of a man believing himself turned into glass, the new covering is a poor fiction incapable of guiding observers through other cutaneous worlds, as his contact is strictly through language. I do not suggest a form of bodily "communication" *per se* absent of spoken or written language itself, but when touch is eliminated—direct contact with human society and culture because of (artificial) barriers—a language of skin becomes debilitated. The glass sheath of Vidriera turns him into a monster of nature as hazily detailed as, for example, the supposed portrait that Cervantes draws of himself in the prologue to the *Novelas ejemplares* [Exemplary Novels].

Just as Cervantes appears in many guises in his *Novelas*—"Cervantes," prologuist, narrator—and is always present yet always diffuse, Vidriera appears in distinct forms with distinct coverings ("skins") but is never fully present. Unlike many characters in the novella, Vidriera is rarely described inside the protective coverings of a house or other structure, with the exception of his visit to shrines in Rome.[6] Buildings as shields have served, for better or worse, Isabela (Clotaldo's home and Queen Elizabeth I's court in *La española inglesa* [The English Spanish Girl]) and Campuzano (the hospital in *El casamiento engañoso* [The Deceitful Marriage]). Other characters of the *Novelas* are definable by the skins they wear and the tales they tell: Ricaredo (*La española inglesa*), dresses as a courtier until his transformation through pilgrimage and captivity, emerging with a rough blue cape of those rescued by the Trinitarians; Carrizales (*El celoso extremeño* [The Jealous Old Man from Extremadura]) has skin that is old and sagging, a man unfit for a child-bride; La Cañizares (*El coloquio de los perros* [The Dialogue of the Dogs]) is described in her repulsive nudity; Campuzano is characterized by his sickly pallor. Each of these situations exemplifies displacement writ large on the skin, a crucial element of this discourse. Characters move from inside to outside, they expose themselves to or protect themselves from the elements, or they reveal or hide their interiority. By speaking of outer coverings and centers we as readers detect attempts both at containment and escape, or push-

---

6   This particular detail may be a function of the novella's picaresque character, as the narrated events of *Rinconete y Cortadillo* take place primarily outside of shelter. Serre articulates that we build houses for biological reasons: "comme une variété de mammifères ou de primates mous qui, après avoir perdu la toison, inventa la maison et la remplit incontinent de boîtes gigognes" [like a kind of mammal or weak primate who, after having lost its fur, built the house and filled it at once with nested boxes] (157; translation my own)].

ing at the edges, or breaking through, or being expelled, or fighting one's way in. These seemingly opposing images populate Cervantes's narratives, easily identifiable as additional sources of tension within the containing "vessel" itself, the narrative and its framework.[7] In a recent essay on *La española inglesa* I argue that skin, in its immediacy, serves as both metaphor for the novella as a whole and as a marker of nationality and faith, especially as the locus for the sense of touch, that which draws the characters into contact with their worlds. The skin of Cervantes's narrative holds together the author's observations of economics and history placed within a hybrid literary genre while skin as revealed (or hidden) becomes a skein, a layered marker or tapestry of transformations through loss and regeneration (of country, of religion, of literal skin) (Ganelin, "Cervantes's").

Readers of Cervantes would not be remiss to conclude that this author, on creating characters who embody the full complement of sensorial experience, has "skin in the game." While this admittedly facile play on words trades on the subject of skin or coverings in *El licenciado Vidriera*, it also alludes to Cervantes's lived experience, the prologue to the *Novelas ejemplares*, and ways to embody a character. Much has been written on Cervantes's fictional portrait presented in the prologue and the descriptive narrative that is part of it. Whether the representation serves as a "signature," however unreliable it may be (Lorenzo 90-92); or part of an "elaborate, concocted tale of an absent engraving that should have substituted for a prologue," which highlights questions attendant upon language and truth (Boyd 58, 67); a faithful representation of Cervantes's likeness (Mancing, "Cervantes" 122-24); or a statement that "this author does write from lived experience" (Gaylord 111), the portrait and Cervantes's various conceits surrounding it signal a literary embodiment. Julien Simon, in his introductory essay to the special issue of the journal *Cervantes*, "Cognitive Cervantes," concludes in what could be a logical extension of Mary Gaylord's summary comment: "The senses, feelings, interplay of minds, psychological development of characters, and their well-defined voices and subjectivities constitute some of the threads of the narrative fabric woven by Cervantes" (11). Just as Cervantes presents himself in the *Novelas*' prologue as an embodied individual yet not quite so—the portrait both remains squarely on the fictional plane and teases us to flesh out the author's human likeness—so he introduces us to myriad characters

---

7 The *entremeses* [interludes] as well as the *comedias* [plays] would be another excellent focus for a sensorial study; theatre, especially in its staged presentation, lends both sensuous and sensual depth to a playtext. See Ganelin, "Confusing Senses."

who explore the contours of being human. The prologue, with its challenging metaphor of an ironic self-effacing "pepitoria" [stew], is located at the edge of the collection yet "covers" it and in a way binds it; its physical placement, as Steven Connor views in another context, grants it a place of empowerment (265). We can begin to see the constellation of possibilities that "skin" and the concomitant sense of touch may generate as we seek to understand how the membranes of fiction relate to the membrane of widely-defined flesh, how Cervantes's characters become "real" and question their relation to society.

El licenciado Vidriera presents an unusual array of skins. In Tomás Rodaja's transformations, Cervantes forces today's readers to join Howes in questioning "immutable order" and the sensory model that the author had inherited. Seventeenth-century Spain is a raucous place in its reflection of vibrant arts coupled with political corruption, economic decline and philosophical conundrums, particularly in questions concerning the fundamental conceptions of human mind and body interaction in a momentous transition toward Cartesianism. *Vidriera*, in its display of bodily segregation, contests the growing belief in separation that had begun to seep into the collective consciousness of those most attuned to cultural shifts and models of being. The notion of a skeptical reader dealing with Cervantes's modernity easily forms part of this questioning, as Steven Wagschal has elaborated, particularly in learning how Cervantes expands "the conditions for the possibility of experience" (152).

Mutability finds its expression from the outset of the novella as one of the prime markers of Tomás Rodaja's identity in what we can call his "outer skin," the socially-encoded clothing he wears.[8] As the two students of noble birth come upon a sleeping Tomás along the banks of the Tormes river, the narrator notes that he is "vestido como labrador" ["dressed like a peasant"] (43; 275). Ensuing descriptions reveal the almost chameleon-like change in, or perhaps protean nature of, this young man. His coverings are central to understanding Tomás's sensorial contact with the world, his path toward knowledge, his conversion to a man of glass, and his final transformation into a soldier. The protagonist's metamorphosis occurs relatively rapidly, a sign of instability established with the first descriptor, which surmises a lowly provenance. When Tomás, taken in by the two traveling students, gives his surname as Rodaja,

---

8   Quotations are from the Sieber edition; all translations of *El licenciado Vidriera* are from "The Glass Graduate," trans. Price. For an elaboration on clothing as skin, see Benthien; she refers to a story by Kafka wherein he calls skin "natural fancy dress" (qtd. in Benthien 111).

the narrator states, "de donde infirieron sus amos, por el nombre y por el vestido, que debía de ser hijo de algún labrador pobre" ["from which his masters inferred (from his name as well as his dress) that he was probably the son of some poor peasant family"] (43; 275). Again we may only *infer* a status in life as it is judged primarily by what covers him. Soon thereafter, "le vistieron de negro" ["they dressed him in the garb of a student"] (43; 275), placing on him a new second skin that itself appears to work magic: "y a pocas semanas dio Tomás muestras de tener raro ingenio" ["and within a few weeks Tomás gave every sign of being unusually intelligent"] (43; 275). Rodaja studies at the Universidad de Salamanca for eight years, an event summarized in a few lines of text (43-44), prior to embarking on his "European tour" at the invitation of Captain Diego de Valdivia. As he prepares to depart Antequera, "habíase vestido Tomás de papagayo" ["Tomás had by now dressed himself in the ostentatious military style"] (47; 277), a colorful portrayal that commentators such as Harry Sieber (47n11) and Juan Bautista Avalle-Arce (108n21) define rightly as "bizarramente" (with panache) and relate it to soldiers' clothing. Yet this is the same moment in the text when the narrator begins to employ the verb "notar" to describe Tomás's gaze at the objects he views in his travels, with a greater reliance on the act of viewing than observing the essence of the objects themselves.[9] "Papagayo" (literally, "parrot," but descriptive of colorful clothing) also anticipates Tomás's change into Vidriera as in the phrase "Hablar como el papagayo. Phrase que vale decir algunas cosas buenas y discretas, sin inteligencia ni conocimiento" [Speak like a parrot. Phrase that means to say some wise and discrete things, but without comprehension or knowledge] (*Diccionario*).[10] Seeing and being seen operate jointly, and the later transformation from bright clothing to glass is one of consistency, as neither permits profound observations, neither allows contact, and both keep a viewer staring—Tomás Rodaja-*cum*-Licenciado Vidriera as object repels any attempt at proximity or crossing the threshold it establishes.

Alterations in Tomás's dress also prepare for and characterize his visit to Italy; Rome appears as a series of sensorial images suggestive of a planned religious peregrination (Conrod 256). Frédéric Conrod's observation points to the internal senses of contemplation as might be practiced in spiritual exercises, yet the text yields little confirmation that the potential depth of these experiences produces any real effect in Rodaja, whose life seems to be lived on the "surface." The descriptions are suggestive as well of unclear objects, of enclosures, of obfuscation: "diamantes engastados en oro" ["diamonds

---

9   Forcione 229ff. develops this idea fully.
10 Translation is mine.

in gold"] (48; 279), referring to houses set against the hillside; the adornments placed by pilgrims on the walls of Our Lady of Loreto shrine, which cover the walls themselves, rendering them unviewable: "no vio paredes ni murallas" ["he could not see the inner nor the outer wall"] (50; 281). By locating a visit to this particular shrine, Cervantes announces Tomás's further movement toward insularity, toward a separation of his interiority from the exterior world. Yet the impossibility of seeing the walls themselves makes of them a layer of "flesh" that hides or displaces the fundamental simplicity of the Virgin Mary's home. Though myriad observations characterize Tomás's travels from his arrival in Antequera (46) to his return to Salamanca (50), the rapidity of the journey imposes a lack of focus concomitant with his self-imposed isolation.[11] It is as if the sites had been seen through a glass darkly: "Now we see only reflections in a mirror, mere riddles, but then we shall be seeing face to face. Now I can know only imperfectly; but then I shall know just as fully as I am myself known" (I *Corinthians* 13:12), an ironic anticipation of Tomás's transformation to glass, and an even more ironic framing for a discussion of his knowledge.[12]

"Vidrio" as the descriptor of Tomás's condition is employed eight times (53-54) once Rodaja recovers physically from the effects of a potion administered to him by the courtesan whose amorous advances Tomás had rejected, yields to the name Licenciado Vidriera, given to him by the seamstress' husband (55), one of the many who posed questions to Vidriera and responded with their own gibes. The word "vidrio" disappears soon after the Licenciado begins his journey as the man of glass although references to his name accumulate. The transition from the descriptor of material ("de vidrio") to a proper name (Vidriera), enshrines or incarnates him. As Richard Kearney argues in his presentation of a "carnal hermeneutics," we need to "revisit the deep and inextricable relationship between *sensation* and *interpretation*" (101). Vidriera, from the perspective of a man of straw-protected glass, spouts "wisdom" yet he cannot take the step from sense to sensibility, does not know how to be tactful. Tact requires contact, as Kearney argues (103), and Vidriera actively rejects flesh on flesh. His turning into glass is the logical consequence of his superficial tourism, to his constant changing of dress,

---

11   This section of the novella does conform to the travel-narrative structure of the period, at least on its surface; Paul Lewis-Smith, for example, contextualizes it as revelatory of Tomás's provincialism or as Cervantes's guide to other young scholars in Valladolid (441).

12   Cervantes's employment of the *Bible* has been ably studied, most recently by Ruth Fine. She does not bring *Corinthians* to bear in this episode.

to his utter rejection of the woman who prepared the poisoned *membrillo* [quince], rendering him unable to engage in a perception of contact itself (Stewart 33).

The passage from observer (even when observed observing) to commentator follows a logical process based on the protagonist's untouchability, itself a cornerstone of what Alban Forcione calls a "diseased form of humor" (269), an implication that the untouchable life is *manqué*. One of the more astute commentaries on Vidriera's affliction as well as on his locutions are from George Shipley, who argues that the figure of the court fool is turned on its head. Licenciado Vidriera is a natural fool, "purely and perfectly irresponsible, ... destitute of reason" (720), quite in line with Forcione's reading of the "seductive attractiveness of dogmatic thinking to humanity" (269) that Cervantes aptly recognized. Vidriera's verbal barbs and his glass surface are of a piece; he speaks the language of the surface with a control of easily-imitated discourse.[13] Glass is the metaphor for the superficial man. The covering impedes touch, hinders direct contact and knowledge (with implications for both "sabiduría" and "conocimiento"), hampers "conveyance into the interior of the subject" (Harvey 2). He weaves a language separated or blocked from the self; his distorted and deficient skin obstructs knowing the self, a prerequisite for knowing anything beyond the self. Vidriera's reaction to any who dared draw near reinforces a concept of false skin as dangerous shield: "grandes gritos que daba cuando le tocaban o a él se arrimaban, por el hábito que traía ..." ["the shrieks he gave when people touched him or came near him, for the clothes he wore"] (73; 305). Cervantes reveals the dangers of shallow thinking and thin narratives. Tomás's decision to carry with him in his earlier travels a Garcilaso "sin comento" ["without notes"] (47; 277) can certainly suggest a well-rounded humanist education (Shipley 729), but this detail can cut two ways: Tomás may be in no need of a guide because his education has provided him with sufficient intellectual judgment to appreciate the poet's artistic accomplishments, yet this "unadorned" Garcilaso stands in contrast to Tomás's frequently superficial Roman holiday: "Todo lo miró y notó y puso en su punto" ["He looked at everything and considered everything carefully"] (49; 281).

---

13   I part company with Shipley where he holds that "[t]he youth developed admirably at home, at school, and on his traveling fellowship, until ... he fell victim of a carnal conspiracy ..." (721). Tomás learns by rote, observes, and views, but never internalizes; he had been separated from society from the outset, never finding a niche as a fully-constituted subject.

Shipley's comments, as well as those by Stephen Rupp, lead neatly to the question of displacement. Rupp focuses on the limitations of satire in the text: "by displacing generic and discursive boundaries, the novella questions conventional patterns of thought and rhetoric" (146). We can take this assertion one logical step further, as it applies as well to the sensual turn introduced at this essay's outset as the novella posits the dangers of displacing another boundary and disrupting the paradigm of a mind-body continuum. By remaining on the surface, by seeing and noting, and finally by protecting himself in straw, Tomás Rodaja/Licenciado Vidriera isolates himself from human company. Mark Paterson offers a cogent synthesis of the philosophical tradition surrounding the sense of touch, and recalls one of Husserl's fundamental assertions: "I perceive *with* my hands" (qtd. in Paterson 30; emphasis in original). Forcione observes how Rodaja opts to abandon Salamanca, accompanies Captain Valdivia but refuses to enlist, and, tellingly, "rejects even the touch of his fellow man" (313). Kearney elaborates by positing that a lack of touch leads to a lack of hospitality (101); "hospitality" and "hostile," in both English and Spanish, have their root in the Latin "hostis," which means both "enemy" and "guest." To extend a hand may be an act of welcoming, a trait missing in Vidriera, and therefore may exemplify his lack of charity. No sensible life is possible without the power of touch (Heller-Roazen 27).

The central portion of the triptych-like structure of *Vidriera* reflects what occurs when touch becomes divorced from the world around us. On the one hand the novella is a cautionary tale written by one fully involved, corporeally, in an active life. Vidriera, however, touches not lest he be touched. The transparency of glass makes it appear to point to accessibility, yet this is but an illusion of substance.[14] Glass creates a distance and eliminates the immediacy of sensual conveyance; as glass is non-porous, it also blocks any sensation that touch produces. For Vidriera, his *real* connection to the world is severed, in his mind, and he ceases to be tactile; tactility is exposure to something other than one's self as well as the negotiation between embodied beings (Kearney 103). He only skims over the folds in the flesh of the world of human sensation.[15] Cervantes makes of Vidriera a standard-bearer for questioning

---

14   I thank Catherine Larson for sharing her perception of this Cervantine irony.

15   This view would appear to differ from Michael Gerli's, but I see points of contact: "Figuratively, [Vidriera] is like glass: superficially he appears invisible and insubstantial, yet he is like that transparent medium capable of transfiguring the objects placed behind it. As an allegory of enlightenment, he is at once peripheral, yet in possession of an inner view" (19). My perspective follows a different path, but I

the rupture in the flow of inside-outside sensory perception, an expression of embodiment against the increasing neo-stoic mind/body dualities that will soon dominate discourse.[16] Skin is the membrane that both separates and protects the individual and conduces sensations to the body (whether human or politic). Paterson argues that touch is "the first sense prior to the differentiation into other sensory modalities" (4). Vidriera's self-protection from cutaneous contact impedes full sensorial possibilities of engagement with the world around him, and his self-defined glass membrane halts skin's function as a conduit, even if only in his mind.

Despite his metamorphoses Vidriera is no Pygmalion. Tomás's decision, once he is cured of his malady, to become a soldier and engage in the fully physical contact of skin, takes place out of sight, rendered as summarily as his years in Salamanca. All we have is the narrator's assurance: "... se fue a Flandes, donde la vida que había comenzado a eternizar por las letras la acabó de eternizar por las armas ... dejando fama en su muerte de prudente y valentísimo soldado" ["(he) went off to Flanders, where ... the life he had begun to make famous by learning he ended by fame in arms leaving behind him, when he died, the reputation of having been a wise and most valiant soldier"] (74; 307).[17] Tomás, even in the evolution from Rodaja to Rueda—smoothing out the edges, attempting to move from a literal slice of life to what he intended to be a well-rounded existence—has always remained a character who cannot become fully embodied in the sense that Isabela or Preciosa become. The exploits of war and Rueda's honorable death are related as succinctly as are his years as a student in Salamanca. That death is told as an event quite distant, however glorious it may have been, and is therefore an extension of Vidriera's malady. Touch is exteroceptive (outward) yet it is proximal (close to the body), and a death in war told from a narrative distance reinforces

---

think that terms like "invisible," "insubstantial," and "peripheral" allow both readings. I was not aware of Gerli's use of "darkened glass" (19) until after I had suggested the oblique reference above to *Corinthians*.

16   Forcione addresses these issues, the question of *desengaño*, the link between Stoicisim and satire, and the evolution toward Quevedo's mordant writings (293-96).

17   Joseph Ricapito's smart summary of the legal profession in Cervantes's time, the social class expectations of those who would practice law, and the difficulties faced by those who attempt to rise above their station (an idea reinforced by and part of the moral setting noted by Huarte de San Juan), all speak to Tomás's coming up against the metaphorical glass ceiling. Even at the risk of such an anachronistic metaphor, Vidriera's believing himself made of glass may be the only possible, if delusional, reaction to such challenges (69-78).

Tomás's detachment from the depth of human experience. Cervantes writes large the "tension between the quotidian immediacy of cutaneous contact and the philosophical profundity of touch" (Paterson 2). Without a literary "tangible flesh" (Kearney 103), there can be no connection to a lived life that the reader can imagine. Susan Stewart has written that "touch and the reciprocal motility of touch are the beginning of agency. Touch is the most important vehicle for our access to reality" (34). Cervantes warns his readers that living life in mere observation, avoiding the human messiness of sustained, intimate contact, reduces us to objects of manufacture ("de vidrio" [of glass]) and never the subject of the glorious messiness of life. The constant and consistent tensions between inside and outside, of gaining knowledge through bodily and sensual experience, are hallmarks of early modern writing within and without Spain, and Cervantes, possibly more than any of his contemporaries, requires us (his readers) to understand the demands of what truly makes us human.

Works Cited

Aristotle. *The Complete Works of Aristotle*. Ed. Jonathan Barnes. Vol. 1. Princeton: Princeton UP, 1984. Print. Bollingen Series LXXI 2.

Benthien, Claudia. *Skin*. Trans. Thomas Dunlap. New York: Columbia UP, 2002. Print.

Boyd, Stephen F. "Cervantes's Exemplary Prologue." *A Companion to Cervantes's* Novelas ejemplares. Ed. Stephen F. Boyd. Woodbridge: Tamesis, 2005. 47-68. Print.

Cervantes, Miguel de. *The Glass Graduate*. Trans. R. M. Price. *The Complete Exemplary Novels*. Ed. Barry Ife and Jonathan Thacker. 2nd ed. Oxford: Aris and Phillips, 2013. 271-307. Print.

———. *Novelas ejemplares*. 2 vols. Ed. Harry Sieber. Madrid: Cátedra, 1990. Print.

———. *Novelas ejemplares*. 3 vols. Ed. Juan Bautista Avalle-Arce. Madrid: Castalia, 1987. Print.

Connor, Steven. *The Book of Skin*. Ithaca: Cornell UP, 2004. Print.

Conrod, Frédéric. "La Roma española y sus resonancias jesuitas en dos *Novelas ejemplares*." *Novelas ejemplares: Las grietas de la ejemplaridad*. Ed. Julio Baena. Newark, DE: Juan de la Cuesta, 2008. 251-64. Print.

Corbin, Alain. *Time, Desire and Horror: Towards a History of the Senses*. Trans. Jean Birrell. Cambridge: Polity, 1995. Print.

Diccionario de autoridades. Tomo V. 1737. Real Academia Española. *Nuevo diccionario histórico del español.* Web. 23 Apr. 2016.

Fine, Ruth. *Reescrituras bíblicas cervantinas.* Madrid: Iberoamericana; Frankfurt: Verveurt, 2014. Print.

Forcione, Alban. *Cervantes and the Humanist Vision: A Study of Four Exemplary Novels.* Princeton: Princeton UP, 1982. Print.

Ganelin, Charles. "Cervantes's Exemplary Sensorium, or the Skinny on *La española inglesa.*" *Beyond Sight: The Other Senses in Iberian Literature.* Ed. Steven Wagschal and Ryan Giles. Toronto: U of Toronto P. Forthcoming.

———. "Confusing Senses and Tirso de Molina's *La celosa de sí misma.*" *Bulletin of Spanish Studies* 90.4-5 (2013): 619-38. Print.

García Santo-Tomás, Enrique. *Espacio urbano y creación literaria en el Madrid de Felipe IV.* Madrid: Iberoamericana, 2004. Print.

Gaylord, Mary Malcolm. "Cervantes' Other Fiction." *The Cambridge Companion to Cervantes.* Ed. Anthony J. Cascardi. Cambridge: Cambridge UP, 2002. 100-30. Print.

Gerli, E. Michael. *Refiguring Authority: Reading, Writing, and Rewriting in Cervantes.* Lexington: UP of Kentucky, 1995. Print.

Harvey, Elizabeth D., ed. *Sensible Flesh: On Touch in Early Modern Culture.* Philadelphia: U of Pennsylvania P, 2003. Print.

Heller-Roazen, Daniel. *The Inner Touch: Archaeology of a Sensation.* New York: Zone, 2007. Print.

Holy Bible. Corinthians I:12-13. *Bible.com.* Web. 10 Nov. 2015.

Howes, David, ed. *Empire of the Senses: The Sensual Culture Reader.* New York: Berg, 2005. Print.

Jablonski, Nina G. *Skin: A Natural History.* Berkeley: U of California P, 2006. Print.

Kearney, Richard. "What is Carnal Hermeneutics?" *New Literary History* 46 (2015): 99-124. Print.

Lewis-Smith, Paul. "Literature and Sin: Moral-Theological Wisdom and Literary Ethics in Cervantes's *El licenciado Vidriera.*" *Modern Language Review* 105.2 (2010): 439-54. *JSTOR.* Web. 10 July 2015.

Lorenzo, Javier. "'En blanco y sin figura:' Prologue, Portrait, and Signature in Cervantes' *Novelas ejemplares.*" *Letras hispanas* 2.2 (2005): 86-101. *Texas SU.* Web. 17 June 2014.

Majid, Asifa, and Stephen C. Levinson. "The Senses in Language and Culture." *Senses & Society* 6.1 (2011): 5-18. Web. 15 Sept. 2015.

Mancing, Howard. "Cervantes as Narrator of *Don Quijote*." *Cervantes: Bulletin of the Cervantes Society of America* 23.1 (2003): 117-40. Print.

———. "Embodied Cognition and Autopoiesis in *Don Quijote*." *Cognitive Approaches to Early Modern Spanish Literature*. Ed. Isabel Jaén and Julien Jacques Simon. Oxford: Oxford UP, 2016. 37-52. Print.

Paterson, Mark. *The Senses of Touch: Haptics, Affects and Technologies*. Oxford: Berg, 2007. Print.

Ricapito, Joseph. *Cervantes's* Novelas ejemplares: *Between History and Creativity*. West Lafayette: Purdue UP, 1996. Print.

Rupp, Stephen. "Soldiers and Satire in *El licenciado Vidriera*." *A Companion to Cervantes's* Novelas ejemplares. Ed. Stephen F. Boyd. Woodbridge: Tamesis, 2005. 134-47. Print.

Serre, Michel. *Les cinq sens: Philosophie des corps mêlés I*. Paris: Bernard Grasset, 1985. Print.

Shipley, George. "Cervantes' Licenciado Vidriera Was No Ordinary Fool." *Bulletin of Hispanic Studies* 82 (2005): 717-31. Print.

Simon, Julien. "Introduction to 'Cognitive Cervantes:' Integrating Mind and Cervantes's Texts." *Cognitive Cervantes*. Ed. Julien J. Simon, Barbara Simerka, and Howard Mancing. Spec. cluster of essays of *Cervantes: Bulletin of the Cervantes Society of America* 32.1 (2012): 11-21. Print.

Stewart, Susan. "Prologue: From the Museum of Touch." *Material Memories*. Ed. Marius Kwint, Christopher Breward, and Jeremy Aynsley. Oxford: Berg, 1999. 17-36. Print.

Wagschal, Steven. "*Don Quixote*, the Skeptical Reader and the Nature of Reality." *Cervantes in Perspective*. Ed. Julia Domínguez. Madrid: Iberoamericana, 2013. 139-54. Print.

Hecho reloj:
Human Clocks, Bodies and Sexuality in Early-Modern Spanish Humorous Literature

Rachel Schmidt
University of Calgary

In his article, "Embodied Cognitive Science and the Study of Literature," Howard Mancing brings to the attention of literary scholars the important corrective understanding that humans "are not machines, but systems, complex interrelated biological organisms that function in context and are in a constant process of (autopoietically) adapting to and dealing with that context" ("Embodied Cognitive Science" 29). Moreover, his article "Embodied Cognition and Autopoiesis in *Don Quixote*" anchors the recent volume *Cognitive Approaches to Early Modern Spanish Literature* by positing the very necessary notion of Theory of Body as the necessary partner to Theory of Mind (38-39). As Mancing so rightly reminds us, "the complete understanding of a work of literature involves a recognition of the biological reality of life" ("Embodied Cognition" 50). Our interpretation of the autopoietic adaptation of the individual—and by extension, the literary character as we understand him or her—is then both a function of our use of Theory of Body and Theory of Mind. In order to know about a literary character, we must know both about their mind and their body. In Mancing's terms, "all knowledge is, at the same time, fully social and fully biological," for the human being exists in constant autopoietic adaptation to the social *and* physical environment ("Embodied Cognition" 45).

The notion of the human machine enters a variety of early-modern Spanish discourses through clock imagery. Using the phrase "hecho reloj" / "made a clock," writers jokingly highlighted the human body's sexual functioning. Unlike other sensorial processes, the phenomenal experience of time corresponds to "internal clocks" that, although based in physiognomy, can also respond to external stimuli. Almost all animal species have naturally occurring circadian rhythms of approximately twenty-four hours that respond to light and dark, and that regulate hormones and body temperature plus rest and activity (Campbell 102). Human fertility responds to light and melatonin, with the number of conceptions (especially of twins) falling in the Arctic Circle during the months of darkness. In the absence of light and dark cues as well as social interactions, humans settle into a body rhythm that is slightly longer than twenty-four hours, with sleeping periods rarely lasting longer than four hours (Campbell 114). The use of the image of the "clock-man" by authors such as Miguel de Cervantes and Francisco de Quevedo shows that they understood the ways in which the "internal" clocks of early-modern Spaniards were being "re-set" by social forces.[1]

The mechanical clock appeared shortly before 1300 CE (Mayr 5), although regimentation of daily life according to hours is generally attributed to the monastic discipline set by the Benedictine rule (Mumford 13). The innovation of the mechanical clock over water clocks or candle clocks is its use of verge-and-foliot escapement, in which the escapement controls the acceleration of two falling weights, such that a steady, constant motion is produced. Toledo built its town clock in 1371, Valencia in 1378, Burgos in 1384, Lérida in 1390, Barcelona after 1393, Sevilla in 1396, Huesca by 1423 and Zaragoza around 1424 (Morales Gómez and Torreblanca Gaspar 455). Town clocks arrived gradually in smaller Castilian towns throughout the sixteenth century, replacing daylight and church bells as the means for marking the hours (Asenjo González 176). In the sixteenth century these clocks moved from church towers to municipal buildings, not always without conflict. For Juan José Morales Gómez and María Jesús Torreblanca Gaspar, the physical removal of the public clock to a civic building mirrors the transition from ecclesiastical time, marked according to liturgical rhythms, to commercially structured units of time, as well as from the rhythms of rural labor, marked by daylight, to urban labor, marked by hours (456).[2] Spring-powered clocks

---

[1] For complaints about the effects of tyrannical clocks in other literatures, see Macey 24-25.

[2] Jacques Le Goff champions the argument for a transition from ecclesiastical time to commercial time, based on the needs of merchants and industry (48-49). Gerhard Dohrn van-Rossum maintains that the rapid spread of the clock and the subsequent regimentation of time occurred for a variety of reasons, including the prestige adhering to the clock tower and the appearance the tower gave of governmental authority and order (126-72).

were invented in the mid-fifteenth century, allowing for the making of portable, compact watches and table clocks (Mayr 8). Personal watches had wheel-based mechanisms requiring winding, and were small enough to be worn as adornment, as evidenced by Carlos V's chiming earrings (Cummins 15).[3]

Town clocks as well as table clocks often incorporated human figures. There exists a sixteenth-century table clock in which the right arm of an automaton figure of Carlos V moves in accordance to the bells, as his figure presides over twelve shields of his imperial territories (Montañés Fontenla 22). Civic or church clocks often included automated human figures that struck a bell with a hammer or mallet. These figures went by the epithet "tardón" (literally, slow one) in Castilian or, as in *La pícara Justina,* "hombre de reloj" [clock-man] (Herrero García 21-22). Before the invention of the mechanical clock and the automata, humans were hired to ring church or civic tower bells. Into the seventeenth century the profession of keeping timepieces well-running was so important that the Spanish monarchs employed a royal clock tender whose duty was to keep all palace clocks in time with each other and the sun (Atienza 208). Continued improvement on mechanical designs of timepieces, as in any technology, can be attributed to the desire to replace human effort with that of a machine (Macey 11). Thus, the clock is an automaton insofar as it stands in for a human being.

The topos of the cosmos functioning as a clock was widespread. Good governance is associated with clocks, as seen in the title of Antonio de Guevara's *Relox de príncipes* [Clock of Princes] (1529), or even when one of Lope's characters in *Servir a Buenos* [To Serve the Good] proclaims that republics are like clocks in a tower or on the chest (Fernández, *Anxieties* 117). Religious poetry incorporates clock imagery, as in Lope de Vega's *estribillo* [a verse repeated in a poem], "Un reloj he visto, Andrés" [I have seen a clock, Andrés],[4] in which the Trinity is described according to clock imagery (Heiple 160). The passing of time, both with regards to passing love and the theme of earthly *desengaño* or disenchantment, finds symbolic expression in poems such as Quevedo's "Reloj de campanilla" [Clock Bell] and Francisco López de Zárate's "Enseñando a un príncipe en un reloj a aprovechar el tiempo, y a ser benigno" [Teaching a prince through a watch to take advantage of time and to be benign]. In López de Zárate's work the human appears as subject to the wear of time, with bodily parts that decay and fail at any moment (Heiple 173). The personification of clocks takes a macabre turn when Quevedo, in-

---

    3   Pocket watches were not available to a bourgeois market until Christian Huygens invented the pendulum watch in 1657.
    4   All translations are mine unless otherwise indicated.

spired by Hieronomo Amalteo, initiates a poetic fashion, lasting until 1681, for the topos of the hour glass in which the ashes of the rejected lover or the rejecting beloved flow ceaselessly through the timepiece (Asensio 18-19).

In humorous texts, the image of the human clock serves to make fun of embodied daily life, as bodily rhythms, social habits and economic interactions are held to new standards by the changes brought about by regimented time. Pedro Calderón de la Barca mocks the owner of a portable clock in his *Entremés del reloj y genios de la venta* [Interlude of the Clock and the Inn Geniuses], making fun of both the rarity of the timepiece and its bearer's obnoxious insistence on measuring time. Among the four "genios" causing laughter at the inn, including a hypochondriac, one boastful of his clothing and another of his hometown Villalpando, it is the one who always pulls out his clock to tell time that merits a title billing. The mule boy Pedro and the maid Juana joke of nightfall by making reference to the appearance of the seven "cabrillas," the stars of the Pleiades, but the clock owner pedantically consults his timepiece, proclaiming that it will soon be 7:30. The joke is on him, as Pedro responds: "¿Siete y media? ¡Jesús! ¿Qué está diciendo? / ¿Quién oyó desatino tan horrendo? / ¿En el reloj cabrillas? ¿Es esfera?" [Seven o'clock? / Jesus! What are you saying? / Who heard such madness? / Are there goats or a sphere in the clock?] (180). The clock is not only unnecessary, but turns its owner into a dullard incapable of witty verbal exchange. For example, the law in Valencia continued to stipulate that the work day was "de sol a sol" [from sun-up to sun-down] (Dohrn van-Rossum 305). Nonetheless, clock hours were introduced there to limit the time for harder labor: starting in 1537, digging and chopping could only be undertaken from 7 a.m. to 5 p.m., and in 1555 from 8 a.m. to 5 p.m. Indeed, the syntagm "hecho reloj" [turned into a clock], is often used in humorous literature to refer to males who are the unwitting marks of deceit, fraud, and exploitation due to their own dulled intellect. The image extends to physical activity similar to that of the automaton rhythmically pounding and chopping--or to the laborers whose work was measured by a clock.

The joke of the human automaton, "hombre de reloj" [clock-man], appears at its most physical in picaresque novels, *entremeses* (humorous one-act plays performed between acts of other plays) and *bailes* or dances. In the *entremés, De ladrones y el reloj* [On Thieves and a Clock] (c. 1625) attributed to Luis Quiñones de Benavente, the *moza*, a lascivious young woman, and the *gracioso*, a stock character that plays the fool, are intent on mugging and robbing a card shark. They plan to do so by making themselves appear like a clock ("que parezcamos reloj") and then giving their target twelve hits ("dar las doce") (210). The joke depends on visualizing a bell, shaped like a pot, which will be rung twelve times by a mallet. Francés de Zúñiga, in his *Crónica burlesca del emperador Carlos V* [Burlesque Chronicle of the Emperor Charles V] (1529), likewise pictures the human figure fighting (or not) in terms of a human clock. Upon arriving at Valladolid, the Emperor meets the sad figures of the town leaders, Juan Rodríguez de Baeza, who seems like a drowsy ass, and the comendador Santiestevan, "que pareçe relox que se le van las pesas abaxo" [who looks like a clock with its weights hanging down] (102). The *pesas,* being the two weights that hang to each side of the gear mechanism in a mechanical clock, express inertia, but also testicles. Enrique Fernández quotes the reference to testicles in a quip from Juan de Timoneda's *Buen aviso y portacuentos* [Good News and Storybook] (1564) about a woman who asked for the time from a castrated man and received this answer from another: "Mala cuenta le puede dar de eso el reloj sin pesas" ["It is not a question to be asked of a clock with no weights"] (118).[5] In all these instances, clock-like parts associated with rhythmic pulsation stand for physical dynamism (or lack thereof). In *La Pícara Justina* (1605), the female narrator clarifies: "¿Saben a qué los comparo yo estos amantes campanudos que hacen apariencias y no ofrecen? Parécenme que son como afinadores de órgano, que le templan y no le tocan; son como hombre de reloj, que amagan a quebrar la campana y solo la hacen sonar ..." [Do you know to what I compare these bell-like lovers that make a show and do not offer? They seem to me like organ tuners that warm it up and do not touch it; they are like the clock-man who fakes breaking the bell and only makes it sound ...] (López de Úbeda 447). Zúñiga, who served as a *bufón de corte,* or court jester, also describes himself in battle as a clock, but in a pun that preserves his sexual virility: "este coronista ... armado parecía hombrezico de relox de San Martín de Valdeyglesias" [this armed chronicler ... looked like the little clock-man of San Martín de Valdeyglesias] (78). Near San Martín de Valdeiglesias stands a sheer cliff, the haunt of current-day rock climbers, called the Peña de Reloj [Clock Cliff]. Our diminutive court jester boasts of a very erect clock.

The well-adjusted clock in love or marital relations was a topos that appeared in serious literature, but satirical and humorous writers took full advantage of images of ill-adjusted, broken or even jerry-rigged clocks to poke fun at sexual relationships. Through the voice of the doctor who participates in the dialogue, Cristóbal Suárez de Figueroa, in *El pasajero* [The Traveler] (1617), recounts the story of an aging married couple. The skeletal wife takes

---

5   Both the quotation and translation are from Fernández, *Anxieties* 118.

to her bed, complaining her husband is having an adulterous affair, but she refuses to accept his amorous advances. In the anecdote, images of food and sex are combined: "En saliendo fuera de casa el infeliz esposo, trataba de almorzar famosamente, aforrando el estómago con tres o cuatro pieles del Baco más resentido. Tras esto, reposaba un poco, enderezando los flacos miembros cuando ambiguo el reloj duda si dará o no las doce" [When the unhappy spouse left the house, he tried to lunch abundantly, filling his stomach with three or four wineskins. Afterwards, he rested a bit, straightening his floppy members, when the ambiguous clock doubts if it will or will not chime twelve] (2.374). His members flaccid upon drinking and the clock hesitating to chime, the husband returns home to his wife, Quintañona, whom he then attempts to seduce with delicacies (2.375). The doctor witnesses the spectacle and pleads with the wife not to be jealous of the husband, whether he has a lover or not. The eighteenth-century *Bayle del amor reloxero* [Dance of the Clockish Love], by Francisco Benegasi y Luxán, actually creates a human clock from different stock characters: Amor [Love], Vejete [Old Man], Dueña [Madame], Valiente [Knave], Hidalgo [Gentleman], Miserable [Beggar], Soldado [Soldier], and three Damas [Ladies]. Under the direction of Amor, each character enacts a part of the clock. For example, the Vejete takes the part of the alarm as he suffers from insomnia; the soldier, who has deserted the army for his lover, plays the screw; and the wise (*cuerda*) woman who left an unfaithful lover plays the *cuerda*, or the clock's cord. The human clock, however, does not work well, never striking more than one, thus disappointing the *hidalgo* by never arriving at the correct time, being lunch time ("la de comer") and the ladies by never striking more than once (2, 49).

In the *Celestina* (1499) Fernando de Rojas highlights the effects of the town clock on commercial and physical aspects of daily life in early-modern Spain. For example, documents show that Teruel's town clock was used in the fifteenth century to organize workdays (Morales Gómez and Torreblanca Gaspar 469). The *Celestina*'s characters are alert to the peals of the town bells, and frequently count their ringing as a group (Fernández, "El reloj" 37). Unlike Calisto, who lives in the elastic time of an enamored noble, and Sempronio, Pármeno, Areúsa and Elicia, who all fail to use time well, Celestina knows how to manage time, valuing its worth to her in business terms (39). Calisto is described as "hecho reloj" when Celestina begins to grease him up for money. As Pármeno whispers to Sempronio while they witness the conversation: "Ya escurre eslabones el perdido: ya se desconciertan sus badajadas. Nunca da menos de doce; siempre está hecho reloj de mediodías" [Now the loser's links are running; now his bell clapper is getting confused. He never chimes less than twelve; he is always a noon kind of clock] (Rojas 148). Given that Calisto is described as a clock, the first two phrases, "escurre eslabones" [the links are running] and "desconciertan sus badajadas" [the bell clappers are ill-timed], refer to devices of a timepiece. The editors of the 2000 edition explain the first phrase as the movement of the chain that releases the mechanism that will chime the hour, and then reference a refrain from Núñez: "Reloj de mediodía, no da menos de doce" [Noon clock, never chimes less than twelve]. Sebastián de Covarrubias lists "badajo" as the term for clapper, adding that the noun "badajadas" [claps] means "necedades" [foolishness] (182). Calisto, *hecho reloj* [turned into a clock], has now become Celestina's mark and will begin to put out money for her—a vision that causes Sempronio to salivate. Medieval and early-modern clocks did not have minute hands, let alone second hands, and thus sported only hour hands. When Sempronio remarks that Calisto always gives twelve, is he referring to an erection?

Popular stories and jokes emphasized the clock as an economical machine that mechanized and measured, giving and putting out, even in criminal economic exchanges. In the sixteenth and seventeenth centuries the joke about the stingy man who does not give out occurs repeatedly, and is based on the image of the worthless clock that does not correctly tell time. Melchor Santa Cruz de Dueñas records the joke thus: "Alabando a un señor que era muy escaso, de virtuoso, y que era tan concertado como un reloj, respondió uno: Reloj que no da, no vale nada" [Praising a tightwad as virtuous, and as so well-timed as a clock, one responded: A clock that doesn't give, is worth nothing] (222).[6] Quevedo's poem known as "Las sacadoras" [The Takers] expresses bald-faced lust to use other humans for monetary gain (Chevalier). The lyrical voice belongs to a female seeking males who will regularly provide her with *cuartos*, this word meaning both coins and quarter hours. The refrain reads: "Yo los quiero relojes / y no muchachos / que me den cada hora / y aun cada cuarto" [I want them as clocks / and not boys / who give every hour / and even every quarter] (Quevedo 1289). She expects regularly timed contributions and exclaims: "Reloj que sin cuartos diere / horas muy bien concertadas, / ése da horas menguadas / ¡triste de la que le oyere! / El que cuartos no tuviere, / si tiene ochavos es harto" [The clock that would not give / very well-timed quarter hours, / that gives measly hours, / oh, sorry

---

6   A similar version of the joke is attributed to Alonso Carrillo by María Pilar Cuartero and Maxime Chevalier (see their edition of Santa Cruz de Dueñas 52). In the same edition, they list multiple occurrences of the joke, a few appearing in Lope de Vega's *La humildad y la soberbia* and *La bella aurora* and Tirso de Molina's *El mayor desengaño,* plus the *Entremés de los relojes* and *Don Pegote* (446).

listener! / He who doesn't have quarters, / if he has eighths, he's irritating] (1289). *Ochavos,* being a coin of lesser value, clearly refer to a man of less economic power. Nonetheless, the man's relative worth might also be sexual, an eighth of an hour being less satisfactory to the woman than a quarter hour.

In his *entremés, El juez de los divorcios* [The Divorce Judge] (1615), Cervantes uses the ill-timed clock imagery to describe failing marriages: "¿Quién diablos acertará a concertar estos relojes, estando las ruedas tan desconcertadas?" [Who in the world will reset these clocks, having wheels so badly timed?] (70). Belén Atienza views the judge who is called upon to fix these faltering clocks as a bad *relojero,* this being the profession of keeping the faulty mechanisms of clocks running well, because he fails to reconcile the couples (212). Both wives complain of husbands who fail to live up to timely desires. Mariana, married to Vejete, first requests that the time limit of marriages be adjusted: "En los reinos y en las repúblicas bien ordenadas, había de ser limitado el tiempo de los matrimonios, y de tres en tres años se habían de deshacer, o confirmarse de nuevo, como cosas de arrendamiento, y no que hayan de durar toda la vida, con perpetuo dolor de entrambas partes" [In well-ordered republics, the time-limits of marriages should be limited, and after every three years they should be undone or reaffirmed, like rental agreements, and should not last a lifetime, with perpetual pain for both parties] (Cervantes 62). The judge does not dismiss out of hand this suggested social engineering, but rather admits that if this "arbitrio," a term used for proposed governmental or societal reforms, could have been put into practice, and especially for money, it already would have been done. According to Covarrubias, the second meaning of *arrendar* is "dar o tomar a renta" [to rent a service for a period of time] (151). To define a fundamental unit of human society, perhaps the most fundamental, in terms of limited term contracts, points toward a modern view of human relationship in which measured time, rather than life events, determines beginnings and endings. Mariana's complaint reveals that she understands marriage as a contractual obligation to render services that are marked by the course of the day as she loses sleep waking up in the middle of the night to give him warm cloths, to adjust him in bed, and to give him syrup so he can breathe ("porque no se ahogue del pecho") [so that his chest not strangle him] (Cervantes 62-3). She slips, however, as she describes the age difference that renders her marriage difficult in traditional temporal terms as her springtime and his winter (62). Upon turning down her request for a divorce, the judge returns to a traditional understanding of marital temporality: "y, pues comistes las maduras, gustad de las duras; que no está obligado ningún marido a tener la velocidad y corrida del tiempo, que no pase por su puerta y por sus días" [since you ate the ripe fruit, enjoy the hard; no husband is obliged to detain the velocity and rapidity of time, that it should not pass through his door and his days] (64). The image of cyclical time, spring leading to fall, would reinforce the traditional notion of life-long marriage, but ripe fruit normally softens. Instead, here it hardens into dried-up fruit, yielding little nourishment and implying hard times for the wife who receives little in return for her care of the aging, withering body of her husband. Despite the bitter aftertaste of the judge's judgement, Mariana is allowed to entertain the notion of marriage as a temporary contract, if only in jest.

The second wife, Guiomar, sues for divorce from her husband, a soldier, because he refuses to submit to a temporally regimented work day, choosing, instead, a day based on leisure. The only exact hour the so-called soldier recognizes is two o'clock, when he appears for lunch. Otherwise, he spends the mornings going to mass or gossiping in the Puerta de Guadalajara, the afternoons in the gaming house, returning home at midnight for dinner—if there is any—, and wanders all night (66). Along with his imprecise hours comes a lack of income, to which the soldier regularly admits, saying that he has no occupation (67). The grounds for which Guiomar requests divorce are telling, for she claims the man before the court is not the man she married, whom she thought was "moliente y corriente" [milling and running] (66). This idiomatic phrase originates in the description of a well-timed waterwheel (Cejador y Frauca 177). Similar to clocks in their operation, water mills ran on the rhythmic motion of wheels, gears, and spars; moreover, water-run clocks were present in Roman and Islamic Iberia. The association between lustful wives and mills needing tending dates to fourteenth-century Castilian proverbs (Shipley 247-48), but is also found in Apuleius's *The Golden Ass*. When one adds Guiomar's insult about her husband's lack of sexual performance to his lack of economically productive activity, it becomes clear why she believes he is not the *molinero* [miller] she thought she married.

Cervantes's divorce-seeking wives seem to suffer from sexual frustration induced by ill-adjusted sexual drives between partners. Mariana, married to the Vejete whose ailing body she spends her physical energy and time tending to, is condemned to a sexless marriage due to the cyclically mismatched time of youth and old age. Guiomar suffers the neglect of her soldier husband who has rejected capitalist time, which should leave him free to spend carefree, lustful moments with her, yet he is off at the inns and gambling halls. The ending to this *entremés*, abrupt and unsatisfactory for the twenty first-century reader, closes with the musicians singing a repetition of the judge's ruling:

"Entre casados de honor, / cuando hay pleito descubierto, / más vale el peor concierto, / que no el divorcio mejor" [In honorable marriages / when there is a clear dispute, / better the worst concert, / than the best divorce] (72). One could imagine a poor performance by the musicians undermining the decision as they themselves played in ill harmony. Nonetheless, the clock image Cervantes explores in this *entremés* does not offer the same recognition of "women's right to pursue sensual satisfaction in human relationships" as one sees in his exploration of similarly unfulfilling marriages in *El celoso extremeño* [The Extremaduran Jealous Husband] and *El viejo celoso* [The Old Jealous Husband] (Martín 198). The judgement casts the women into the mechanized, measured world of regimented time and weighty judges where voices calling for sensual pleasure will receive no sympathetic hearing.

Lewis Mumford, in addition to linking the regimentation of time to the rise of modern capitalism, also notes its mixed effects on bodily life. Although it is perhaps helpful to maintain certain functions, such as eating and defecation, the worker's regimented day has led to the deterioration of modern sexuality, since the "strength of the impulse itself is pulsating rather than evenly recurrent: here habits fostered by the clock or the calendar may lead to dullness and decay" (270). Scientific studies of infertility show that disrupted circadian rhythms do more than just put a damper on sex lives; they actually decrease fertility. Increased rates of melatonin have been found in the blood of men suffering from infertility and have been posited as a possible explanation for the phenomenon (Karasek et al.). A recent study links irregular sleep to infertility due to the interruption of the circadian-controlled release of hormones stimulating ovulation (Russo et al.). The Crown of Castile showed signs of demographic crisis around 1560, and Spain was pushed into negative population growth by 1600, a trend that would not reverse until the middle of the eighteenth century (Alvar Ezquerra 47-8). Factors contributing to the decline included famine, epidemics, and emigration to the Americas as well as the expulsion of the *moriscos* (38-41, 57-9). Increasing urbanization of the remaining population caused declining birth rates, with fewer marriages and births (63). Alfredo Alvar Ezquerra comments that there would have been birth control "practices," but not methods, in the urban centers. Was urban life in early-modern Spain, with its shortage of young, productive men in marriages coupled with sexual and mercantile economies based on mechanized time, contributing to this decline? The gendering of the "hombre de reloj" / "clock-man" has only one exception that I have found, in the description in *La pícara Justina* of the female innkeeper who makes a pleasant sound as the money received from guests rings in her purse: "mas si un huésped se le escapa sin pagar, da el golpe en vago, desconciértase el reloj y arma un ruido del diablo" [but if she lets a guest escape without paying, the clock gets discombobulated and sets off a diabolical noise] (López de Úbeda 317). This "clock-woman" is subject to the same commercial regimentation as the "clock-man." Thus, the exception proves the rule, the rule of mechanized, commercial time over the human body.

Works Cited

Alvar Ezquerra, Alfredo. "La población española: Siglos XVI al XVIII." *La sociedad española en la Edad Moderna*. Ed. Antonio Domínguez Ortiz and Alfredo Alvar Ezquerra. Madrid: Istmo, 2005. 17-81. Print.

Asenjo González, María. "El ritmo de la comunidad: Vivir en la ciudad, las artes y los oficios en la Corona de Castilla." *La vida cotidiana en la Edad Media: VIII Semana de Estudios Medievales: Nájera, del 4 al 8 de agosto de 1997*. Logroño: Instituto de Estudios Riojanos, 1998. 169-200. Print.

Asensio, Eugenio. "Reloj de arena y amor en una poesía de Quevedo (fuentes italianas, derivaciones españolas)." *Dicenda: Cuadernos de filología española* 7 (1988): 17-32. Print.

Atienza, Belén. "El juez, el dramaturgo y el relojero: justicia y lectura como ciencias inexactas en *El juez de los divorcios* de Cervantes." *Bulletin of the Comediantes* 56.2 (2004): 193-217. Print.

Benegasi y Luxán, Francisco. *Obras lyricas, jocoserías que dexó escritas*. Madrid: Juan de San Martín, 1746. Print.

Calderón de la Barca, Pedro. *Entremeses, jácaras y mojigangas*. Ed. Evangelina Rodríguez and Antonio Tordera. Madrid: Castalia, 1982. Print.

Campbell, Scott S. "Circadian Rhythms and Human Temporal Experience." *Cognitive Models of Psychological Time*. Ed. Richard A. Block. Hillsdale: Lawrence Erlbaum, 1990. 101-18. Print.

Cejador y Frauca, Julio. *Diccionario fraseológico del Siglo de Oro (Fraseología o estilística castellana)*. Ed. Abraham Madroñal and Delfín Carbonell. Barcelona: Ediciones del Serbal, 2008. Print.

Cervantes, Miguel de. *Entremeses*. Ed. Eugenio Asensio. Madrid: Castalia, 1987. Print.

Chevalier, Maxime. "Cuentecillos y chistes tradicionales en la obra de Quevedo." *Centro Virtual de Cervantes*. n.d. Web. 8 Apr. 2015.

Covarrubias, Sebastián de. *Tesoro de la lengua castellana o española*. Ed. Martín de Riquer. Barcelona: Ad Litteram, 2003. Print.

Cummins, Genevieve. *How the Watch Was Worn: A Fashion for 500 Years.* Woodridge, Suffolk, UK: Antique Collectors' Club, 2010. Print.

Dohrn-van Rossum, Gerhard. *History of the Hour: Clocks and Modern Temporal Orders.* Trans. Thomas Dunlap. Chicago: U of Chicago P, 1996. Print.

Fernández (Fernández Rivera), Enrique. *Anxieties of Interiority and Dissection in Early Modern Spain.* Toronto: U of Toronto P, 2015.

———. "El reloj, la hora y la economía del tiempo en *La Celestina.*" *Celestinesca* 34 (2010): 31-40. Print.

Heiple, Daniel L. *Mechanical Imagery in Spanish Golden Age Poetry.* Potomac: José Porrúa Tarranzas, 1983. Print.

Herrero García, Miguel. *El reloj en la vida española.* Madrid: Roberto Carbonell Blasco, 1955. Print.

Karasek, M., M. Pawlikowski, B. Nowakowska-Jankiewicz, H. Kolodziej-Maciejewska, J. Zielenewski, D. Cieslak, and F. Leidenberger. "Circadian Variations in Plasma Melatonin, FSH, LH, and Prolactin and Testosterone Levels in Infertile Men." *Journal of Pineal Research* 9.2 (1990): 149-57. *Wiley Online Library*. Web. 27 Apr. 2015.

Le Goff, Jacques. *Time Work and Culture in the Middle Ages.* Trans. Arthur Goldhammer. Chicago: U of Chicago P, 1980. Print.

López de Úbeda, Francisco. *La pícara Justina.* Ed. Bruno Mario Damiani. Potomac: Studia Humanitatis, 1982. Print.

Macey, Samuel L. *The Dynamics of Progress: Time, Method, and Measure.* Athens: U of Georgia P, 1989. Print.

Mancing, Howard. "Embodied Cognition and Autopoiesis in *Don Quixote.*" *Cognitive Approaches to Early Modern Spanish Literature.* Ed. Isabel Jaén and Julien Jacques Simon. Oxford: Oxford UP, 2016. 39-51. Print.

———. "Embodied Cognitive Science and the Study of Literature." *Cognitive Cervantes.* Ed. Julien J. Simon, Barbara Simerka, and Howard Mancing. Spec. cluster of essays of *Cervantes: Bulletin of the Cervantes Society of America* 32.1 (2012): 25-69. Print.

Martín, Adrienne Laskier. *An Erotic Philology of Golden Age Spain.* Nashville: Vanderbilt UP, 2008. Print.

Mayr, Otto. *Authority, Liberty, and Automatic Machinery in Early Modern Europe.* Baltimore: Johns Hopkins UP, 1986. Print.

Montañés Fontenla, Luis. *Museo español de antigüedades.* Madrid: Roberto Carbonell Blasco, 1964. Print.

Morales Gómez, Juan José, and María Jesús Torreblanca Gaspar. "Tiempo y relojes en Teruel en el siglo XV." *Aragón en la Edad Media* 8 (1989): 449-74. Print.
Mumford, Lewis. *Technics and Civilization*. New York: Harcourt, Brace and World, 1963. Print.
Quevedo, Francisco de. *Poesía original completa*. Ed. José Manuel Blecua. Madrid: Planeta, 1981. Print.
Quiñones de Benavente, Luis. *Nuevos entremeses atribuidos a Luis Quiñones de Benavente*. Ed. Abraham Madroñal Durán. Kassel: Edition Reichenberger, 1996. Print.
Rojas, Fernando de. *La Celestina: Tragicomedia de Calisto y Melibea*. Ed. Francisco J. Lobera, Guillermo Serés, Paloma Díaz-Mas, Carlos Mota, Íñigo Ruiz Arzálluz, and Francisco Rico. Barcelona: Crítica, 2000. Print.
Russo, Kimberly A., Janet L. La, Shannon B. Z. Stephens, Matthew C. Poling, Namita A. Padgaonkar, Kimberly J. Jennings, David J. Piekarski, Alexander S. Kauffman, and Lance J. Kriegsfield. "Circadian Control of the Female Reproductive Axis Through Gated Responsiveness of the RFRP-3 System to VIP Signaling." *Endocrinology* 156.7 (July 2015): 2608-18. *Endocrine Society*. Web. 27 Apr. 2015.
Santa Cruz de Dueñas, Melchor. *Floresta española*. Ed. María Pilar Cuartero and Maxime Chevalier. Barcelona: Crítica, 1997. Print.
Shipley, George A. "A Case of Functional Obscurity: The Master Tambourine Painter of *Lazarillo*, Tratado VI." *MLN* 97.2 (Mar. 1982): 225-53. *JSTOR*. Web. 30 Apr. 2015.
Suárez de Figueroa, Cristóbal. *El pasajero*. 2 vols. Ed. María Isabel López Bascuñana. Barcelona: PPU, 1988. Print.
Zúñiga, Francés de. *Crónica burlesca del Emperador Carlos V*. Ed. José Antonio Sánchez Paso. Salamanca: Universidad de Salamanca, 1989. Print.

De lo que se come se cría:
Diet and Procreation in Early Modern Spain

Isabel Jaén
Portland State University

BOOKSTORES TODAY ARE REPLETE with publications on what to eat to feel good and how to prevent and fight cancer and other diseases with the help of superfoods such as broccoli or kale.[1] Food is a tool at our disposal, a tool to preserve and shape our bodies.[2] A remarkable example of how our societies view the connection between food and the shaping of an organism is the blog "Entremujeres" [Among Women] of *Clarín*, one of the main newspapers in Argentina, which provides future mothers with "tricks" to choose the sex of their babies, including dietetic recommendations such as eating legumes, cold meats, fish and fruits if they wish male offspring and dairy, chard, or oatmeal, if they desire a girl. According to the blog, their advice is based on biochemical studies carried out during the 1980s, which demonstrate that a high proportion of potassium and sodium in the diet along with a decrease in calcium and magnesium favor the sperm Y, while the opposite relationship favors the sperm X (Elustondo). Interestingly, *Clarín*'s recommendations in the twenty-first century are not far from those that phy-

---

[1] It is important to note that, as Nina L. Etkin reminds us, "Until the recent and rapidly escalating interest in functional foods and supplements, since the 1980s ... foods were regarded as virtually chemically inert, thus of no salience to disease processes" (3).

[2] On the sociological complexity surrounding the relationship between nourishment and the body, see McIntosh (chapter 6). For a more recent study on the connection between food, medicine, and culture, see Chen, among others. On food, cooking, medicine, and habit during the sixteenth and seventeenth centuries, see Valles Rojo.

sicians would offer in sixteenth-century Spain, although the main purpose of early modern precepts is that children male and not female may be born, as declared in Juan Huarte de San Juan's *Examen de ingenios* [Examination of Men's Wits].[3]

The connection between health, food, and society is indeed a very old one, entering early modernity via Galen's interpretation of the Hippocratic writings along with Judaic-Arabic medicine, eclecticism that is reflected in the writings of Huarte and other doctors of his time.[4] Here, I shall focus specifically on how Huarte gathers and turns this tradition into his practical project of helping the king to perfect the republic by offering parents advice on how to beget (male) wise children and, later on, direct them to the profession for which they will be most capable according to the nature of their wits. This is a matter of great importance, as Huarte enunciates in the first *proemio* (prologue) of his *Examen*, dedicated to Philip II:

> Para que las obras de los artífices tuviesen la perfección que convenía al uso de la república, me pareció, Católica Real Majestad, que se había de establecer una ley: que el carpintero no hiciese obra tocante al oficio del labrador, ni el tejedor del arquitecto, ni el jurisperito curase, ni el médico abogase; sino que cada uno ejercitase sola aquel arte para la cual tenía talento natural, y dejase las demás. (149)

> To the end that artificers may attain the perfection requisite for the use of the commonwealth, me thinketh, Catholic royal Majesty, a law should be enacted that no carpenter should exercise himself in any work which appertained to the occupation of a husbandman, nor a tailor to that of an architect, and that the advocate should not minister physic, nor the physician play the advocate, but each one exercise only that art to which he beareth a natural inclination, and let pass the residue. (76)

Hence, according to Huarte, the republic needs not only capable citizens but citizens that carry out the jobs for which they are apt. These capable citizens (wits) belong by default to the male sex, since females are naturally unable wits because of their humid and cold temperament, necessary to bear chil-

---

3   English translations of Huarte come from Rocío Sumillera's edition of the early modern translation by Richard Carew, unless otherwise noted.

4   In addition to these medical views, we find during the period a wide array of manuals and treatises on food, whose principles also permeate fictional discourses (see Nadeau).

dren. Consequently, "Los padres que quisiesen gozar de hijos sabios y que tengan habilidad para letras han de procurar que nazcan varones; porque las hembras, por razón de la frialdad y humidad de su sexo, no pueden alcanzar ingenio profundo" ["Those parents who seek the comfort of having wise children and such as are towards for learning, must endeavour that they may be born male, for the female, through the cold and moist of their sex, cannot be endowed with any profound judgement"] (627; 292).[5]

Huarte lists a series of recommendations, based on the humoral, anatomical, and embryological science of his time, to succeed in giving birth to sons and not daughters:

> Una de las cuales es comer alimentos calientes y secos; la segunda, procurar que se cuezgan bien en el estómago; la tercera, hacer mucho ejercicio; la cuarta, no llegarse al acto de la generación hasta que la simiente esté cocida y bien sazonada; la quinta, tener cuenta con su mujer cuatro o cinco días antes que le venga la regla; la sexta, procurar que la simiente caiga en el lado derecho del útero. Las cuales guardadas como diremos, es imposible engendrarse mujer. (631)

> One of which is to eat meats hot and dry; the second, to procure that they make good digestion in the stomach; the third, to use much exercise; the fourth, not to apply themselves unto the act of generation until their seed be well ripened and seasoned; the fifth, to company with the wife four or five days before her natural course is to run; the sixth, to procure that the seed fall in the right side of the womb, which being observed (as we shall prescribe) it will grow impossible that a female should be engendered. (294)

Huarte offers the sociological observation that higher social classes tend to bring to the world more females than males, since noble and rich people, "comen y beben lo que su estómago no puede gastar" ["they eat and drink that which their stomach cannot digest"] (633; 295). Eating in moderate quantities is, thus, paramount to keeping the organism balanced, maximizing the chances to beget male offspring. Even more important is eating the

---

[5] Although Huarte distinguishes three degrees of humidity and coldness in women, considering that women in the first degree (less humid and cold) possess some level of ability and wisdom, all women are by default unable wits, since those qualities are associated with heat and dryness, corresponding to the male temperament.

right foods before the couple engages in the act of generation, to ensure that the seed or sperm has the right temperature and humidity to become a male fetus. But what are then the "right" foods for this purpose?

As Etkin remarks in *Edible Medicines*, Galenic medicine was based on the opposites hot-cold and wet-dry and "[f]oods as well as medicines were assigned a valence along these continua" (49). In accordance with this tradition, Huarte points to the intrinsic qualities of food, stressing the importance for obtaining male offspring of ingesting dry and hot viands, such as honey and white wine. There is a danger, however, in producing a very hot and dry seed for generation: "siendo la simiente muy caliente y seca, hemos dicho muchas veces atrás que por fuerza se ha de engendrar un varón maligno, astuto, caviloso y con inclinación a muchos vicios y males. Y tales hombres como éstos, si no se van a la mano, son peligrosos en la república ..." ["the seed being hot and dry we have often heretofore affirmed it followeth of force that there be born a man malicious, wily, cavilling, and addicted to many vices and evils, and such persons as these (unless they be straightly curbed) bring great danger to the commonwealth"] (Huarte 632; 295).

According to Huarte, the solution to avoid this danger resides in ingesting foods that are temperate (slightly less hot and dry). Temperate meats can be produced by roasting or by seasoning them with some spices. These meats include hens, partridges, turtles, doves, thrushes, blackbirds, and goats (632). Such dietetic diligences are key: as we have discussed, for the benefit of the republic, males (and not females) must be conceived but the seed that will produce these males should ideally be temperate (not too hot and not too dry).

Why is a temperate seed so important for generation? Let us go back for a moment to Huarte's humoral sex/gender continuum in the *Examen*, where we read that there are three possible temperaments that the male constitution admits. Men can be hot and dry, hot and humid, or temperate. Huarte defines these three different temperaments with a set of physical and, more importantly, mental characteristics, referring to the faculties favored in each one: "el hombre que se mostrare agudo en las obras de la imaginativa terná calor y sequedad en el tercer grado; y si el hombre no supiere mucho, es señal que con el calor se ha juntado humidad, la cual echa siempre a perder la parte racional; y confirmarse ha más si tiene mucha memoria" ["the man who showeth himself prompt in the works of the imagination should be hot and dry in the third degree. And if a man be of no great reach, it tokeneth that with his heat much moisture is united, which always endamageth the reasonable part, and this is the more confirmed if he be good of memory"] (620; 287-88).

Of all possible male constitutions, the temperate is the most perfect, since:

> el calor no excede a la frialdad, ni la humidad a la sequedad, antes se hallan en tanta igualdad y conformes como si realmente no fueran contrarias ni tuvieran oposición natural. De lo cual resulta un instrumento tan acomodado a las obras del ánima racional, que viene el hombre a tener perfecta memoria para las cosas pasadas, y grande imaginativa para ver lo que está por venir, y grande entendimiento para distinguir, inferir, raciocinar, juzgar y eligir. (574)

> the heat exceedeth not the cold, nor the moist the dry, but are found in such equality and conformity as if really they were not contraries, nor had any natural opposition. Whence resulteth an instrument so appliable to the operations of the reasonable soul, that man commeth to possess a perfect memory of things passed, and a great imagination to see what is to come, and a great understanding to distinguish, infer, argue, judge and make choice. (258)

This perfect temperament is the one that suits the ruler of the republic. It is, however, a very rare one; most human beings are intemperate, due to inhabiting intemperate regions, being subject to the seasons, going to the different ages (with their different temperatures), and eating hot or cold foods (170). In the context of this process of becoming progressively intemperate as we age, Huarte's recommendations to attempt to produce a temperate seed and, thereby, temperate offspring are particularly relevant and reveal an understanding of the dynamics between nature (what we are born with) and nurture (how the environment changes us as we develop).

The centrality of temperance in Huarte's treatise has its origins in both physiological and moral beliefs; it responds to the Renaissance elaboration of the Hippocratic-Galenic tradition as well as to the emphasis that humanism places on self-control, advocated among others by Juan Luis Vives.[6] A temperate man not only is a healthy organism but also an individual that

---

6   Accordingly, in this article I will employ the term "temperance," depending on the context, both in a medical and a moral sense, to signify balance (as the noun form of temperate) and self-control.

has conquered his lower passions in favor of his rational soul.[7] As Huarte states, echoing the Galenic ideology that the faculties of the soul follow the temperaments of the body, the laws of soul and those of the body demand "una mesma cosa" [the same thing] and, thereby, "dijo bien Galeno que al médico pertenecía hacer un hombre, de vicioso, virtuoso; y que los filósofos morales hacían mal en no aprovecharse de la medicina para conseguir el fin de su arte, pues en alterar los miembros del cuerpo hacían obrar a los virtuosos con suavidad" [Galen stated correctly that it was the task of the physician to turn a vicious man into a virtuous one; and that moral philosophers were mistaken in not profiting from medicine to attain their ends, since altering the members of the body would cause the virtuous to behave gently] (255; my translation).

At this point, it is important to remember that the whole Huartian project of discovering the natural ability of wits with the purpose of placing citizens in the right occupation is essentially a moral-practical one. If everyone does the work for which he is naturally capable, the commonwealth will be better served. In addition to the republic's responsibility of placing citizens where they can be more useful, citizens carry the responsibility of adopting habits that help them be virtuous. Thus, the correspondence between body (natural temperament) and soul (habit and behavior) has both an individual and a public site of realization. Citizens must exercise for the republic the same virtuosity that they exercise for themselves. The first step in attaining this virtuosity via a temperate lifestyle is precisely, a temperate generation.

Continuing with the dietetic diligences that couples must observe for an optimal generation of male offspring, Huarte recommends accompanying roasted temperate meats with white bread: "El pan con que se comiere ha de ser candial, hecho de la flor de harina, masado con sal y anís; porque el rubial es frío y húmedo, como adelante probaremos, y para el ingenio muy prejudicial" ["The bread with which the same is eaten should be white, of the finest meal, seasoned with salt and aniseed, for the brown is cold and moist (as we will prove hereafter) and very damageable to the wit"] (632; 295). White bread was already considered nutritionally superior by the Romans (Tannahill 91) and the preserving and medicinal properties of salt were very well known to ancient societies.[8] Bread must be "*masado con sal*[9] porque ningún alimento de cuantos usan los hombres hace tan buen entendimiento como

---

    7   See Book III of Vives's *De anima et vita*, translated by Carlos G. Noreña as *The Passions of the Soul*.
    8   On the properties, use, and history of salt, see Laszlo.
    9   Emphasis in the original.

este mineral" ["'seasoned with salt' because none of all the aliments which a man useth bettereth so much the understanding as doth this mineral"] (648; 304).

The drink to accompany the meals must be white wine but "aguado en la proporción que el estómago lo aprobare; y el agua con que se ha de templar, conviene que sea dulce y muy delicada" ["watered in such proportion as the stomach may allow thereof, and the water with which it is tempered should be very fresh and pure"] (632; 295).[10] Wine is described in the *Examen* as an ambivalent food:

> por ser tan vaporable y sutil, hace que él y los demás alimentos vayan crudos a los vasos seminarios y que la simiente irrite falsamente al hombre sin estar cocida y sazonada. Y, por tanto, loa Platón una ley que halló en la república de los cartaginenses por la cual prohibían que el hombre casado, ni su mujer, no bebiesen vino el día que se pensaban llegar al acto de la generación, entendiendo que este licor hacía mucho daño a la salud corporal del niño y que era bastante causa para que saliese vicioso y de malas costumbres. (633)

> for this liquor in being so vaporous and subtle occasioneth that the other meats together therewith pass to the seed-vessels raw, and that the seed falsely provoketh a man ere it be digested and seasoned. Whereon Plato commendeth a law enacted in the Carthaginian commonwealth which forbade the married couple that they should not taste of any wine that day when they meant to perform the rights of the marriage bed, as well ware that this liquor always bred much hurt and damage to the child's bodily health, and might yield occasion that he should prove vicious and of ill conditions. (295-96)

However, Huarte further specifies, "si se bebe con moderación, de ningún manjar se hace tan buena simiente (para el fin que llevamos) como del vino blanco, especialmente para dar ingenio y habilidad, que es lo que más pretendemos" ["if the same be moderately taken, so good seed is not endangered of any meat (for the end which we seek after) as of white wine, and especially to give wit and ability, which is that whereto we pretend"] (633; 296). Through

---

   10   Because of this vaporous quality, wine was often watered in early modern meals, "to prevent it from fuming and rising into the head, causing dizziness" (Albala 97).

this resolved ambivalence, Huarte emphasizes once more for his readers the importance of temperance.

Moreover, parents not only can choose through an adequate diet the sex of their offspring but they can also predetermine the faculties that will be predominant in their future child.[11] To that end, if the couple intends to bring to the world a child of great *entendimiento* [understanding], apt to learn and exercise the disciplines of theology, natural and moral philosophy, and the law, they must also know that "Las perdices y francolines tienen las (sic) mesma sustancia y temperamento que el pan candial, el cabrito y el vino moscatel; de los cuales manjares usando los padres ... harán los hijos de grande *entendimiento*" ["Partridges and francolins have a like substance, and the self temperature with bread of white meal, and kid, and muscatel wine. And if parents use these meats ... they shall breed children of great understanding"] (648-49; 304; emphasis in original).

If they wish to beget a child of great memory, whose wit would be appropriate for the study of grammar, languages, or arithmetic, among the disciplines that rely on this faculty, "coman, ocho o nueve días antes de que se lleguen al acto de la generación, truchas, salmones, lampreas, besugos y anguilas; de los cuales manjares harán la simiente húmida y muy glutinosa. Estas dos calidades dijimos atrás que hacían la memoria fácil para recebir, y muy tenaz para conservar las figura[s] mucho tiempo" ["let them eight or nine days before they betake themselves to the act of generation eat trouts, salmons, lampreys, and eels, by which meat they shall make their seed very moist and clammy. These two qualities (as I have said before) make the memory easy to receive and very fast to preserve the figures a long time"] (649; 304-05).

In case parents seek a male of great imagination, a faculty essential for the arts and sciences that consist of figure, correspondence, harmony, and proportion, such as poetry, the practice of medicine, astrology, the government of the republic, the art of warfare, painting, writing, reading, being a gracious and witty man, etc. (396), Huarte explains:

> De palomas, cabrito, ajos, cebollas, puerros, rábanos, pimienta, vinagre, vino blanco, miel, y de todo género de especias, se hace la simiente caliente y seca y de partes muy delicadas. El hijo que de estos alimentos se engendrase será de grande *imaginativa*; pero falto de entendimiento, por el mucho calor, y falto de memoria, por la mucha sequedad. Éstos suelen

---

11   On the right correspondence between temperaments/faculties and the professions, see chapter VII in Huarte.

ser muy perjudiciales a la república porque el calor los inclina a muchos vicios y males, y les da ingenio y ánimo para poderlo ejecutar; aunque, si se van a la mano, más servicios recibe de la imaginativa de éstos que del entendimiento y memoria. (649)

By pigeons, goats, garlic, onions, leeks, rapes, pepper, vinegar, white wine, honey, and all other sorts of spices, the seed is made hot and dry, and of parts very subtle and delicate. The child who is engendered of such meat shall be of great imagination, but not of like understanding by means of the much heat, and he shall want memory through his abundance of dryness. These are wont to be very prejudicial to the commonwealth, for the heat inclineth them to many vices and evils, and giveth them a wit and mind to put the same in execution. Howbeit if we do keep them under, the commonwealth shall receive more service by these men's imagination than by the understanding and memory of the others. (305)

The faculty of imagination in the *Examen* is also ambivalent: it is essential to ruling but it can be quite detrimental to the republic. As we read above, in order to unravel this apparent contradiction, Huarte specifies that those wits in which this faculty is prominent must be kept under control. Once more it is the principle of temperance that guides the precepts included in his treatise.

Finally, parents who seek to beget "un hijo gentil hombre, sabio y de buenas costumbres" ["prompt, wise, and of good conditions"] (651; 306) need to eat, six days in advance, goat milk, regarded by doctors as one of the most delicate aliments available to man (651; 306). It must be, however, boiled with honey in order to add the lacking element of fire to its composition (it naturally possesses the other three elements: earth through its cheese, water through whey, and air through its butter). This perfect aliment will produce a temperate seed and, thereby, a balanced child of great understanding and no lack of memory or imagination.

As I have discussed, the ingestion of selected roasted and spiced meats— accompanied by bread seasoned with salt and by watered white wine in moderation—along with that of goat milk boiled with honey, offers couples the highest probability of conceiving a temperate male. To these dietetic precepts, Huarte adds his recommendations on exercising, waiting for the seed to be mature enough to conceive, and ensuring that it falls in the right side of the womb. It is important to note that diet remains, nonetheless, central to his eugenics.

When it comes to following these recommendations—although both members of the couple contribute their seed and should in principle follow them equally—women, as bearers of the site of generation, carry a heavier responsibility. For instance, after intercourse, they need to position their body in a manner that ensures that the seed falls on the right side of the womb (of higher temperature due to its proximity to the liver, the right kidney, and the right seed-vessel): "Lo cual hará la mujer fácilmente recostándose sobre el lado derecho después de pasado el acto de la generación, la cabeza baja y los pies puestos en alto. Pero ha de estar un día o dos en la cama; porque el útero no luego abraza la simiente, hasta pasadas algunas horas" ["Which the woman shall easily accomplish by resting on her right side when the act of generation is ended, with her head down and her heels up. But it behoveth her to keep her bed a day or two, for the womb doth not straightways embrace the seed but after some hours space"] (640; 301).[12] She must also avoid standing right after copulation: "El ponerse luego en pie la mujer, pasado el acto de la generación, es muy peligroso; y, así, aconseja Aristóteles que haga primero evacuación de los excrementos y urina, porque no haya ocasión de levantarse" ["That a woman rise up straightways on her feet so soon as the act of generation hath passed is a matter very perilous. Therefore, Aristotle compelleth that she beforehand make evacuation of the excrements and of her urine to the end she may have no cause to rise"] (641; 301).

As in the case of men, women must wait until the seed is ripe for conception to be possible.[13] Peter Garnsey explains in *Food and Society in Classical Antiquity*, that according to Greco-Roman medical beliefs, the sexual appetites of females, particularly of young age, needed to be controlled and their marriages were often postponed until a later age. Control was also exercised through their diets, by keeping their food intake low and preventing them from drinking wine (102). Garnsey further points that:

> Doctors were concerned to limit the food consumption of females, whether rich or poor, young or mature. This discussion is about needs of

---

12   On the classical antecedents of the belief of male generation taking place from seed coming from the right testes and being deposited on the right side of the uterus, see chapter 3 in Sassi.

13   Huarte reminds readers that waiting for the female seed to mature is an essential provision, demonstrated by the fact that "las mujeres públicas, por no aguardar que su simiente se cueza y madure, jamás se hacen preñadas" ["common harlots never conceive because they stay not till the seed be digested and ripened"] (637; 298).

women, but those needs are seen through the eyes of males and reflect the higher status and superior power of men. Women are judged to need less food than men, but their needs are defined by men and largely in the interests of men and of the male-dominated society as a whole. The desired ends are achieved through the systematic supervision and control of women from childhood to adulthood. (103)

Food in the household was allocated according to these beliefs and forms of social regulation, which would place females at a nutritional disadvantage (Garnsey 111). This ideology of physiological and moral frugality as expressed in the female diet—particularly during her upbringing and education as a young woman—was also emphasized by early modern thought, as illustrated by Vives in his treatise *De institutione feminae christianae* [The Education of a Christian Woman], where he offers dietetic guidance based on fasting and moderation.[14] These precepts respond to the pedagogical belief that control must be exercised over the female since her first years, due to the inferiority and fragility of both her body and mind.

Regarding the role and ability of the female body in procreation, Renaissance medicine of Hippocratic heritage is guided by the same principle of temperance. The fertile woman is one who has a temperate womb, since "las mujeres que tienen los vientres fríos no conciben, ni las que los tienen muy húmidos, ni muy calientes y secos" ["women who have their belly cold cannot conceive, no more than such as are very moist or very cold and dry"] (611; 281). In their humid and cold natures women are subject to three degrees. Women in the second degree are fertile and beautiful; their beauty acting as the signal that Nature conferred to them the fit temperature to procreate (618).

Indeed, having the adequate temperament and, thereby, the ability to procreate was of particular importance for females. As María Cruz de Carlos Varona reminds us, "Both royalty and the aristocracy regarded motherhood as the most esteemed status for women who had not taken religious vows" (151) and the female ability to bear children was present and praised through representations of maternity such as portraits displaying eggs and other symbolic elements, an example of which is Luis de Morales's *Nacimiento de la Virgen* [Birth of the Virgin] (166-67).[15] On the other hand, "one of the worse

---

14 See chapter VII in Fantazzi's edition of Vives's treatise.

15 Eggs were an important component of the diet of the pregnant woman, as well as white meat, recommended during the days prior to the birth to aid in expulsing the baby (Carlos Varona 166). It is also interesting to note that pigeon eggs were

things that could happen to a woman was her inability to give her husband children and thus the necessity to accept his bastards" (164). Maternity could be a source of happiness or distress depending on the particular social context.

In early modernity, women are not viewed as simply passive receptors of the male seed that will produce the generation, as Aristotle erroneously thought.[16] In this regard, Huarte stresses in his treatise the Hippocratic view that both male and female sperm can be either forming agent or aliment of the new human being: "Porque muchas veces la simiente de la mujer es de mayor eficacia que la del varón; y cuando acontesce así, hace ella la generación y la del marido sirve de alimento. Otras veces la del varón es más potente y prolífica, y la de la mujer no hace más que nutrir" ["For many times, the seed of the woman is of greater efficacy than that of the man, and when this betideth, she maketh the generation and that of the husband serveth for aliment. Otherwhiles, that of the husband is more mighty, and that of the wife doth nought else than nourish"] (662; 312). This metaphor of sperm as food reaffirms the centrality of nutrition in the early modern view of procreation, while extending the role of nourishing to both sexes.

In spite of the fact that either one of the parents can act as motor or coadjutant of the generation—hence the importance of both members of the couple following dietary recommendations—male sperm and female sperm do not produce the same result when being the generating cause: If the female seed acts as the generating agent and the male as the aliment, the result will be an unable wit, whereas a male forming seed and a female seed aliment will produce a wise child: "en saliendo el hijo discreto y avisado, es indicio infalible de haberse hecho de la simiente de su padre; y si es torpe y nescio se colige haberse formado de la simiente de su madre" ["when the child proveth discreet and prompt, the same yieldeth an infallible token that he was formed of his father's seed. And if he shew blockish and untoward, we infer that he was formed of the seed of his mother"] (666; 314).[17] The female sperm, thus, possesses an inferior status as generating power.

---

regarded in the Hispanic tradition as an aphrodisiac due to being more humid and hotter than chicken eggs (Ibn Zuhr 55) and, thus, also played a role in procreation.

16   As Huarte explains, Aristotle thought of female sperm as "un poco de agua sin virtud ni fuerzas para engendrar" ["a little water without virtue or force for generation"] (662; 312).

17   On the Galenic view of sperm and how it is interpreted in the Middle Ages, see also Arikha 81-82.

Although according to the anatomical knowledge described by Galen in his treatise *On the Usefulness of the Parts*, and echoed by Huarte, male and female reproductive organs were almost identical—they were in fact regarded as the reverse version of each other—the female body was considered imperfect due to being colder (Galen 628). Female sperm is regarded in early modernity as inferior due, besides low temperature, to the smaller size of the female testes, which must remain inside the body so heat won't disperse the nutriment that the fetus needs: "Forthwith, of course, the female must have smaller, less perfect testes, and the semen generated in them must be scantier, colder, and wetter (for these things too follow of necessity from the deficient heat)" (Galen 631). This anatomical belief takes us back to the humoral classification of females as cold and wet, and, thereby, the owners of imperfect wits that must be kept away from exercising the main roles involved in keeping healthy the republic, ideally by ensuring a male offspring.

As I have exposed, the ideology of shaping the republic by shaping the wits that conform it rests on a complex interrelation of physiological and moral beliefs. In this sense, Huarte embraces and embodies the humanist longing for virtue while engaging in a project whose pragmatism transcends medical philosophy, becoming a tool for social regulation.

Works Cited

Albala, Ken. *Eating Right in the Renaissance*. Berkeley: U of California P, 2002. Web. 1 Mar. 2014.

Arikha, Noga. *Passions and Tempers: A History of the Humours*. New York: Ecco, 2007. Print.

Carlos Varona, María Cruz de. "Giving Birth at the Habsburg Court: Visual and Material Culture." *Early Modern Habsburg Women: Transnational Contexts, Cultural Conflicts, Dynastic Continuities*. Ed. Anne J. Cruz and Maria Galli Stampino. Farnham: Ashgate, 2013. 151-74. Print.

Chen, Nancy N. *Food, Medicine, and the Quest for Good Health: Nutrition, Medicine, and Culture*. New York: Columbia UP, 2009. Print.

Elustondo, Georgina. "¿Cómo elegir el sexo del bebé?" *Entremujeres* n.d.: N.p. *Clarín*. Web. 1 Mar. 2014.

Etkin, Nina L. *Edible Medicines: An Ethnopharmacology of Food*. Tucson: U of Arizona P, 2006. Print.

Galen. *On the Usefulness of the Parts of the* Body. Trans. Margaret Tallmadge May. Vol. 2. Ithaca: Cornell UP, 1968. Print.

Garnsey, Peter. *Food and Society in Classical Antiquity*. Cambridge: Cambridge UP, 1999. Print.

Huarte de San Juan, Juan. *Examen de ingenios para las ciencias*. Ed. Guillermo Serés. Madrid: Cátedra, 1989. Print.

———. *The Examination of Men's Wits*. Trans. Richard Carew. Ed. Rocío G. Sumillera. London: Modern Humanities Research Association, 2014. Print.

Ibn Zuhr, Abū Marwān Abd Al-Malik. *Kitāb al-ag̱diya (Tratado de los alimentos)*. Ed. Expiración García Sánchez. Madrid: CSIC, 1992. Print.

Laszlo, Pierre. *Chemins et savoirs du sel*. Paris: Hachette, 1998. Print.

McIntosh, Wm. Alex. *Sociologies of Food and Nutrition*. New York: Plenum P, 1996. Print.

Nadeau, Carolyn A. *Food Matters: Alonso Quijano's Diet and the Discourse of Food in Early Modern* Spain. Toronto: U of Toronto P, 2016. Print.

Sassi, Maria Michela. *The Science of Man in Ancient Greece*. Chicago: U of Chicago P, 2001. Print.

Tannahill, Reay. *Food in History*. New York: Stein and Day, 1973. Print.

Valles Rojo, Julio. *Cocina y alimentación en los siglos XVI y XVII*. Valladolid: Junta de Castilla y León, 2007. Print.

Vives, Juan Luis. *The Education of a Christian Woman: A Sixteenth-Century Manual*. Ed. and trans. Charles Fantazzi. Chicago: U of Chicago P, 2000. Print.

———. *The Passions of the Soul: The Third Book of* De anima et vita. Trans. Carlos G. Noreña. Lewiston: Edwin Mellen P, 1990. Print.

Se le secó el celebro: Food as an Empathetic Response in *Don Quixote*

Carolyn A. Nadeau
Illinois Wesleyan University

In 2012 Howard Mancing, together with Julien Simon and Barbara Simerka, edited a special cluster of the *Bulletin of the Cervantes Society of America*, *Cognitive Cervantes*.[1] In this volume they brought together a series of articles that represents some of the most exciting work being done with the application of cognitive science to the study of literature.[2] In his own essay, Mancing provides a thoughtful overview of the work being done from its beginnings in the mid-twentieth century through today and explains that "cognitive approaches to literature is now a fully established and rapidly growing field of literary study" (55). One of the areas of study includes emotion and empathy and it is this particular branch of cognitive studies that serves as a point of departure to explore responses to Don Quixote's mental break.

Following in the footsteps of Galen, Avicenna, Dioscorides, and Hispanic Muslim and Jewish doctors like Averroes and Maimonides, early modern physicians took a more scientific stance as they began dispelling the theologically-charged popular attitudes that mental illness served as punishment for a moral defect or sin against God. In *El ingenioso hidalgo don Quijote de la Mancha* [The Ingenious Gentleman Don Quixote of La Mancha], Cervantes reflects this modern sensitivity to mental health by explaining in

---

[1] See Simon, Simerka, and Mancing.
[2] For more on cognitive literary studies, see Jaén and Simon, *Cognitive Literary*; Aldama. For scholarship that focuses on early modern Spain, see Jaén and Simon, *Cognitive Approaches*.

scientific terms the cause for his protagonist's mental break.³ Drawing from the established theory of humors, he includes various indicators of heat and exhaustion that effectively dried up Alonso Quijano's brain and led to his mental break. But, more than the cause itself, I am drawn to the fascinating way in which Cervantes develops responses to the illness. Once his mental instability is identified, most characters in part I of the novel empathize with the protagonist and feel a sense of responsibility for helping to find a cure. Others respond with an outright dismissal of the illness or worse, with, what neuroscientists would call today, an "aversive emotional response."⁴ A common empathetic response developed throughout the novel is to offer food and water to restore humoral balance and mitigate the, often times, violent outbreaks that Don Quixote suffers. Alonso Quijano's niece and housekeeper; his friends, the priest and the barber; and others across La Mancha describe the role of food in curing Don Quixote. The author also implicitly makes this connection in part I when Don Quixote delivers his most lucid speeches, on the Golden Age and on arms and letters, after having dined well, first among sheep herders and later among those at the inn.

The reactions to the protagonist's mental state in part II of *Don Quixote* become even more complex as characters not only respond to what they witness but also to what they have read. In her article, "A Theory of Narrative Empathy," Suzanne Keen defines empathy as "a vicarious, spontaneous sharing of affect, [that] can be provoked by witnessing another's emotional state, by hearing about another's condition, or even by reading" (208). In Cervantes's masterpiece, the characters' responses to what they witness, hear, and read display a wide range of emotions from the empathy Maritornes shows Sancho after he has been blanketed and humiliated at the inn in part I to the cruel jokes the duke and duchess play on Don Quixote when he is a guest at their palace in part II.

In the very first line of part II of the novel, the priest and barber remind the niece and housekeeper to provide their ailing friend, Don Quixote, with good food: "dándole a comer cosas confortativas y apropiadas para el corazón

---

   3   Carlos Castilla del Pino searched CORDE (*Corpus diacrónico del español*) for the use of *locura* and *loco* in the novel, which appear 78 and 89 times respectively. He also notes that throughout all his work, Cervantes includes *locura* 182 times (59).

   4   In her article, "A Theory of Narrative Empathy," Suzanne Keen explains that contemporary neuroscientists can observe an individual's mirror neuron system to better understand how one reacts to others' actions and reactions. In effect, they can, to a certain extent, quantify the experience of empathy. For information on the controversy regarding the mirror neuron system, see Hickok; Gallese et al.

y el celebro" ["give him food to eat that would strengthen and fortify his heart and brain"] (II.41; 459).[5] Later, the housekeeper exaggerates the number of eggs used in restoring her master's humors and aiding in his recovery: "para hacerle volver algún tanto en sí, gasté más de seiscientos huevos" ["to bring him back to himself a little, I used more than six hundred eggs"] (II.85; 497).[6] For the housekeeper and niece and for the priest and barber, alimentary measures are key to their empathetic response to assist in recovering Don Quixote's mental health. This essay, then, seeks to join the dialogue on the treatment of madness in *Don Quixote* by focusing on how Cervantes writes about recognizing and responding empathetically to incidences of mental illness, specifically through the alimentary measures characters choose in an effort to restore his sanity.

Before examining the humane responses to witnessing mental illness or the use of foodstuffs to treat it that are present in the text, a few words on the state of treating the mental ill in early modern Spain are appropriate.[7] The issue is complex because on the one hand, Spain was a trailblazer within Europe for treating mental health patients and advancing positive conditions for them. But, on the other hand, records of unfavorable living conditions and inhumane treatments are repeatedly found in early modern medical records.[8] Valencia was the first European city to open a hospital for the mentally ill in 1409, followed by Zaragoza, 1425; Seville, 1436; Barcelona, 1481; and Toledo, 1483 (Lampérez y Romea 255).[9] In Zaragoza, the hospital's goals were four-fold: "recoger a los insensatos, evitar los insultos a que se hallan expuestos, mejorar su situación y procurar restablecerles el

---

   5   All citations from *Don Quixote* are from the edition by Murillo and refer to part and page. The translations of *Don Quixote* are from Edith Grossman's edition and translation of the novel, citing page only.

   6   Primary medical sources confirm that eggs were thought to be effective in treating both mental and physical illnesses. See Laguna, II.36-38; Méndez Nieto, especially p. 487; Lobera de Ávila 81-82. For an excellent secondary source, see Cruz Cruz 208-10.

   7   For an extensive study on the history of health care for mental illness, see Aguado Díaz. Belén Atienza also provides an excellent overview of madness in early modern Spain (1-55).

   8   For further information on the treatment of the mentally ill in Zaragoza, see Baquero; in Valencia, Tropé; in Seville, López Alonso; and for an overview of Spain, González Duro.

   9   In his *History of Madness*, Michel Foucault surmises that Spain may have been the first to open hospitals for the mentally ill due to the historic ties with the Arab world (117).

juicio" [gather up the insensate, avoid the insults to which they are regularly subjected, improve their situation, and procure to regain their sanity] (Baquero 35).[10] By the mid-sixteenth century the hospital was regularly caring for some 200 mentally ill in addition to 500 physically ill and 200 abandoned babies (Baquero 50).

In terms of the patients' diet, institutions certainly understood the tacit connection between food and health. However, in writing about the mentally ill in Seville, Carmen López Alonso reports that in a 1642 document lack of access to food was one of the leading causes of death along with exposure to the cold (147). Records for both Zaragoza and Seville do indicate that mentally ill patients ate regular meals that included daily meat consumption. Recounting the quantities of meat for every 100 patients in Zaragoza, Baquero reports that, "A los locos les daban doce libras de carne por la mañana y cuatro por la tarde y, además, las patas, cabezas sin seso y vísceras de las reses sacrificadas" [The insane received twelve pounds of meat in the morning and four in the afternoon, as well as, feet, heads without the brain, and other viscera of slaughtered cattle] (51).[11]

For patients given to violent outbursts, methods of restraint were certainly employed. Tropé recounts "la multiplicidad de los medios de sujeción utilizados pone de manifiesto los límites de la terapéutica entonces aplicada: en algunos casos, al no poder curar a los locos, se les hace callar (bozales) o se les inmoviliza por la fuerza (grilletes, collares, cadenas, esposas)" [The variety of restraining methods used makes evident the limitations of the then applied therapy. In some cases, when it was not possible to cure the insane, they were silenced (muzzles) or forcibly immobilized (shackles, collars, chains, handcuffs)] (Tropé 242).

These less than favorable conditions are what inspired John of God—the now patron saint of hospitals, nurses, and patients—to establish hospitals for both physically and mentally ill patients that quickly became famous for their moral treatment of patients, in particular the mentally ill who were treated with kindness and patience (Rumbaut 33). One biographer explains that, "a combination of charity, intuition, hard work, perseverance and ne-

---

10   This and other translations in the essay, except those for *Don Quixote,* are my own.

11   In addition to organ meats, whose quantity is unspecified, sixteen pounds of meat per 100 patients amounts to approximately 2.5 ounces of meat each day for each patient, the equivalent of a jar of baby food. In Seville, records from 1690 show that 5.3 ounces for each patient, over double the amount of meat consumed when compared with the records from Zaragoza (qtd. in López Alonso 148).

cessity allowed Juan de Dios to achieve a functional institution that looks modern even by present standards, and revolutionary by the standard of his day" (Rumbaut 33). John of God's model quickly spread throughout Spain and the rest of Europe. In 1571 the Brothers Hospitallers of St. John of God became a congregation, fought in the Battle of Lepanto, and by the end of the sixteenth century had opened dozens of new hospitals in Spain, Italy, other parts of Europe, and in the New World (Rumbaut 38-39).[12] With the overlap both at Lepanto and later in Madrid, where Antón Martín established the Hospital de San Juan de Dios around the corner from where Cervantes resided, it is highly probable that Cervantes was familiar with John of God's legacy of the humane treatment of the mentally ill.[13]

Regarding the cause of Don Quixote's madness, critics have primarily cited his melancholic and/or choleric temperament, but have also written on the excessive exposure to heat, his diet, and of course, his intense reading of books of chivalry.[14] Within the pages of the novel, whether acknowledg-

---

[12] Today the Catholic Order the Brothers Hospitallers of Saint John of God is "the only one in the world that takes care of mental and neurological patients in such a comprehensive way" (Rumbaut 41).

[13] Antón Martín's hospital was quickly absorbed by the large-scale project of amalgamating eleven hospitals in Madrid (1580s), many of which were run by confraternities, to be transferred to the administration of the Royal Council. Only a few years later, chronicler Quintana wrote that the project had been a mistake because it was easier to treat the ill in a small environment of twenty patients than in a larger one designed for hundreds (Huguet-Termes 75).

[14] In her monograph, Teresa Soufas notes that, "the overwhelming majority of Renaissance scientists, physicians, and philosophers associate insanity and mania with some form of melancholia" (19). Dale Shuger categorizes into three groups how critics have treated the theme of madness in the novel. The *hard school* understands the novel as a comic work and questions of psychology are secondary to the novel's greater purpose. In contrast, other critics, like Rafael Salillas and later Soufas, have made psychology the primary focus of their research and use either early modern or contemporary medical theories to explain the mental break that Alonso Quijano experiences but do not delve into madness as a primary force in the novel. However, a third group of critics, including Shuger, do exactly this. For these critics, madness provides an opportunity to examine the world and offer critiques of a society steeped in hypocrisy. While many critics emphasize universal aspects of a world gone mad, and here Shuger notes both Foucault and Bakhtin (3-5), she examines the multiple discourses of madness in early modern Spain and uses archival evidence to support her argument that Cervantes's construction of madness is grounded in, "the dynamics of madness he might have seen in his own society" (6). For specific scholarship on mental illness in the novel, also see Johnson; Boruchoff; McCrea; Herrera; Heiple.

ing his melancholy and choleric temperament or not, almost everyone who meets or hears about his exploits rapidly realizes that Don Quixote is not of sound mind and responds accordingly. Some, like the first innkeeper, respond with kindness, in this case, by offering him practical advice as he continues on his adventures (I.89-90; 31). Others, like the travelling merchants on the road to Toledo, are less patient and actually leave him beaten and broken as they proceed on their journey (I.101-02; 40-41). And, to be clear, at no time is the notion of committing Don Quixote to an asylum ever raised, as Avellaneda so mistakenly suggests in his apocryphal version.

Other characters in the novel recognize that Don Quixote's mental breaks are sporadic in nature. The priest, in explaining Don Quixote's predicament to Cardenio (I.381; 257), and the narrator, after Don Quixote's famous speech on the defense of arms and letters (I.471; 333), reiterate this idea. For medical authorities, insanity was certainly not limited to permanent states but also encompassed those who experienced short-term bouts. The medieval intellectual and physician Maimonides explains well these conditions: "no era loco sólo aquel que iba completamente desnudo, rompía objetos y arrojaba piedras, sino que aquel que tenía el espíritu extravagante y cuyos pensamientos se enredaban siempre acerca de un mismo tema, aunque hablase y preguntase normalmente en los demás campos, era un inepto y había que ponerlo entre los locos" [The crazy person was not just the one who ran around naked, broke things, and threw rocks, but also the one who had an eccentric spirit and whose thoughts were always fixated on a single idea even if he spoke and posed normal questions about something else, he was incompetent and had to be placed with the insane] (qtd. in González Duro 114).

In both parts I and II, long-term responses of those who witness his insanity focus on returning Don Quixote home and restoring his health. Even strangers, like Dorotea and Don Fernando, enter into his fantasy world to assist in this noble task. For short-term responses to alleviate his madness Cervantes understood that water would diminish these temporal bouts of insanity. Before his departure, the niece insists that after a frenzied episode, he would be restored with a jug of cold water (I.107; 44). After securing the famed Mambrino helmet/barber's basin, Don Quixote and Sancho eat well and drink fresh stream water which, as the narrator explains, eliminates both choleric and melancholic temperaments (I.257; 157), and Cardenio, whose madness was instigated by the alleged betrayal of his beloved, is pacified as he sits next to a cool, babbling brook (I.329-31; 214-17).

The narrative thread of empathizing (or not) with Don Quixote's mental condition continues through the end of part I when the narrator reiterates the importance of bringing him home to cure him: "dieron orden para que ... pudiesen el cura y el barbero llevársele, como deseaban, y procurar la cura de su locura en su tierra" ["they devised a scheme that would ... allow the priest and barber to take him back with them, as they desired, and treat his madness at home"] (I.554; 403). Even the cannon, who only briefly meets the crazed knight, expresses his concern for Don Quixote's fate as he requests that the priest inform him of his progress toward recovery once they return home (I.602; 443).

Cervantes's position on the treatment of the mentally ill, as seen in the humane responses to Don Quixote's own madness, aligns with the practices instituted by Juan de Dios and the Brothers Hospitallers and that were also expressed in the writings of Juan Luis Vives. In his treatise on the poor, Vives writes about the disgraceful treatment of the mentally ill and includes a more humane alternative to helping them recover:

> Apliquense a cada uno caritativa y seriamente los remedios necesarios; unos necesitan de confortativos y alimentos; otros de un trato suave y afable para que se amansen poco a poco como las fieras; otros de enseñanza; habrá algunos que necesiten de castigo y prisiones, pero úsese de esto de modo que no sea motivo de enfurecerse más; ante todas cosas, en cuanto sea posible, se ha de procurar introducir en sus ánimos aquel sosiego con que fácilmente vuelve el juicio y la sanidad al entendimiento. (115)

> Give to each one the necessary remedies charitably and seriously; some require comfort and food; others, a gentle and kind handling that slowly calms them like taming a wild animal; others through learning; still others may need punishment and imprisonment but use this (method) in a way that does not further aggravate them. Above all and as much as possible, one must try to introduce into their souls that calm that easily restores their reason and health and understanding.

In his *History of Mental Psychology*, Gregory Zilboorg notes the foresight of Vives's humanitarian approach to the mentally ill when he writes that, "present-day psychiatry, particularly hospital (intramural) psychiatry, would find nothing to add to or subtract from Vives's statement, except, of course, the chains" (188). In the novel, Don Quixote's friends want nothing more than to return him home where family and friends can do what Vives suggests, restore his reason, health, and understanding. This reaction is reiterated during the episode of Cardenio when the shepherds actively try to seek him out and bring him to a nearby village to cure him (I.289; 181). When lucid, Cardenio himself acknowledges their acts of kindness and Don Quixote, too, reaches out to Cardenio to alleviate his pain (I.290; 182).

But, not everyone was sympathetic to Don Quixote's situation. Several travellers who pass by the inn had no patience for his exploits. In fact, when officers of the Holy Brotherhood realized Don Quixote was the one who had freed the galley slaves, they are determined to arrest him. However, the priest, using the weight of the law behind him, convinces them otherwise: "no tenían para qué llevar aquel negocio adelante, pues aunque le prendiesen y llevasen, luego le habían de dejar por loco" ["they had no need to proceed with the matter, for even if they arrested him and took him away, they would have to release him immediately because he was a madman"] (I.548; 398).[15] When the goatherd Eugenio does not hesitate to point out his madness, Don Quixote responds violently; food becomes his literal weapon as he proceeds to hit the goatherd with a loaf of bread, to which the goatherd responds in kind and initiates a chaotic scene right on top of the food, dishes, and cloths: "quebrando platos, rompiendo tazas y derramando y esparciendo cuanto en ella estaba" ["breaking plates, shattering cups, and spilling and scattering everything that was on it"] (I.597; 439).

In the first chapter of part II, food returns to the text as a remedy for mental illness in the barber's tale of the madman of Seville, in which the only time in the novel contemporary images of a hospital for the mentally ill are described.[16] It is no surprise that the barber narrates this story, first, because barbers played a central role working in conjunction with doctors and hospital administrators to care for the mentally ill. In her description of the Hospital General in Valencia, Tropé recounts that barbers were the ones most likely to perform medical procedures like bloodletting and purging of

---

15   This perspective was maintained by the Inquisition as Sara Nalle, in her case study of Bartolomé Sánchez, reports that "Inquisitors quickly applied the principle of the insanity defense to dismiss such cases" (147). For more on insanity as a legal defense and its treatment in *Don Quixote*, see Byrne 74-82.

16   Other critics have analyzed this episode including Rebecca Gould, who examines it in terms of the metaphysical conditions of Don Quixote's hunger, and Maurice Molho, who writes about this episode along with those of the two crazed men of the prologue to understand better characteristics of schizophrenia and their relationship to writing the novel.

mentally ill patients (256). Hence, the barber would be more familiar with anecdotes similar to the one he shares with Don Quixote.

Not only in terms of contemporary medical practices but also in terms of Cervantes's own narrative thread, the barber's tale at the start of part II links the novel to his enchanter role in prophesizing Don Quixote's return home at the end of part I. When Don Quixote is restrained in his bed and then enclosed in a cage (practices common to mental asylums), it is the barber who pronounces his treatment of returning home and marrying Dulcinea, thus echoing barbers' responsibilities of medical treatments in contemporary hospitals. Ten years later, Cervantes appropriately begins the second part of the novel with another barber's tale. His second story involves a licentiate whose relatives had committed him to a madhouse. When approved for release, the patient asks to say goodbye to some of the others who are restrained in individual cells. As he turns to one of the encaged madman, he assures him that he will regularly send him good food to eat: "Yo tendré cuidado de enviarle algunos regalos que coma, y cómalos en todo caso; que le hago saber que imagino, como quien ha pasado por ello, que todas nuestras locuras proceden de tener los estómagos vacíos y los celebros llenos de aire" ["I will be sure to send you some good things to eat, and eat them you must, for I say that I believe, as one who has experienced it himself, that all our madness comes from having our stomachs empty and our heads full of air"] (II.46; 463). In his promise to his fellow patient (which in the end cannot be fulfilled because he was confirmed crazy and never released) he implies how inadequate food at mental hospitals is and reiterates the all important link between food and health.

Don Quixote fully understands that food will help cure him: "Hiciéronle a don Quijote mil preguntas, y a ninguna quiso responder otra cosa sino que le diesen de comer y le dejasen dormir, que era lo que más le importaba" ["They asked Don Quixote a thousand questions, but the only answer he gave was that they should give him something to eat and let him sleep, which was what he cared about most"] (I.109; 45). When he awakens and discusses chivalric works with the priest, he begins to get worked up and again insists that he eat: "tráiganme de yantar, que sé que es lo que más me hará al caso" ["bring me something to eat, since I know that is what I need most at present"] (I.123; 54). His housekeeper would have done well to have a domestic manual like *Livro de receptas de pivetes, pastilhas e vvas perfumadas y conserbas* [Book of Recipes for Incense, Tablets and Perfumes, and Preserves], which includes recipes for curing the insane with such diverse ingredients as fennel, culantro, nettles, rue, pennyroyal, ox tongue, and vulture liver (64r-64v). In

Discursos medicinales (1606-09), Juan Méndez Nieto also writes about the central role food plays in curing the mentally ill: "que coma el enfermo más de lo que solía en salud, engorde y se le humedezca el çelebro y hábito de todo el cuerpo, por razón del mucho y tenplado alimento, porque en esto está la essençia y mayor parte de su cura y remedio" [the ill person should eat more than when he is healthy, he should gain weight and his brain and the habit of his entire body should become more moist on account of the great quantity of mild food, because this is the essence and main part of his cure and remedy] (478).

When a person was institutionalized, food remedies were designed to combat illnesses specifically related to heat and dryness. Nicolas Monardes, for example, prescribed different edible flowers, camphor, and sandalwood (qtd. in Valles Rojo 360). Other patients, who were experiencing excessive lethargy or in a catatonic state, would be administered syrup or a cordial of sugar and high-proof spirits (Tropé 265). Hospital records have daily entries on medicine prepared for the ill that included burdock, borage syrup, poppy, absinth, henbane, black nightshade, nightshade, and hellebore, but rarely do they specify which products were used for which patients (Tropé 266-67).

Internal medicine, though not often specified, included sugar and aromatic resins (Tropé 249). Saffron, mastic, spikenard and fennel were used for cleansing bile from the system (Tropé 263); purgatives and laxatives were common as well. Tropé explains, for example, that to eliminate bile, agarikon and rhubarb were administered and vegetable extracts like Mediterranean buckthorn were also commonplace (263). Classic medical manuals support the treatments that Tropé has recorded from the Valencia records. In Andrés Laguna's annotation of Dioscorides's entry on agarikon, he writes, "Purga los humores flemáticos y coléricos, descarga el celebro, aviva el sentido, alivia los nervios, y músculos ... sirve contra la gotacoral, y antiguos dolores de la cabeza [It purges the phlegmatic and choleric humors, gets the brain going, awakens the senses, soothes the nerves and muscles ... it is effective against epilepsy and long-standing headaches] (III,3).

Cervantes is certainly aware of Laguna's masterpiece as he owned a copy of it as well as a number of other medical texts (Eisenberg 284). In fact, Don Quixote references Laguna's masterpiece to express how hungry he is: "Tomara yo ahora más aína un cuartal de pan, o una hogaza y dos cabezas de sardinas arenques, que cuantas yerbas describe Dioscorides, aunque fuera el ilustrado por el doctor Laguna" ["Now I would rather have a ration of bread or a large loaf and a couple of sardine heads than all the plants described by Dioscorides or commented on by Dr. Laguna"] (I.226; 132).

Don Quixote's famous balsam of Fierabras includes ingredients—rosemary, oil, wine, and salt—that, when blended together, assisted in calming epileptic attacks associated with the mentally ill as well as general nervous attacks and jaundice, yellowed skin being yet another characteristic of Don Quixote. Dioscorides explains the multiple benefits of rosemary when taken with oil and wine: "es util contra la gota coral. ... Bebese con vino, y pimienta contra la amarillez llamada ictericia. Administrada en forma de uncion con azeyte, provoca sudor, y sirve al espasmo, y rupturas de nervios" [It is useful for epilepsy. ... Drunk with wine and black pepper, it prevents the yellowness called jaundice. Administered as an ointment with oil it induces sweat, and is useful for spasms and nervous breakdowns] (III.82). When Don Quixote drinks this electuary, the narrator confirms that he awoke "aliviado y sano" ["cured and healthy"] (I.211; 120).

In part II of *Don Quixote,* food takes on an even more important role than in part I.[17] From their first encounter with the Knight of the Wood, Don Quixote and Sancho meet a series of people from all social classes, essentially, everyone with whom they come in contact—country gentlemen, innkeepers, a duke and duchess (although here food motifs operate in negative terms), international pilgrims, shepherds, bandits, urban aristocracy, and other travelers—who open their homes or their travel packs to them, break bread together, and share in the adventures of the errant knight. In the famous Barataria episode when Sancho becomes governor, the doctor Pedro Recio's insistence on consuming certain foodstuffs while rejecting others draws on contemporary humoral theory to legitimize his claims. Finally, after Don Quixote and Sancho depart from the duke and duchess' palace, food motifs shift from descriptions of actual meals to discussions of sustenance and here, after being trampled by bulls, Don Quixote expresses his feelings of defeat and desire to die in terms of starvation, the complete absence of food:

> Come, Sancho amigo—dijo don Quijote—: sustenta la vida, que más que a mí te importa, y déjame morir a mí a manos de mis pensamientos y a fuerzas de mis desgracias. Yo, Sancho, nací para vivir muriendo, y tú para morir comiendo ... al cabo al cabo, cuando esperaba palmas, triunfos y coronas, granjeadas y merecidas por mis valerosas hazañas, me he visto esta mañana pisado, y acoceado, y molido, de los pies de animales inmundos y soeces. Esta consideración me embota los dientes, entorpece las muelas, y entomece las manos, y *quita de todo en todo la gana del co-*

---

17   For more on the significant role of food in part II of *Don Quixote,* see Nadeau.

mer, de manera, que pienso dejarme morir de hambre, muerte la más cruel de las muertes. (II.482; my emphasis)

"Eat, Sancho my friend," said Don Quixote, "sustain life, which matters to you more than to me, and let me die at the hands of my thoughts and by means of my misfortunes. I, Sancho, was born to live by dying, and you to die by eating; ... and when I have expected the palms, triumphs, and crowns that were earned and deserved by my valorous deeds, I have seen myself this morning trampled and kicked and bruised by the feet of filthy and unclean animals. This thought dulls my teeth, blunts my molars, numbs my hands, and *completely takes away my desire for food, and so I think I shall let myself die of hunger,* the cruelest of all deaths." (842-43; my emphasis)

In this dialogue with Sancho and through the use of food motifs, Don Quixote expresses for the first time his intense disenchantment and desire to die. Sancho encourages his master to eat and sleep and thus Don Quixote renews his spirits but his capacity to maintain his fantasy begins to wane and with it, his desire to eat or will to live.

Talk of disillusionment and death fill the final pages of the novel. The food images that had both enriched his journey and revealed characters' empathetic nature (or not) as they responded to what they had read, heard, and witnessed first-hand, have come full circle. As Don Quixote arrives home, the priest and the barber urge him to rest and eat well (II.585; 932) while the niece and housekeeper feed and pamper him (II.586; 933). After Don Quixote pronounces his last will and testament, he remains alive for a final three days and in that time, the narrator, through images of eating and drinking, stresses that his family and friends tried to go on with their lives: "Andaba la casa alborotada; pero, con todo, *comía la Sobrina, brindaba el Ama,* y se regocijaba Sancho Panza; que esto del heredar algo borra o templa en el heredero la memoria de la pena que es razón que deje el muerto" ["The house was in an uproar, but even so *the niece ate, the housekeeper drank*, and Sancho Panza was content, for the fact of inheriting something wipes away or tempers in the heir the memory of the grief that is reasonably felt for the deceased"] (II.591; 938; my emphasis). As Don Quixote breathes his last breath, food, seen throughout the novel as an empathetic response to repairing Don Quixote's mental health, is reduced to its most basic, biological level. In a single image of eating and drinking, those closest to Don Quixote, the niece and the housekeeper, know they must go on living in the face of their tragic loss.

Works Cited

Aguado Díaz, Antonio León. *Historia de las deficiencias*. Madrid: Escuela Libre Editorial, 1995. Print.

Aldama, Frederick Luis, ed. *Toward a Cognitive Theory of Narrative Acts*. Austin: U of Texas P, 2010. Print.

Atienza, Belén. *El loco en el espejo: Locura y melancolía en la España de Lope de Vega*. New York: Rodopi, 2009. Print.

Baquero, Aurelio. *Bosquejo histórico del hospital real y general de Nuestra Señora de Gracias de Zaragoza*. Zaragoza: Consejo superior de investigaciones científicas, 1952. Print.

Boruchoff, David. "On the Place of Madness, Deviance, and Eccentricity in *Don Quijote*." *Hispanic Review* 70.1 (2002): 1-23. Print.

Byrne, Susan. *Law and History in Cervantes' Don Quixote*. Toronto: U of Toronto P, 2012. Print.

Castilla del Pino, Carlos. *Cordura y locura en Cervantes*. Barcelona: Península, 2005. Print.

Cervantes, Miguel de. *Don Quixote*. Trans. Edith Grossman. New York: Harper Collins, 2003. Print.

———. *El ingenioso hidalgo don Quijote de la Mancha*. Ed. Luis Andrés Murillo. 2 vols. Madrid: Castalia, 1978. Print.

Cruz Cruz, Juan. *Dietética medieval*. Huesca: La Val de Onsera, 1997. Print.

Eisenberg, Daniel. "La biblioteca de Cervantes." *Studia in honorem prof. M. de Riquer*. Vol. 2 Barcelona: Quaderns Crema, 1987. 271-328. Print.

Foucault, Michel. *History of Madness*. Trans. Jonathan Murphy and Jean Kalpha. Ed. Jean Khalfa. New York: Routledge, 2006. Print.

Gallese, Vittorio, Morton Ann Gernsbacher, Cecilia Heyes, Gregory Hickok, and Marco Iacoboni. "Mirror Neuron Forum." *Perspectives on Psychological Science* 6.4 (2011): 369-407. Print.

González Duro, Enrique. *Historia de la locura en España: Tomo I Siglos XIII al XVII*. Madrid: Temas de Hoy, 1994. Print.

Gould, Rebecca. "Modernity, Madness, Disenchantment: Don Quixote's Hunger." *Symplokē: A Journal for the Intermingling of Literary, Cultural and Theoretical Scholarship* 19.1-2 (2011): 35-53. Print.

Heiple, Daniel. "Renaissance Medical Psychology in *Don Quijote*." *Ideologies and Literature* 2.9 (1979): 65-72. Print.

Herrera, Enrique. "La locura quijotesca." *Hispanic Journal* 25.1-2 (2004): 9-29. Print.

Hickok, Gregory. "Eight Problems with the Mirror Neuron Theory of Action Understanding in Monkeys and Humans." *Journal of Cognitive Neuroscience* 21.7 (2009): 1229-43. Print.

Huguet-Termes, Teresa. "Madrid Hospitals and Welfare in the Context of the Hapsburg Empire." *Health and Medicine in Hapsburg Spain: Agents, Practices, Representations.* Ed. Teresa Huguet-Termes, Jon Arrizabalaga, and Harold J. Cook. London: Wellcome Trust Centre for the History of Medicine at UCL, 2009. 64-85. Print.

Jaén, Isabel, and Julien Jacques Simon, eds. *Cognitive Literary Studies: Current Themes and New Directions.* Austin: U of Texas P, 2012. Print.

———, eds. *Cognitive Approaches to Early Modern Spanish Literature.* New York: Oxford UP, 2016. Print.

Johnson, Carroll B. *Madness and Lust: A Psychoanalytical Approach to* Don Quixote. Berkeley: U of California P, 1983. Print.

Keen, Suzanne. "A Theory of Narrative Empathy." *Narrative* 14.3 (2006): 207-36. Print.

Laguna, Andrés. *Pedacio Dioscorides Anazarbeo, annotado por el doctor Andrés Laguna, medico dignissmio de Julio III, pontífice máximo nuevamente ilustrado, y añadido, demonstrando las figuras de plantas, y animales en estampas finas, y dividido en dos tomos.* 6 vols. 1555. Madrid: Alonso Balbas, 1733. Print.

Lampérez y Romea, Vicente. *Arquitectura civil española de los siglos I a XVIII.* Madrid: Editorial Saturnino Calleja, 1922. Print.

Livro de receptas de pivetes, pastilhas e vvas perfumadas y conserbas. Sixteenth century. MS. 1462. National Library of Spain, Madrid. Print.

Lobera de Ávila, Luis. *El banquete de nobles caballeros.* San Sebastian: R&B Ediciones, 1996. Print.

López Alonso, Carmen. *Locura y sociedad en Sevilla: Historia del Hospital de los Inocentes (1436?-1840).* Seville: Diputación Provincial Sevilla, 1988. Print.

Mancing, Howard. "Embodied Cognitive Science and the Study of Literature." *Cognitive Cervantes.* Ed. Julien J. Simon, Barbara Simerka, and Howard Mancing. Spec. cluster of essays of *Cervantes: Bulletin of the Cervantes Society of America* 32.1 (2012): 25-69. Print.

Méndez Nieto, Juan. *Discursos medicinales.* Salamanca: Universidad de Salamanca, 1989. Print.

McCrea, Brian. "Madness and Community: *Don Quixote*, Huarte de San Juan's *Examen de ingenios* and Michel Foucault's *History of Insanity*." *Indiana Journal of Hispanic Literatures* 5 (Fall 1994): 213-24. Print.

Molho, Maurice. "Para una lectura psicológica de los cuentecillos de locos del segundo *Don Quijote*." *Cervantes: Bulletin of the Cervantes Society of America* 11.1 (1991): 87-98. Print.

Nadeau, Carolyn. "A Gastronomic Map of *Don Quixote* Part 2." *eHumanista/Cervantes* 4 (2015): 140-58. U of California Santa Barbara. Web. 2 Nov. 2016.

Nalle, Sara Tilghman. *Mad for God: Bartolomé Sánchez, the Secret Messiah of Cardenete*. Charlottesville: U of Virginia P, 2001. Print.

Rumbaut, Ruben D. *John of God: His Place in the History of Psychiatry and Medicine*. Miami: Ediciones Universal, 1978. Print.

Salillas, Rafael. *Un gran inspirador de Cervantes: El doctor Juan Huarte de San Juan y su* Examen de ingenios. Madrid: Imprenta a cargo de Eduardo Arias, 1905. Print.

Simon, Julien J., Barbara Simerka, and Howard Mancing, eds. *Cognitive Cervantes*. Spec. cluster of essays of *Cervantes: Bulletin of the Cervantes Society of America* 32.1 (2012). Print.

Shuger, Dale. *Don Quixote in the Archives: Madness and Literature in Early Modern Spain*. Edinburgh: Edinburgh UP, 2012. Print. Edinburgh Critical Studies in Renaissance Culture.

Soufas, Teresa Scott. *Melancholy and the Secular Mind in Spanish Golden Age Literature*. Columbia: U of Missouri P, 1990. Print.

Tropé, Hélène. *Locura y sociedad en la Valencia de los siglos XV al XVII*. Valencia: Diputaciò de Valencia, 1994. Print.

Valles Rojo, Julio. *Cocina y alimentación en los siglos XVI y XVII*. [Valladolid]: Junta de Castilla y León, 2007. Print.

Vives, Juan Luis. *El tratado del socorro de los pobres*. Valencia: Prometeo, n.d. Print.

Zilboorg, Gregory. *A History of Medical Psychology*. New York: Norton, 1941. Print.

Fear and Torture in La Mancha: The Embodied Memories of Sancho Panza

Massimiliano Adelmo Giorgini
Independent scholar

To investigate literature from the perspective of embodied cognition is to ignore the increasingly distant echo of voices declaring the author dead and insisting that there is nothing beyond the text itself. Samuel Taylor Coleridge foresightedly noted in the early nineteenth century that "text must not be taken without the context" (227)—and to this end, it is only logical that the living, breathing, feeling human being who pens the words be considered the greatest single element of the context of the art we read. While it can be argued that to extend cognitive and affective analyses to literary characters is to ascribe embodiment to a fictional entity and therefore assert a biological context upon a physically nonexistent concept, the truth is that the human who writes the sentences in which the invented personalities exist creates these characters based upon a theory of mind no less real than that which the author would use in social interactions with people of flesh and blood, and similarly forms these characters with actions and gestures which serve as triggers for the writer's own mirror neurons in the recognition of the affective states of individuals he/she encounters in daily life—an internal construction of an imagined physical other which Howard Mancing calls a "Theory of Body" (38). Therefore, the study of the same process in reverse—examining indicators of the affective states and the theory of mind of literary characters to arrive at the possible aims or thoughts of the author during their creation—is a valid and worthwhile endeavor which could lead to a new or deeper understanding of the text, even with complete awareness that the full knowledge of the intentions of any writer living or dead is an impossibility. For this reason and with these methods, this study investigates the affective signs of fear manifested by Sancho Panza during his encounter with Clavileño, and considers the possible environmental triggers which activate this underlying affective state suggested by those signs. These potential triggers are considered alongside the historical religious and political context of the author to suggest a possible pain trauma event from Sancho's past—perhaps even one connected to the era's inquisitorial spectre of control.

In chapter 41 of *Don Quixote II*, the magical wooden horse Clavileño the Swift is brought to the estate of the duke and duchess so that Don Quixote and Sancho Panza may fly to Candaya. In that mythical land, the Cervantine knight is expected to engage in singular combat with the evil enchanter Malambruno in order to lift the curse of beardedness from the Countess Trifaldi and her dueñas. Following several protests from Sancho Panza with regard to taking part in the adventure, Don Quixote observes that "desde la memorable aventura de los batanes ... nunca he visto a Sancho con tanto temor como ahora" [Not since the memorable adventure of the fulling mills have I ever seen Sancho as fearful as now] (II.41: 364).[1] If Don Quixote is correct, what precisely could it be about riding on Clavileño that frightens Sancho so? Sancho himself gives some insight into his aversion to mounting the wooden steed in chapter 40 of *Don Quixote II*, just after learning of Clavileño from the Countess Trifaldi:

> ¡Bueno es que apenas puedo tenerme en mi rucio, y sobre un albarda más blanda que la mesma seda, y querrían ahora que me tuviese en unas ancas de tabla, sin cojín ni almohada alguna! Pardiez, yo no me pienso moler ... (II.40: 359)

> I can barely stay on my donkey, and that's on a saddle softer than silk, and now they want me to sit on haunches made of planks, without even a cushion or a pillow! By God, I don't plan to thrash myself ...

Through Sancho's own explanation, it is obvious that it is the rough tactile sensation which he would experience on his buttocks by being seated on the wooden hindquarters of Clavileño which most disturbs him. Indeed, Sancho goes so far as to equate mounting Clavileño to *molerse* [thrashing oneself]—

---

[1] All citations from *Don Quixote* are from the edition by Allen and refer to part, chapter, and page. All English translations are the author's unless otherwise noted.

an indication of the degree of pain he imagines possible through the contact of his own body with the boards that make up the magical horse's back.

Furthermore, Sancho's repeated protests against the idea of riding on the back of Clavileño throughout much of chapters 40 and 41 of *Don Quixote II* touch repeatedly on the perceived hardness of the surface upon which he is expected to sit. Following Don Quixote's suggestion that Sancho lash himself 500 times "a buena cuenta de los tres mil y trecientos azotes a que estás obligado" [as a good start towards the three thousand three hundred lashings to which you are obligated] (II.41: 364), Sancho once again brings up the discomfort of his proposed mount in protest: "¿Ahora que tengo de ir sentado en una tabla rasa, quiere vuestra merced que me lastime las posas?" [Now that I must go seated upon a flat plank, your grace wants me to hurt my buttocks?] (II.41: 364-65). Even the narrator mentions the squire's complaints regarding his equine accommodations when the reluctant rider finally does mount Clavileño:

> De mal talante y poco a poco llegó a subir Sancho, y, acomodándose lo mejor que pudo en las ancas, las halló algo duras y no nada blandas, y pidió al duque que ... le acomodasen de algún cojín o de alguna almohada ... porque las ancas de aquel caballo más parecían de mármol que de leño. (II.41: 366)

> With a bad attitude and little by little Sancho eventually mounted, and, accommodating himself the best he could on the haunches, he found them rather hard and not a bit soft, and he asked the duke ... to please give him some cushion or pillow ... because the haunches of that horse seemed more like marble than wood.

Upon hearing this request, the Countess Trifaldi informs Sancho that Clavileño does not tolerate wearing any such trappings, and suggests that the squire ride sidesaddle, "que así no sentiría tanto la dureza" [so that he would not feel the hardness so much] (II.41: 366).

The repeated protests on the part of Sancho constitute a sort of fear-avoidance method, which Asmundson, Norton, and Vlaeyen describe as "behaviors that postpone or prevent exposure to an aversive situation or activity" (11). Significantly, Carroll Izard and Silvan Tomkins point out that "since the memory of pain does not 'hurt,' it cannot produce learning or avoidance behavior" on its own, and therefore it is only via the co-presence of a negative affect, such as fear, that anticipatory avoidance behavior can be motivated (86). Therefore, in the case of Sancho's response to being pushed to ride on Clavileño, the fear in the squire sensed by Don Quixote must truly exist in Sancho for that memory of pain—whatever its source—to inspire such adamant avoidance behavior. Izard and Tomkins explain the relationships between fear, pain and avoidance behavior:

> For a burned child to learn to shun the flame, he must first learn to connect the flame with the combined responses of pain and fear. Then, after the flame is no longer burning him, he must connect the flame or his memory with the fear response so that perception of flame induces fear. ... After these events, the following sequence is possible: perception or memory of flame → fear → awareness of relationship between flame, pain, and fear → anticipatory avoidance behavior. (86)

In the case of Sancho, then, the perception or memory of the hard wooden surface itself acts as does the flame in the example given by Izard and Tomkins. But how could such an otherwise seemingly neutral object be encoded alongside fear in the memory of an individual?

While fear is a complicated affect in which several subcortical structures of the brain play important roles in ways that function outside of the realm of individual experience (Fisher 62), there is no doubt that memory of trauma has an especially powerful connection to the development of learned fear (118). Indeed, as Katz, Page, Fashler, Rosenbloom, and Asmundson point out, research has "shown a relationship between the fear circuitry and the experience of pain" (141). As these same researchers also observe, "the neural circuitry of fear conditioning significantly overlaps with the neural circuitry involved in both PTSD and pain" (141). Taking these findings into account, it would seem that Sancho's direct reference to the pain and discomfort he believes he would experience when seated upon the wooden horse combined with the fear pointed out by Don Quixote might well be rooted in a real trauma from his past.

In the case of the recollection of past trauma connected to a real experience of pain, two types of memory can act simultaneously to trigger the affect of fear: body memory and cognitive memory. Johnston, Campbell-Yeo, Fernandes and Ranger point out that "body memory of past events or trauma (physical, emotional, or sexual) can be stored in the fascia, similarly to neural storage" (5). While it is impossible to objectively quantify the physiological characteristics of a fictional character, we can reasonably assume that the intensity of the avoidance behavior Sancho demonstrates (which is rooted in the fear sensed by Don Quixote) is indicative of a reaction at least initially connected primarily to a cognitive memory of pain, and then most likely joined by a trauma memory in the body of a past pain event at the time the squire reluctantly mounts Clavileño. Indeed, Sancho's historical pain experience may have led not only to the fear and resulting avoidance behaviors when faced with Clavileño, but this very same fear resultant from the original trauma could also amplify the squire's perception of pain or discomfort when forced to seat himself upon the wooden horse. Furthermore, the fear and the recollection of the past trauma in conjunction are capable of a negative sensation in the present. As Esther Cohen explains, "most humans familiar with pain carry the memory within them as a permanent mark and therefore fear its recurrence. At the same time, memory and fear magnify, and sometimes even cause pain" (37). In the situation considered here, Sancho might well experience real physical pain in the present as a result of the combination of the fear affect and the memories triggered in him by this encounter.

The indications of Sancho's fear reaction are not only detectable in his own words, however. As mentioned earlier, Don Quixote notes that he has never seen Sancho this fearful since the night of the fulling mills (II.41: 364). Furthermore, just after the observation by Don Quixote of what he perceives to be Sancho's strong negative affect towards mounting Clavileño, the would-be knight adds that "si yo fuera tan agorero como otros, su pusilanimidad me hiciera algunas cosquillas en el ánimo" [if I were as superstitious as others, his pusillanimity would give me shivers in my soul] (II.41: 364). The emotional mirror neuron system described by Giacomo Rizzolatti and Corrado Sinigaglia allows one to recognize emotive states in others at the visceromotor level without "automatically being induced to feel compassion" for them (191). Indeed, while Don Quixote recognizes and understands the fear reaction of Sancho, he himself wishes to distance himself from those who might be sucked into the empathic reaction so fully as to be overtaken by that external affect—he cognizes Sancho's fear, but does not allow himself to feel compassion for him. Further, it is also possible that the protagonist believes that if he is infected with Sancho's fear that Don Quixote himself will also begin to suffer his pain. In fact, Rizzolatti and Lisa Vozza have asserted that "il dolore è un'emozione che sappiamo riconoscere in modo diretto negli altri. Quando vediamo qualcuno colpito dal dolore abbiamo l'impressione di sentire anche noi quella stessa sensazione" [pain is an emotion that we can recognize in a direct manner in others. When we see someone stricken with pain we have the impression of feeling that same sensation ourselves] (66). Therefore, Sancho's fear and pain memory are not only encoded into his own words when faced with the wooden horse, but also sensed and reflected in Don Quixote's observations of Sancho—enough so to directly state that he will not allow himself to feel the same fear felt by his squire.

If indeed Sancho's fear, avoidance behaviors and increased sensitivity to pain when confronted with the idea of mounting Clavileño do derive from some significant body memory, what might the nature of that original event be? Thus far, we have considered as a possible source experience some historical pain event from Sancho's past. Indeed, according to Thomas Fuchs, "the most indelible impression in body memory is caused by trauma, that is, the experience of a serious accident, of rape, torture, or threat of death" (17). While all of these represent disquieting possibilities in the history of the squire which would seem to potentially align with (if not explain in and of themselves) the pain event postulated thus far, unless it is feasible to single out just one of these experiences it does not bring this investigation much closer to gaining a significantly deeper understanding of the source of Sancho's unexpectedly disproportionate affect in this adventure.

Some light is cast upon what could be the nature of Sancho's historical pain event through a consideration of factors that can trigger memory reactivation. According to Elizabeth Behnke, "the most fundamental principle of reactivation is similarity," in that a traumatic body memory is most often initiated by the resemblance of the current situation to a painful experience of the past. As Behnke explains, "the original situation as a whole may be reactivated by the current presence of part of it," with the net effect that the individual re-experiences the emotions and even physical sensations of the past event, to the degree that "the fear and pain are conjured up again" (89). Therefore, one possible explanation for Sancho's words and behavior when faced with the wooden horse could be that there exists in his past some traumatic pain experience which is similar in some significant manner to his encounter with Clavileño.

Continuing a path followed in prior research, at this point the study examined the possibility that Miguel de Cervantes was encoding subversive references between the lines of this adventure, using Sancho's inordinate fear reaction and avoidance behavior to point to some unspecified pain event— with the intention of eluding censors while alluding to a specific abuse or injustice in order to issue an anti-inquisitorial critique.[2] Given the aforementioned fear and other indicators of an unspecified historical pain event in

---

2   See Giorgini, "Cervantes" 164; Giorgini, "Drawing" 342-43.

Sancho's reaction to Clavileño, the most obvious target of Cervantes's potential recrimination would be some element of the well-documented use of torture by the agents of the Inquisition (Green 65-88).

As it turns out, Adhémar Esmein explains that one of the principal methods of inquisitorial interrogations included questioning under torture as the subject was "stretched naked upon a wooden horse, to which he was bound" (137). Esmein further states that there existed variations of such devices named after equines which could produce greater or lesser torment for those being questioned. As Esmein puts it, "a gradation was imported into the tortures by having two patterns of wooden horse, the 'little' and the 'big horse'" (137). Indeed, in regard to the use of the wooden horse for torture, Samuel Chandler writes in *The History of Persecution, from the Patriarchal Age, to the Reign of George II* that the Inquisition employed "two different forms of the antient [sic] Eculeus" (214), while John Ward describes several forms of the *equuleus*, all of which were "in some measure made like a horse," and states that beyond the equine-like form, what all had in common was that "on the equuleus the torture was applied in order to extort confession" (382). The *equuleus* was also known in Italian as the "cavalletto" ("little horse") and in English as the "Spanish Donkey," for its infamous association with the torture methods of the Inquisition (Brewer xliii). One version of the *equuleus* is essentially what is known as the "rack" in English. It is a flat wooden table with a cross bar on it, and the victim is placed upon it so the cross bar crosses laterally under the dorsal side of the victim between the shoulders and the lower back. The victim's legs and arms are all tied with heavy rope that is then stretched to tension away from the center of the body, creating ever greater pressure of the crossbar against the dorsal side of the victim as the tension of the ropes is increased. The other form of the *equuleus* employed by the Inquisition:

> was a wooden machine of torture, which was a species of impalement. The victim was made to sit on a sharp-pointed conical box, and in order to give weight to his body, and force the point of the seat further in, heavy weights were attached to the hands and feet of the sufferer. (Brewer xliii)

This same Spanish donkey had a range of variation of design, as the manufacture of each instrument was of local provenance. Another version of this instrument "is an upright plank, the top end beveled on both sides like the point of a cold chisel, or like an inverted V. The offender sat astride this upright plank, with heavy weights attached to his feet" (MacDonald 18). While the devices described thus far were given the name "horse" in one form or another, the descriptions may not seem especially equine. However, inquisitors did also often embellish the instrument in a way that accentuated the characteristics of its name. As Geoffrey Abbott explains about one common configuration of the *equuleus*, "a further bizarre touch was the addition of a carved horse's head and tufted tail, accessories which, hardly surprisingly, failed to raise a laugh from the unfortunates who were sentenced to ride the appliance" (325). While the inquisitorial policy on the use of the Spanish donkey was primarily as a means of extracting truthful confessions to supplement additional evidence and witness testimony, it did also often "result in an unintentional death, depending on the stamina" of the interrogated (Abbott 325). Most interesting to the specific case of Sancho's encounter with Clavileño is the latter version of the Spanish donkey, as its especially highlighted resemblance to a horse rings most similar to the wooden horse commissioned by the duke and duchess. Furthermore, however, Sancho's affective fear reaction to the possible tactile sensation that Clavileño would cause to his buttocks corresponds to the findings of Fuchs, who explains that "the former pains of a torture victim may reappear in a present conflict and correspond exactly to the body parts that were exposed to the torture" (18).

Sixteenth-century theologian and historian Phillipus von Limborch describes the use of the wooden horse torture device by the Spanish Inquisition (222-23), citing the specific case of Englishman William Lithgow, who was accused of being a Protestant heretic and "was expofed to the moft cruel Torments upon the Wooden Horfe" (223). Lithgow survived the ordeal and wrote a detailed memoir of his travels titled *The Totall Difcourfe, Of the Rare Aduentures, and painefull Peregrinations*, first published in 1614 (Schelling 303) and expanded in 1632 in which he describes the experience in great detail (461-75) and calls the machine upon which he was tortured a "Pottaro" (463). This "Pottaro" is quite likely Lithgow's attempt to phonetically reproduce the Spanish term "potro" [colt]. 1611's *Tesoro de la lengua castellana, o española* by Sebastián de Covarrubias Orozco lists one definition of "potro" as "caballo nueuo" [young horse] and the other as "cierto inftrumento de madera para dar tormento, del nombre Latino *equuleus*, que es como diminutivo de *equus*, y de alli tomò nombre de 'potro'" [a certain instrument of torture, from the Latin word *equuleus*, which is a diminutive of *equus*, from which it took the name "colt"] (594).

Awareness of the torture device known as the "potro" was not limited to historians, grammarians and the tortured, however. Indeed, the word was also part of the cultural milieu, as evidenced by Francisco de Quevedo's reference to the inquisitorial tool in his novel *El buscón* when protagonist Pablos states: "Muchas veces me hubieran llorado en el asno, si hubiera cantado en el potro" [They would have made me mourn on a donkey many times, if I had sung on the *colt*] (102). As Pura Fernández and Juan Pedro Gabino explain in their edition to *El buscón*, this means that had Pablos confessed his sins on the "potro," they would have punished him many times by whipping him as he rode through the streets on a donkey's back (71n30).

Such open, although oblique, literary reference to torture is not limited to Quevedo, however—it also appears in *Don Quixote I*, chapter 22—during the adventure of the *galeotes* [galley slaves]. When Don Quixote asks the crime of one of the galley slaves, the knight is informed that the prisoner's crime was being "músico y cantor" [a musician and singer] (308), which the convict himself explains by stating that "quien canta una vez llora toda la vida" [he who sings once mourns all his life] (308). Upon hearing this suggestive explanation, Don Quixote states that he does not understand, causing one of the guards to explicitly expound that "a este pecador le dieron tormento y confesó su delito" [they tortured this sinner and he confessed his crime] (308). But if torture is so overtly discussed in novels by major authors of the period—and directly explained within the pages of *Don Quixote*—what need would there be to so subtly insinuate its existence through an indirect reference such as Clavileño?

In considering this question, one major possibility is that although mentions of a wooden horse have ceased to trigger overt connections to torture in modern day readers, and therefore seem inordinately subtle, the implications may have been immediate and hilarious to Cervantes's contemporaries. What may have seemed such an obvious mention of a torture device in conjunction with Sancho's protests could well have been just one more opportunity for *schadenfreude* at the squire's expense, similar in nature to the 3,300 "azotes" [lashes] which the squire is expected to give himself in order to disenchant Dulcinea in *Don Quixote II*, chapter 35. Still, the fact remains that in this adventure there is no speaker similar to the guard in the adventure of the galley slaves who plainly states that the prisoner was tortured. So for what reason might Cervantes have chosen to refer to torture so much more obliquely in the case of Sancho's encounter with Clavileño?

One answer to this question could lie in the nature of the offenses which led to the torture in both of the aforementioned literary references—in both cases the tortures resulted from crimes prosecutable in the secular courts. However, matters were quite different where the inquisitorial courts were concerned. While the details of criminal trials were public knowledge, inquisitorial procedures and details of trials were shrouded in silence. As John F. Chuciak IV explains:

> Not only the Inquisition's officials and ministers but also the accused, any accusers, and all of the witnesses for both the defense and the prosecution swore an oath of secrecy. The suspected heretic at the very first audience with the inquisitors vowed to … keep secret not only his own case but also everything that he might see or hear while in the tribunal … and any violations of this oath of secrecy earned the suspect one hundred or two hundred lashes. (31)

Perhaps no other evidence illustrates the generalized fear to criticize or even mention the Inquisition better than the well-known Golden Age Spanish proverb "¡Del Rey y la Inquisición, Chitón!" [About the King and the Inquisition, hush up!], which implies equivalence between such statements and treason (Puigblanch 168). Indeed, in regard to this saying, Ryan Prendergast states that "it not only alludes to the need for self-censorship but also clearly demonstrates the prominence of the Spanish Inquisition in the early modern Spanish cultural imaginary" (117). While Prendergast acknowledges that it would have been impossible for the Inquisition to effectively enforce its rules throughout all of Iberia, he argues that through its reputation the Holy Office was able "to create a fear-inspiring and haunting presence" which was able to impose its will via a "specter of control" (117). Might such a specter of control explain why Cervantes writes clearly of the penal process for criminal issues in *Don Quixote I*, chapter 22, yet seems to follow the "¡Chitón!" admonition with regards to the relationship between Sancho Panza and Clavileño? Is it possible that Sancho's tangible fear was rooted in anxiety about potential torture by the Inquisition, or perhaps even in the memories of his own experience in the torture chambers of the Holy Office?

One revelatory response by Sancho to Countess Trifaldi's several entreaties to the squire that he mount Clavileño is that "yo no soy brujo" [I am not a warlock] (II.41: 363). The term "brujo," being the masculine form of "bruja," can mean male witch (or "warlock"), but equally signifies enchanter, sorcerer, or necromancer. Covarrubias defines the term in Cervantes's era as: "Bruxa, bruxo, cierto genero de gente perdida y endiablada, que perdido el temor a Dios, ofrecen sus cuerpos y ſus almas al demonio a trueca de vna libertad vicioſa, y libidinoſa" [Witch, warlock, a certain type of degenerate and diabolical people, who having lost the fear of God, offer their bodies and their souls to the devil in exchange for a depraved and libidinous freedom] (153). Further, in language that almost mirrors that of Sancho, who states that unlike brujos, he is not one "para gustar de andar por los aires" [to enjoy going about through the air] (I.41: 363), Covarrubias explains that brujos "van por los ayres" [go through the air] (154). Covarrubias adds that these brujos unite in gatherings where the devil appears to them and they give him allegiance, "negando la fanta Fe" [denying the Holy Faith] (153) and scorning "nueftro Redentor Iefu Chrifto, y fus fantos Sacramentos, como largamente lo efcriue el Malleus Maleficarum" [our Redeemer Jesus Christ, and his Holy Sacraments, as written about at length in the *Malleus Maleficarum*] (153).

The *Malleus Maleficarum* was a fifteenth-century manual for properly identifying, questioning, trying, and ultimately punishing witches written by German Catholic Inquisitor Heinrich Kramer under the pen name Institoris (Broedel 12-22).[3] Following the publication of the *Malleus Maleficarum* in Spain in 1486, the Spanish Inquisition began to approach practitioners of witchcraft as heretics, due to the fact their beliefs were contrary to the teachings of the Catholic Church (Rawlings 129). Matters changed significantly in 1526 when the Supreme Council of the Inquisition in Spain stopped permitting the capital punishment of witches without its prior approval, effectively ending the practice of witch-hunting for over 70 years (Henningsen 9-10).[4] Indeed, the authority of Kramer's text was itself challenged when "in 1538 the Spanish Inquisition cautioned its members not to believe everything the *Malleus* said, even when it presented apparently firm evidence" (Peters 241). Matters looked even worse for the relevance of the *Malleus* following the publication by Juan Wiero, a book-length attack on Kramer's book titled *Sobre los artificios del diablo* [On the artifices of the devil] in 1563. However, a series of defenses of the *Malleus* followed Wiero's criticism, culminating in theologian Martín del Río's censure of Wiero's text in *Disquisitionum magicarum libri sex* in 1599 (Lara Alberola 73-74). Indeed, despite the cautions by

---

3   While many of the editions published within Kramer's lifetime credited Jacob Sprenger as co-author, all of these were after Sprenger's death. It is believed by most authorities on the *Malleus Maleficarum* that Kramer simply wished to accord the text the prestige promised by the involvement of Sprenger, who was the former dean of theology of the University of Cologne, and that Sprenger at best had little to do with it, and even more likely, would have objected to the bulk of the content (Broedel 18-19).

4   Despite this policy, some witch-burnings still occurred in Barcelona and Zaragoza due to a loophole allowing local inquisitors to proceed in the event of unanimous inquisitorial court decisions (Henningsen 10).

the Supreme Council of the Inquisition to not take the text too closely to its word, the *Malleus* continued to have major influence on the views of witchcraft in popular, literary and theological spheres throughout the Golden Age (Lara Alberola 305). Such an environment was conducive for yet a new wave of witch hunts to occur at the turn of the seventeenth century, and indeed on the day of November 7, 1610 in the city of Logroño, 31 men and women were tried for witchcraft. Of these, 18 were either burned alive, burned dead, or died in prison awaiting judgment (Pavlac 155). The witch-craze of 1610-12 reached such proportions that even Inquisitor Alonso Salazar Frías felt the need to stress to the Supreme Council of the Inquisition that a case of mass hysteria had taken hold and that there were likely no witches to be found among the 2,000 people accused of witchcraft at the time (Henningsen 50-57; Lara Alberola 95). In such a context, Sancho's declaration that he is not a "brujo" is far from being innocuous—*Don Quixote II* was published only three years after the end of the Logroño witch hysteria (and this scene likely written much earlier), and the topic could not possibly have been merely comical in an environment in which witches were still hunted, even if at a more moderate pace.

Beyond Sancho's disavowal of witchcraft and air travel, there is another interesting parallel between the *Malleus* and the Clavileño adventure. Kramer describes how one type of witch, the necromancer, is "often carried for a long time through the air by evil spirits to faraway places," and adds that such necromancers sometimes "persuade others to do the same, and carry them along on a horse (which is not really a horse, but an evil spirit in that shape)" (Kramer 135). While the similarities between *Don Quixote* and other books of chivalry often touch on subjects that would be considered fantasy in the modern day, the *Malleus* in 1615 was still considered a valid tool in the arsenal of the very serious subject of witch hunting—and because witchcraft was most often considered a form of heresy (Broedel 124), this was the territory of the Inquisition (Tutino 19-20).[5]

While the original aim of the Inquisition up to the middle of the sixteenth century was to rid the Iberian Peninsula of "acts of Jewish, Islamic and Protestant heresy," the focus from 1560-1614 became "to correct the unorthodox beliefs and behavioural practices of the Old Christian" (Rawlings

---

[5] It was technically possible, according to the *Malleus* and inquisitorial law, to be a witch and not a heretic, as "heresy, after all, is a matter of belief, and the devil does not care if witches reject Christianity in their hearts or not." Rather, the devil's concern is the behavior of the witch, because "that is all that is needed to ensure damnation" (Broedel 124).

114). The focus of the Inquisition also shifted from major acts or statements of heresy to minor errors of interpretation or the utterance of blasphemous statements (Rawlings 115). Indeed, "in the majority of cases ... subject to prosecution" the offenses were "symptomatic of the naïve mentality, bordering on ignorance, of the masses rather than any deliberate attempt to offend Catholic teachings" (Rawlings 114). The environment in rural areas developed to the point that villagers had to carefully consider their speech—and from this "arose the widespread advice of the time: *que mirase lo que dice*, or 'watch what you say'" (Versluis 16). In such a tense context, it should not be surprising that uneducated villagers might wish to frame all of their speech within the safety of folk sayings and proverbs—perhaps explaining, in part, why a rustic bumpkin like Sancho Panza might wish to avoid original sentence constructions and word choices and speak as much as possible in familiar idioms.[6]

Because the populace was prone to witch-hunts and even unintentional sacrilegious statements were often reported as possible signs of heresy, it should not be surprising that more than a third of all inquisitorial investigations originated from ingenuous questions or expressions of incredulity with regard to articles of faith, such as doubting Mary's virginity or God's omnipotence (Rawlings 114; Haliczer 296). Worse, as Henry Charles Lea explains, was that unlike in the case of criminal offenses, no one was granted immunity from torture by the Inquisition when the charge was heresy. Lea states that "nobles were subject to it and so were ecclesiastics of all ranks" (13). Even age provided no exemption, as senior citizens and children were both often taken to the *potro*, as happened in the cases of eighty-year-old Isabel de Jaén and "a boy of ten or eleven" named Joan de Heredia in 1607 (14). Logically, this reality means that it would have been completely possible for a young Sancho Panza to have uttered some remark questioning the credibility of the notion of a virgin birth, ultimately leading to his questioning and eventual torture by the Inquisition for heresy. Such a situation might also help explain Sancho's preferred choice of mount—because among the consequences for those convicted of heresy, they were also forbidden "to ride on horseback—a mule, or donkey, was the utmost to which they could aspire" (Roth 113).

---

6   In "Profit Maxims: Capitalism and the Common Sense of Time and Money," David Norman Smith discusses the use of proverbs for social, economic and political indoctrination purposes behind the wall of the safety and familiarity of such sayings, and notes that Erich Fromm even linked the increased use of such folk sayings directly to the influence of authoritarianism (29-74).

When the Spanish Inquisition was in its early years, torture was relatively uncommon. As E. William Monter notes, "when the Holy Office was at its most severe point, it rarely tortured anyone: for example, among more than 2,000 *conversos* tried at Valencia before 1530, only twelve were tortured" (75). However, Monter also points out that of those conversos being tried, "hundreds of them were executed" (75). The preferred methodology slowly evolved as the goals of the Holy Office became more centered on discovering the truth of the beliefs of the accused heretics with the goal of possibly saving their souls. Therefore, by the beginning of the seventeenth century execution was much less likely, but once the Inquisition opened an investigation into heresy it was virtually impossible to avoid torture. However, this torture was not considered a punishment per se, but rather an investigative tool to assist in finding the full truth of the beliefs of the accused. In fact, even when suspected heretics openly confessed to any and all crimes of which they were accused, they were still expected to give a complete accounting of the details and motivations for their offenses under torture (Kamen 242). Of all of the available methods of torture to the inquisitors, "the most important of these—the central mechanism of the inquisitorial process, it might be said, was the *potro* (literally 'colt' or 'horse')" (Kerrigan 172). In fact, while the Medieval Inquisition and the early Spanish Inquisition from the beginning through the majority of the sixteenth century employed a host of torture techniques and instruments, the *potro* "was virtually the only torture method used by the tribunal in the seventeenth century" (Kamen 439). In light of this, Sancho's declaration that "yo no soy brujo" [I am not a warlock] (II.41: 363) could be taken as more than just an explanation of why the squire would not wish to ride through the air—but rather as a protestation that as he is not a *brujo* he does not deserve to be put upon the wooden horse.

Once Sancho relents and reluctantly agrees to mount Clavileño, the squire does so with a dramatic flair:

Diciendo 'a Dios,' se dejó vendar los ojos, y, ya después de vendados, se volvió a descubrir, y, mirando a todos los del jardín tiernamente y con lágrimas, dijo que le ayudasen en aquel trance con sendos paternostres y sendas avemarías, porque Dios deparase quien por ellos los dijese cuando en semejantes trances se viesen. (II.41: 366)

Saying, 'to God,' he allowed his eyes to be blindfolded, and, after being blindfolded, he uncovered them again, and looking at everyone in the garden tenderly and with tears in his eyes, he asked that each of them help him in his time of danger with some Our Fathers and Hail Marys so that God would provide someone to say these for them if ever they found themselves in similar peril.

Certainly this statement most closely resembles a hero or martyr's last words, rather than the string of sometimes senseless proverbs most typical of the ignorant rustic's utterances. Don Quixote himself makes a similar observation when he follows these words with the question: "¿Estás puesto en la horca por ventura, o en el último término de la vida, para usar de semejantes plegarias?" [Are you by chance on the gallows, or in the final moments of your life, in order to plead in such a way?] (II.41: 366). Indeed, Sancho's words, as observed by the would-be knight, only make logical sense in this context if the squire believes he is putting his own health and life at risk.

The fact that Sancho is blindfolded as he mounts Clavileño is further indication that what he is about to experience is a form of torture. Blindfolding is even now a common technique of interrogators to increase the fear and feeling of helplessness experienced by the subject being interrogated. Similar methods have been used even quite recently, in places as recognizable to modern readers as Abu Ghraib or Guantanamo Bay. But the technique is far from new, and was also commonplace during the time of the Spanish Inquisition. For example, in the case of the high-profile interrogation of Don Pedro de Lerma by inquisitors, de Lerma was blindfolded immediately before being subjected to torture (Vidal Manzanares 359). Further, one member of an expeditionary force to eliminate Protestants describes first-hand the torture and killing of 88 Lutheran heretics in June 1561 on direct orders of the Spanish Inquisition. Prior to administering punishment to the heretics, the force grabbed them "uno por uno poniéndoles una venda en los ojos" [one by one putting a blindfold over their eyes] (Cantú 255). If Sancho had indeed been investigated by the Inquisition for heresy at some point earlier in life, being pushed to now mount a wooden horse while blindfolded could not possibly fail to trigger both body trauma memories and fear avoidance behaviors. In this case, it would indeed be heroic of Sancho to agree to mount Clavileño and confront whatever may come. In such a light, his martyr's speech and appeal for prayers from all present is altogether befitting.

If Cervantes truly created Sancho with the subtle implication that he may have had such a past as an accused heretic and suffered torture on the *equuleus*, to what end might he have intended such a background? One possibility lies within the reference to witchcraft when Sancho initially refuses to mount Clavileño—specifically, the statement he makes that he is not a warlock who enjoys going about in the air. With this declaration, he attempts to dispel the notion that he deserves to be put on the wooden horse. While the entreaty here is directed primarily at the duke and duchess, it begs the question of to whom the entreaties would need be directed in the case of the *equuleus*. If the warlock or necromancer, doing the work of Satan, fashions an evil spirit into a horse to whisk away innocent souls and turn them into witches, and the dukes, as part of their mean-spirited, elaborate practical joke, fashion a horse out of boards to fool Don Quixote and Sancho into believing they fly through the air, then who or what is the *maleficus* ("witch," but also most literally the compound word "evildoer") who builds wooden horses to take victims—possibly including Sancho—to a world of pain, all in the name of God? It would be difficult in this context of Sancho's inordinate fear reaction when faced with a wooden horse —a response most typical of pain trauma memory, and an affective state which is also reflected in Don Quixote's recognition of that fear—to not consider how such a trauma memory associated with an equine made of lumber may well have derived from having been tortured on the *potro*. Further, Sancho's almost obsessive use of folk sayings and proverbs in place of original sentences could well belie an underlying anxiety or fear of saying the wrong thing—an extreme obedience to the admonition *"que mirase lo que dice"* to avoid interrogation by the Inquisition. Such fears considered in the social and political context of Cervantes, and, in turn, the literary character of his creation, lead to the very real possibility that the youthful Sancho may have inadvertently questioned or negated an article of faith and therefore have been investigated—*id est*, tortured—by the agents of the Inquisition. In this case, the obvious answer to the question of the identity of the *maleficus* who builds wooden horses upon which to torture innocents is that it is the Inquisition itself.

Works Cited

Abbott, Geoffrey. *Execution: A Guide to the Ultimate Penalty*. Chichester: Summersdale, 2012. Print.

Asmundson, Gordon J. G., Peter J. Norton, and Johan W. S. Vlaeyen. "Fear-Avoidance Models of Chronic Pain: An Overview." *Understanding and Treating Fear of Pain*. Ed. Gordon J. G. Asmundson, Johan W. S. Vlaeyen, and Geert Crombez. Oxford: Oxford UP, 2004. 3-24. Print.

Behnke, Elizabeth. "Enduring: A Phenomenological Investigation." *Body Memory, Metaphor and Movement*. Ed. Sabine C. Koch, Thomas Fuchs,

Michela Summa, and Cornelia Müller. Amsterdam: John Benjamins, 2012. 83-104. *ProQuest Ebrary*. Web. 1 Nov. 2016.

Brewer, Ebenezer Cobham. *A Dictionary of Miracles: Imitative, Realistic, and Dogmatic*. Philadelphia: J. B. Lippincott, 1894. *Princeton U*. Web. 1 Nov. 2016.

Broedel, Hans Peter. *The* Malleus Maleficarum *and the Construction of Witchcraft: Theology and Popular Belief*. Manchester: Manchester UP, 2003. Print.

Cantú, César. *Historia universal: Épocas XV y XVI. Tomo V*. Trans. Nemesio Fernández Cuesta. Madrid: Gaspar y Roig Editores, 1856. *Google Books*. Web. 1 Nov. 2016.

Cervantes, Miguel de. *El Ingenioso Hidalgo Don Quijote de la Mancha*. Ed. John J. Allen. 25th ed. 2 vols. Madrid: Cátedra, 2005. Print.

Chandler, Samuel. *The History of Persecution, from the Patriarchal Age, to the Reign of George II*. London: Charles Atmore and J. Craggs, 1813. *Archive.org*. Web. 1 Nov. 2016.

Chuciak IV, John F. *The Inquisition in New Spain, 1536—1820: A Documentary History*. Baltimore: Johns Hopkins UP, 2012. Print.

Cohen, Esther. *The Modulated Scream: Pain in Late Medieval Culture*. Chicago: U of Chicago P, 2010. Print.

Coleridge, Samuel Taylor. "No. 15. Thursday, November 30, 1809." *The Friend: A Series of Essays*. London: Gale and Curtis, 1812. 225-32. *Archive.org*. Web. 1 Nov. 2016.

Covarrubias Orozco, Sebastián de. *Tesoro de la lengua castellana, o española*. Madrid: Luis Sánchez, 1611. *Universidad Complutense de Madrid*. Web. 1 Nov. 2016.

Esmein, Adhémar. *A History of Continental Criminal Procedure*. Boston: Little, Brown, and Co, 1913. *Harvard U*. Web. 1 Nov. 2016.

Fisher, Sebern F. *Neurofeedback in the Treatment of Developmental Trauma: Calming the Fear-Driven Brain*. New York: Norton, 2014. Print.

Fuchs, Thomas. "The Phenomenology of Body Memory." *Body Memory, Metaphor and Movement*. Ed. Sabine C. Koch, Thomas Fuchs, Michela Summa, and Cornelia Müller. Amsterdam: John Benjamins, 2012. 9-22. *ProQuest Ebrary*. Web. 1 Nov. 2016.

Giorgini, Massimiliano A. "Cervantes Lands a Left Hook: Baiting the Inquisition with Ekphrastic Subversion." *Cognitive Cervantes*. Ed. Julien J. Simon, Barbara Simerka, and Howard Mancing. Spec. cluster of essays of *Cervantes: Bulletin of the Cervantes Society of America* 32.1 (2012): 163-99. Print.

———. "Drawing Between the Lines: Ekphrasis and the Subversion of Inquisitorial Prohibition in *Don Quixote.*" *Escrituras silenciadas: El paisaje como historiografía*. Alcalá de Henares: Universidad de Alcalá, 2013. 337-60. Print.

Green, Toby. *Inquisition: Reign of Fear*. New York: Thomas Books, 2009. Print.

Haliczer, Stephen. *Inquisition and Society in the Kingdom of Valencia, 1478-1834*. Berkeley: U of California P, 1990. Print.

Henningsen, Gustav. "The Witchcraft Policy of the Spanish Inquisition." *The Salazar Documents: Inquisitor Alonso de Salazar Frías and Others on the Basque Witch Persecution*. Ed. Gustav Henningsen. Leiden: Brill, 2004. 7-13. *ProQuest Ebrary*. Web. 1 Nov. 2016.

Izard, Carroll E., and Silvan S. Tomkins. "Affect and Behavior: Anxiety as a Negative Affect." *Anxiety and Behavior*. Ed. Charles D. Spielberger. New York: Academic P, 1966. 81-128. Print.

Johnston, Celeste, Marsha Campbell-Yeo, Ananda Fernandes, and Manon Ranger. "Neonatal Pain." *Treatment of Chronic Pain by Integrative Approaches*. Ed. Timothy R. Deer, Michael S. Leong, and Albert L. Ray. New York: Springer, 2015. 271-84. Print.

Kamen, Henry. *The Spanish Inquisition: A Historical Revision*. 4th ed. New Haven: Yale UP, 2014. Print.

Katz, Joel, M. Gabrielle Page, Samantha Fashler, Brittany N. Rosenbloom, and Gordon J. G. Asmundson. "Chronic Pain and the Anxiety Disorders: Epidemiology, Mechanisms and Models of Comorbidity, and Treatment." *Mental Health and Pain: Somatic and Psychiatric Components of Pain in Mental Health*. Ed. Serge Marchand, Djéa Saravane, and Isabelle Gaumond. Paris: Springer-Verlag, 2013. 119-56. Print.

Kerrigan, Michael. *Dark History of the Catholic Church: Schisms, Wars, Inquisitions, Witch Hunts, Scandals, Corruption*. London: Amber Books, 2014. Print.

Kramer, Heinrich [Institoris]. *The Malleus Maleficarum*. Ed. P. G. Maxwell-Stuart. Manchester: Manchester UP, 2007. Print.

Lara Alberola, Eva. *Hechiceras y brujas en la literatura española de los Siglos de Oro*. Valencia: Publicacions de la Universitat de València, 2010. Print.

Lea, Henry Charles. *A History of the Inquisition of Spain*. Vol. 3. New York: Macmillan, 1922. *Penn SU*. Web. 1 Nov. 2016.

Limborch, Phillipus Van. *The History of the Inquisition, as It Has Subsisted in France, Italy, Spain, Portugal, Sicily, Sardinia, Milan, Poland, Flanders, Etc. With a Particular Description of its Secret Prisons, Modes of Torture,*

Style of Accusation, Trial, Etc. Trans. Samuel Chandler. Vol. 1. London: J. Gray, 1731. *UCLA*. Web. 1 Nov. 2016.

Lithgow, William. *The Totall Difcourfe, Of the Rare Aduentures, and painefull Peregrinations of long nineteene Yeares Trauayles, from Scotland, to the moſt Famous Kingdomes in Europe, Aſia, and Affrica*. London: Nicholas Okes, 1632. *Universidad Complutense de Madrid*. Web. 1 Nov. 2016.

MacDonald, George Everett. *Thumbscrew and Rack: Torture Implements Employed in the XVth and XVIth Centuries for the Promulgation of Christianity*. New York: Truth Seeker, [1894]. *U of Michigan*. Web. 1 Nov. 2016.

Mancing, Howard. "Embodied Cognition and Autopoiesis in *Don Quixote*." *Cognitive Approaches to Early Modern Spanish Literature*. Ed. Isabel Jaén and Julien Jacques Simon. Oxford: Oxford UP, 2016. 37-52. Print.

Monter, E. William. *Frontiers of Heresy: The Spanish Inquisition from the Basque Lands to Sicily*. Cambridge: Cambridge UP, 1990. Print.

Pavlac, Brian A. *Witch Hunts in the Western World: Persecution and Punishment from the Inquisition through the Salem Trials*. Westport: Greenwood P, 2009. Print.

Peters, Edward. "Superstition, Magic and Witchcraft on the Eve of the Reformation." *Witchcraft and Magic in Europe, Volume 3: The Middle Ages*. Ed. Karen Jolly, Catharina Raudvere, and Edward Peters. London: Athlone P, 2002. 238-45. Print.

Prendergast, Ryan. *Reading, Writing, and Errant Subjects in Inquisitorial Spain*. Surrey: Ashgate, 2011. Print.

Puigblanch, Antonio. *The Inquisition Unmasked: Being an Historical and Philosophical Tremendous Tribunal, Founded on Authentic Documents; and Exhibiting the Necessity of its Suppression, as a Means of Reform and Regeneration*. Trans. William Walton. Vol. 2. London: Baldwin, Cradock, and Joy, 1816. *Google Books*. Web. 1 Nov. 2016.

Quevedo, Francisco de. *La vida del Buscón llamado don Pablos*. Ed. Pura Fernández and Juan Pedro Gabino. Madrid: Ediciones Akal, 1996. Print.

Rawlings, Helen. *The Spanish Inquisition*. Oxford: Blackwell P, 2006. Print.

Rizzolatti, Giacomo, and Corrado Sinigaglia. *Mirrors in the Brain: How Our Minds Share Actions and Emotions*. Trans. Frances Anderson. Oxford: Oxford UP, 2008. Print.

Rizzolatti, Giacomo, and Lisa Vozza. *Nella mente degli altri: Neuroni specchio e comportamento sociale*. Bologna: Zanichelli Editore, 2008. Print.

Roth, Cecil. *The Spanish Inquisition*. New York: Norton, 1964. Print.

Schelling, Felix Emmanuel. *English Literature during the Lifetime of Shakespeare*. New York: Henry Holt, 1910. *Archive.org*. Web 1 Nov. 2016.

Smith, David Norman. "Profit Maxims: Capitalism and the Common Sense of Time and Money." *Globalization, Critique and Social Theory: Diagnoses and Challenges*. Ed. Harry F. Dahms. Bingley: Emerald, 2015. 29-74.

Tutino, Stefania. *Shadows of Doubt: Language and Truth in Post-Reformation Catholic Culture*. Oxford: Oxford UP, 2014. Print.

Versluis, Arthur. *The New Inquisitions: Heretic-Hunting and the Intellectual Origins of Modern Totalitarianism*. Oxford: Oxford UP, 2006. Print.

Vidal Manzanares, César. *Grandes Procesos de la Inquisición: Seis Relatos Prohibidos*. Barcelona: Planeta, 2005. Print.

Ward, John. "Of the Equuleus or Wooden Horse of the Ancients." *The Philosophical Transaction of the Royal Society of London, from their Commencement in 1665, to the Year 1800. Vol. 7. 1724-1734*. London: C. and R. Baldwin, 1809. 381-83. *Google Play*. Web. 1 Nov. 2016.

III. Author and Protagonist: Inside the Mind of a Genius

The Unbearable Simulacrum of Being: Staging Ontology in Calderón de la Barca's *Great Stage of the World* and Charlie Kaufman's *Synecdoche, New York*

BRUCE R. BURNINGHAM
Illinois State University

IN ONE OF WILLIAM SHAKESPEARE'S most famous and oft-quoted passages, the character of Jacques from *As You Like It* declares: "All the world's a stage, / And all the men and women merely players" (2.7.139-40). Of course, while this passage represents the most famous articulation of the trope of the world as stage, it is neither the first nor the only expression of this idea. The late-medieval *Dance of Death*, while by no means presuming the kind of metatheater articulated by *As You Like It*, certainly anticipates Shakespeare's sense of human beings as performers of their respective social roles on the stage of life and whose ultimate performance becomes simply dancing with death on (final) command. Likewise, the late-medieval English morality play *Everyman* stages the progress of its title character on a journey towards death in which he is abandoned one by one by his all-too-allegorical "friends" named Beauty, Strength, Knowledge, Good Works, etc. The lack of metatheatricality during the medieval period notwithstanding, metatheatricality certainly becomes a driving force as the centuries progress until we finally arrive at such twentieth-century texts as Luigi Pirandello's 1921 stage play *Six Characters in Search of an Author* and Peter Weir and Andrew Niccol's 1998 film *The Truman Show*.

Of course, perhaps the most literal interpretation of the metaphor of the world as stage belongs to Pedro Calderón de la Barca's best-known *autosacramental*, his seventeenth-century *Great Stage of the World* (*El gran teatro del mundo*). This cosmic *auto* opens with a divine character named "El Autor" ["Director" in the English translation] who calls the world into existence and announces his intention of using this world as a great stage on which to test the mettle of his mortal actors. Consequently, as "Autor" (in both Spanish senses of the word; that is, as both "author" and "theatrical impresario"), he distributes a number of archetypal roles among his actors—the Rich Man, the Poor Man, the King, the Peasant, Discretion, Beauty, etc.—and then sends them off to perform their parts. More importantly, he tells them that, if they play their parts well, he will reward them with a place at his Holy Table at the end of the performance. Throughout this play-within-a-play, then, this "Autor" places himself in a prominent position just outside this great stage of the world in order to watch his actors' performance, at the very end of which, after all the actors have played their parts and have been summoned to exit the stage, the *auto* culminates with a scene in which the "good" actors are rewarded with the Eucharist.

How did we get from *Everyman* to *As You Like It*, from *The Dance of Death* to *The Great Stage of the World*? William Egginton, in his book *How the World Became a Stage* offers an explanation. Discussing Saint Genesius, the patron saint of actors, Egginton notes that Genesius is said to have converted to Christianity while playing the role of a Christian martyr before the Roman emperor Diocletian in the late third century CE, and because of this spontaneous conversion actually became a Christian martyr himself. Comparing this legend to its representation in a play by Lope de Vega, Egginton remarks:

> The medieval performance of Genesius's death *could not* have been staged in the metatheatrical style of [Lope], because that style is the essence of a completely different cultural practice than that of medieval spectacle—namely, theater. Theater, in turn, is itself the central cultural practice of a different world from that of the Middle Ages, a world in which the most fundamental of phenomena, the very experience of the space one inhabits, had radically changed. For lack of a better word, we have chronocentrically called this world modern. With this book I am hoping that we will change that, and simply call it *theatrical*. (2; emphasis in original)

For Egginton, metatheatricality is modernity, and modernity is simply theatricality itself—an idea intended to replace theories of subjectivity. "Theatricality," he says, "does much of the work that subjectivity purports to do without suffering from its theoretical incoherence or lack of specificity" (124).

Which brings us to Charlie Kaufman's *Synecdoche, New York*, perhaps the most ambitious staging of "theatricality" since Calderón. Released in 2008, *Synecdoche, New York* represents Kaufman's directorial debut after writing the screenplays for a series of critical acclaimed postmodern films such as *Being John Malkovich*, *Eternal Sunshine of the Spotless Mind*, and *Adaptation*. As with these earlier films, *Synecdoche, New York* explores the interrelated questions of existence, subjectivity, memory, creativity, and death; what Colm O'Shea calls the "Theater of the Self." Indeed, Frank P. Tomasulo perceptively connects *Adaptation* to *As You Like It* by titling a major segment of his essay "All the world's a (sound)stage" (166), while David LaRocca argues that Kaufman's entire body of work is dedicated to exploring our "inner alterity," to tracing the ways in which "we are others to ourselves—separated, divided, alienated" (8). In this last regard, David L. Smith characterizes *Synecdoche, New York* itself as nothing less than "an essay on the simultaneous futility and inevitability of our attempts to become ourselves, to live before we die, to transcend our own shortcomings" (242-43).[1]

The film narrates (more or less) the life story of a theater director named Caden Cotard (played by Philip Seymour Hoffman). The film is divided—like Calderón's *Great Stage of the World*—into two large segments, one substantially longer than the other. In the first segment, which lasts approximately 40 minutes, we meet Caden and his family, which includes his wife Adele Lack (played by Catherine Keener) and his four-year-old daughter Olive (played by Sadie Goldstein). Caden is in the process of directing Arthur Miller's *Death of a Salesman* at a local Schenectady playhouse. Meanwhile, Adele, a painter who creates portraits so tiny that they require jewelers magnifying lenses to be viewed, is finishing up work on a collection of paintings that are scheduled to be exhibited in Berlin. Shortly after the opening of his play, Adele disinvites Caden to accompany her to Germany, preferring instead to take her friend Maria (played by Jennifer Jason Leigh), as well as Olive. Caden will spend the rest of the film desperately trying to become reunited with Adele and Olive as weeks turn into years and years turn into decades. The second segment of the film, which lasts approximately one hour and twenty minutes, follows Caden (who has won a so-called MacArthur "genius grant") as he creates a truly monumental piece of theater in an abandoned warehouse in New York City. Caden describes his concept for this evolving piece of theater to his cast at the start of their very first rehearsal:

---

[1] On the representation of ontology in Kaufman's films, see D'Aquino; Deming; Falzon; Hagberg; Landy; Uyl; Von der Ruhr.

We'll start by talking honestly, and out of that a piece of theater will evolve. I'll begin. I've been thinking a lot about dying lately. ... Regardless of how this particular thing works itself out, I *will* be dying. And so will you. And so will everyone here. [Pause.] And that ... that's what I want to explore. We're all hurtling towards death. Yet, here we are for the moment, alive. Each of us know we're gonna die, but each of us secretly believing we won't. (00:41:30+)

From this stated point of departure, Caden and his ever-growing company of actors spend the rest of their lives (and the rest of Kaufman's film) rehearsing and performing this ontology, with Caden wandering about the increasingly massive set, critiquing everything he sees. At one point, he stops an actor on the metatheatrical sidewalk and tells him not to walk a certain way because real "people don't walk like that" (01:28:21+).

If Caden's complete directorial control is reminiscent of that of Calderón's "Autor" in *The Great Stage of the World*, such similarities are perhaps inevitable given the subject matter.[2] Nevertheless, *Synecdoche, New York* also contains a number of subtle clues that suggest that Kaufman may have been deliberately thinking of Calderón. About an hour into the film, the character of Claire Keen (played by Michelle Williams)—who Caden had originally cast as Linda Loman in his production of *Death of a Salesman*, who Caden eventually married after Adele left him, and who Caden has now cast to "play" herself in his own Great Stage of the World—mentions that she once played Bernarda Alba in a production of Lorca's well-known play (01:08:00+). Likewise, visually invoking Jorge Luis Borges's essay "Magias parciales del *Quijote*" ["Partial Enchantments of the *Quixote*"], in which Borges describes a "perfect" map of England that includes every detail no matter how miniscule, which then implies that this perfect map would also have to include a perfect map of England that included a perfect map of England that included a perfect

---

2   While not as blatantly allegorical as in such precursor texts as *Everyman*, *The Dance of Death*, and *The Great Stage of the World*, the character names in *Synecdoche, New York* are often just as meaningful. Doreen Alexander Child notes that the surname of "Dr. Gravis" refers to a word that means "actively poisonous or intensely noxious," while the surname of Michele Keen "which is in direct opposition to his wife's name Lack, suggests exactly what Caden needs in his life: someone who is warm, alert, impassioned, and devoted" (137). Edward Lawrenson, for his part, indicates that "If Adele Lack is defined by her absence, it's worth noting that Caden Cotard's surname refers to a medical condition [Cotard's syndrome] whose sufferers have a high awareness of their impending mortality" (29).

map of England and so on and so on unto infinity (55; 46), Kaufman creates a momentary sight gag in which a neighborhood map of the warehouse district includes a flap underneath which there is a smaller version of this neighborhood map, that also includes a little flap underneath where there is an even smaller version of this neighborhood map, etc.[3] Moreover, during one particular funeral scene an actor uncannily resembling Pedro Almodóvar appears as one of the extras on the set (and if it is not actually Almodóvar—which may very well be the case—this extra still evokes Almodóvar's recognizable silhouette). All of which is to say, *Synecdoche, New York* contains a number of subtle nods toward the Hispanic tradition, thus tying this film to Calderón's own metatheatrical exploration of human existence whether Kaufman intended such an intertextuality or not. And within this intertextuality, Caden Clotard clearly emerges as a godlike Calderonian "Autor" hovering over and controlling the individual lives of his metatheatrical actors.

Having said this, however, *Synecdoche, New York* differentiates itself substantially from *The Great Stage of the World* in two particular ways. First, while Caden certainly recognizes his godlike authority over the piece of theater that is emerging inside his rented warehouse, he is not—in stark contrast to Calderón's all-powerful and confident divine Director—without his own existential self-doubts. At one point, Caden says to his cast:

> I won't settle for anything less than the brutal truth. Brutal. Brutal. Each day I'll hand you a scrap of paper; it'll tell you what happened to you that day: you found a lump in your breast, you looked at your wife and saw a stranger, etc. ... I'm not excusing myself from this either. I will have someone play me, to delve into the murky, cowardly depths of my lonely, fucked up being. And he'll get notes too, and those notes will correspond to the notes that I truly receive, everyday, from my God. (01:02:10+)

True to his word, Caden hires an actor named Sammy Barnathan (played by Tom Noonan) to "play" him within the world of this monumental theater piece. But, like the infinite regress of Borges's maps, casting a second Caden soon creates a third Caden because it becomes apparent that someone needs to be cast to play "Sammy" (who then, of course, is assigned to play a new level of "Caden").[4]

---

3   On other connections between Borges and Kaufman, see DasGupta 444; Deming 193; Hyde.

4   In his study of *Adaptation*, Kirk Boyle points out that in coming at the notion of "totality" from a different direction Kaufman not only includes the evolution

Second, in contrast to *The Great Stage of the World*—which, as previously noted, conceives of two distinct spaces, one celestial and one terrestrial—*Synecdoche, New York* does not posit (at least not ultimately; at least not so it thinks) a transcendent space beyond Kaufman's Great Stage of the World. When death finally comes to Caden at the end of the film, there is no cosmic Director on hand to reward him for his performance. Instead, Kaufman offers us a slow fade to white and an abrupt suspension of his soundtrack. In some ways, *Synecdoche, New York* ends much like the final episode of HBO's gangster series *The Sopranos* (whose abrupt blackout has been interpreted by some to suggest that Tony Soprano is simply wacked while sitting in a restaurant booth.) For the remainder of this essay I'd like to examine Caden's death scene a little more closely, but before doing so, a few comments on its complex montage are in order.

Roughly twenty minutes before the end of the film, Caden (as he has done so many times before) claims to have finally figured out the play he is directing, and he comes to this epiphany while attending the funeral of Sammy (who has committed suicide): "I know how to do it now. There are nearly thirteen million people in the world. ... And none of those people is an extra. They're all leads in their own stories. They have to be given their due" (01:40:00+). Almost immediately thereafter, within the infinite regress of Cadens that the film implies, a new actor playing Caden repeats this line in a slightly different iteration. Viewers with a keen ear for the American theater will recognize in this doubly repeated phrase echoes from a central speech in *Death of a Salesman* in which Linda tells her son: "[Willy Loman is] a human being, and a terrible thing is happening to him. So attention must be paid. He's not to be allowed to fall into his grave like an old dog. Attention, attention must be finally paid to such a person" (939).[5]

Perhaps in order to deliberately comment on this well-known line from *Death of a Salesman*, Kaufman restages this sequence one final time after the character of Millicent (played by Dianne Wiest) offers to take over the sec-

---

of all life on planet earth as part of the film's narrative, but also pointedly shows the birth of the metafictional "Charlie Kaufman," screenwriter of the metafictional film named *Adaptation* (9). In this last regard, *Synecdoche, New York*'s ever-multiplying Cadens represent both a repeat performance and a variation on a theme (even if *Adaptation*'s Charlie is the product of billions of years of evolution, while *Synecdoche, New York*'s multiple Cadens always seem to simply spring into existence *in medias res*).

5   On the connection between *Death of a Salesman* and *Synecdoche, New York*, see also Davers.

ond-tier Caden role. In this latest iteration of the sequence, a new actor now playing "Sammy" (playing the third-tier Caden) says, "None of those people are extras. They're all leads in their own stories;" at which point the Millicent/Caden interrupts the rehearsal and says, "This ... this is ... this is tedious. This is nothing." She then proceeds to walk into the meta-scene currently underway in order to give some new direction to the meta-actors. This new directorial intervention inspires what becomes, perhaps, the film's most important set piece in which the "attention must be paid" philosophy of *Death of a Salesman* is interrogated in a long, soaring "prayer" (complete with organ music) delivered by the meta-Preacher:

> [E]ven though the world goes on for eons and eons, you are only here for a fraction of a fraction of a second. Most of your time is spent being dead or not yet born. But while alive, you wait ... in vain ... wasting years ... for a phone call or a letter or a look from someone or something to make it all right. And it never comes ... or it seems to, but it doesn't really. So you spend your time in vague regret, or vaguer hope that something good will come along, something to make you feel connected, something to make you feel whole, something to make you feel loved. (01:46:20+)

But this brings us back to Caden's death scene. Having assumed the role of Caden, Millicent essentially takes over the entire production of Caden's Great Stage of the World, with the aging, sickly Caden himself slowly fading away. Millicent/Caden completely disappears from our view and becomes only a voiceover that we hear as she speaks directly to Caden from within an earpiece that he is asked to wear as he wanders around an increasing desolate warehouse stage:

> What was once before you—an exciting, mysterious future—is now behind you. Lived, understood, disappointing. You realize you are not special. You have struggled into existence and are now slipping silently out of it. This is everyone's experience. Every. Single. One. The specifics hardly matter. Everyone is everyone. So you are Adele, Hazel, Claire, Olive. You are Ellen. All her meager sadnesses are yours. All her loneliness. The gray, straw-like hair. Her red, raw hands: it's yours. It is time for you to understand this. [CADEN stops to contemplate his dead, theatrical "other."] Walk. As the people who adore you stop adoring you. As they die. As they move on. As you shed them. As you shed your beauty, your youth. As the world forgets you. As you recognize your transience. As

you begin to lose your characteristics one by one. As you learn there is no one watching and there never was. You think only about driving, not coming from any place, not arriving any place. Just driving, counting off time. Now you are here; it's 7:43. Now you are here; it's 7:44. Now you are ... gone. (01:55:30+)

The problem with this ending is twofold. First, it turns out to not really be the ending. Had Caden died at this precise moment—had the film abruptly gone to black here like the final episode of *The Sopranos*—Kaufman's posited lack of transcendence might have been confirmed. However, the film contains one final scene in which Caden encounters one of the few remaining actors still alive on the set. Caden sits down next to this unnamed actor on an abandoned couch and shares a few final moments with her, placing his head on her shoulder for comfort, before finally being directed by the Millicent voiceover to "die." And as part of this shared moment, Caden admits to the unnamed actor that his project has been a failure: "I feel like I've disappointed you terribly;" to which she replies, "Oh no. I am so proud of you" (00:59:10+). Such a statement, of course, undermines the entire ethos of the previous two long speeches quoted above because it unwittingly demonstrates that there has, indeed, been someone watching Caden's life.[6] Moreover, this person is now on hand to finally provide the affirmation, the connectedness, the wholeness, the love, and indeed the redemption that the Preacher has said will never come. The second problem with this final scene is that it reintegrates into Kaufman's film a transcendence that he has sought to banish. The voiceover Millicent has become Calderón's omniscient and omnipresent "Autor" who stands somewhere outside the mise-en-scene looking in. Additionally, the slow fade to white that Kaufman intends as a representation of Caden's fading mortality is itself transcendent. And thus, at the very end of the film, while *Synecdoche, New York* does not explicitly show us an afterlife, it nevertheless unintentionally suggests one by having Caden essentially go "into the light."

Now, in fairness to Kaufman, much of this is predetermined by the conventions of Hollywood cinema (and one could certainly riff at length here on Kaufman himself as a divine "Autor" whose contract with Sony Pictures Corporation severely constrains the free will of Caden and company). Be

---

6   For instance, when Sammy first comes to audition for the role of "Caden," he tells Caden that he has been watching him for twenty years—a claim borne out by the fact that we catch glimpses of Sammy watching Caden from the very beginning of the film.

that as it may, the line "there is no one watching and there never was" is significant, especially within the context of Egginton's "theatricality," which, he says, "is constitutive of a particular historical form of interpersonal relations and of self-consciousness itself. ... [A]lmost always we are acting, playing our lives out before an audience we cannot see" (Egginton 18-19). For Egginton, the modern is the theatrical. But what such a concept implies, then, is that the "post-modern" should therefore be "post-theatrical." And so far, I don't think that we have quite figured out what "post-theatricality" might entail. In his essay "Simulacra and Simulations" Jean Baudrillard suggests that we have entered a phase of "hyperreality": "Simulation is no longer that of a territory, a referential being or a substance. It is the generation by models of a real without origin or reality" (169). At one point, Caden even suggests that the name for his Great Stage theater piece is *Simulacra*. But, if he (and/or Kaufman above him) is indeed glossing Baudrillard, what this implies is that the theatrical space inside the warehouse should be entirely self-contained, with no connection to the larger New York and no anticipated external audience for the performance. But there clearly is a connection between one New York and the other, between the larger and smaller stages; which is perhaps why Caden eventually abandons the title *Simulacra* (and why Kaufman himself adopts *Synecdoche*).

But therein lies the even larger problem. Any representation must necessarily involve a synecdoche: the part standing in for a larger whole. Thus, when Calderón stages his *Great Stage of the World*, he must necessarily posit an internal stage space of the representation (the performance space of the Rich Man, the Poor Man, etc.) and an external space (the audience space of his divine Director) from which to view the representation. But then, there must also necessarily exist a third level of external space—the space of Calderón's own audiences—from which to view the entire *autosacramental*, and a fourth-level of external space—Calderón's posited God's-eye vantage point of the world—from which to view Calderón, his actors, and his audiences. Such a chain of infinite regress, of course, necessarily posits a heretical fifth-level of space sitting above God himself, and sixth-level, and seventh-level, etc. *Synecdoche, New York* plays with this idea in the other direction by showing us up to three Cadens at a time, and therefore implies (but refrains from trying to show us) the full chain of infinite regress in which the Cadens (as characters) would multiply forever in one direction, while the Cadens (as directors, including Kaufman himself) would forever multiply in the other direction.

Of course, as several critics—including Doreen Alexander Child—have commented, such a chain of infinite regress going in both directions at once is ultimately impossible to represent (140). Representation is, therefore, always synecdoche; always partial, never complete, never whole. Such a recognition—which Barbara Simerka and Christopher Weimer have commented on (98)—is something Kaufman himself has acknowledged (Child 140, 143). Such a recognition also informs Richard Deming's summation of *Synecdoche, New York*: "To represent the world is to be flung outside it, to live apart in the hope of making its fugitive, impossible meanings into something" (206). But, ultimately, such a recognition is precisely why Kaufman cannot stage Caden's death without "staging" Caden's death, without shifting Millicent from one level of representation to the next level higher up. Without this rhetorical move, along with the inevitable recognition that we occupy a viewing space just above Millicent, there can be no *Synecdoche, New York*, no film to watch. In sum, then, Kaufman cannot stage ontology without *staging* ontology. Jacques Derrida has famously said that "*there is nothing outside of the text* [there is no outside-text; *il n'y a pas de hors-texte*]" (158; original emphasis and brackets). He is right, of course, if what he means is that there is no way for any of us to get outside our own level of representation. Nevertheless, Kaufman's cinema does call into question the "wholeness" suggested by Derrida's famous dictum; for what *Synecdoche, New York* and *The Great Stage of the World* (and *The Truman Show* and *Stranger Than Fiction* and *The Purple Rose of Cairo*) demonstrate is that there is *always* someone else watching. As Peter Brook reminds us, "watching" is the essence of theater.[7] And thus, if there is some kind of "post-theatrical" world out there, a world without synecdoche, a world without an endless chain of observers, such a world is ultimately unrepresentable.

Works Cited

Adaptation. Dir. Spike Jonze. Screenplay by Charlie Kaufman. Perf. Nicolas Cage, Meryl Streep, and Chris Cooper. Columbia, 2002. Film.
Baudrillard, Jean. *Selected Writings*. Ed. Mark Poster. 2nd ed. Palo Alto: Stanford UP, 2001. Print.

---

7   "I can take any empty space and call it a bare stage. A man walks across this empty space whilst someone else is watching him, and this is all that is needed for an act of theatre to be engaged" (9).

Being John Malkovich. Dir. Spike Jonze. Screenplay by Charlie Kaufman. Perf. John Cusack, Cameron Diaz, Catherine Keener, and John Malkovich. Universal, 1999. Film.

Borges, Jorge Luis. "Magias parciales del *Quijote*." *Otras inquisiciones*. Madrid: Alianza, 1989. 52-55. Print.

———. "Partial Enchantments of the *Quixote*." Trans. Ruth L. C. Simms. *Other Inquisitions, 1937-1952*. Ed. James E. Irby. Austin: U of Texas P, 1964. 43-46. Print.

Boyle, Kirk. "Reading the Dialectical Ontology of *The Life Aquatic with Steve Zissou* Against the Ontological Monism of *Adaptation*." *Film-Philosophy* 11.1 (2007): 1-32. Print.

Brook, Peter. *The Empty Space*. New York: Atheneum, 1984. Print.

Calderón de la Barca, Pedro. *El gran teatro del mundo/El gran mercado del mundo*. Ed. Eugenio Frutos Cortés. Madrid: Cátedra, 1997. Print.

———. *The Great Stage of the World: An Allegorical Auto Sacramental*. Trans. George W. Brandt. Manchester: Manchester UP, 1976. Print.

Child, Doreen Alexander. *Charlie Kaufman: Confessions of an Original Mind*. Santa Barbara: Praeger, 2010. Print.

D'Aquino, Antonella. "The Self, the Ideal, and the Real: The Artistic Choice of Three Creative Minds: Fellini, Allen, and Kaufman." *Italica* 84.2-3 (2007): 556-77. Print.

DasGupta, Sayantani. "*Being John Doe Malkovich*: Truth, Imagination, and Story in Medicine." *Literature and Medicine* 25.2 (2006): 439-62. Print.

Davers, Rebecca. "'I Know How to Do the Play Now:' A Part of Willy Loman in *Synecdoche, New York*." *Arthur Miller Journal* 6.2 (2011): 25-45. Print.

Deming, Richard. "Living a Part: *Synecdoche, New York*, Metaphor, and the Problem of Skepticism." *The Philosophy of Charlie Kaufman*. Ed. David LaRocca. Lexington: UP of Kentucky, 2011. 193-207. Print.

Derrida, Jacques. *Of Grammatology*. Trans. Gayatri Chakravorty Spivak. Baltimore: Johns Hopkins UP, 1974. Print.

Egginton, William. *How the World Became a Stage: Presence, Theatricality, and the Question of Modernity*. Albany: SUNY P, 2003. Print.

Eternal Sunshine of the Spotless Mind. Dir. Michel Gondry. Screenplay by Charlie Kaufman. Perf. Jim Carrey, Kate Winslet, and Kristen Dunst. Focus Features, 2004. Film.

Everyman. In *Twenty-Three Plays: An Introductory Anthology*. Ed. Otto Reinert and Peter Arnott. New York: Little Brown, 1978. 87-108. Print.

Falzon, Christopher. "On *Being John Malkovich* and Not Being Yourself." *The Philosophy of Charlie Kaufman*. Ed. David LaRocca. Lexington: UP of Kentucky, 2011. 46-65. Print.

Hagberg, Garry L. "The Instructive Impossibility of Being John Malkovich." *The Philosophy of Charlie Kaufman*. Ed. David LaRocca. Lexington: UP of Kentucky, 2011. 169-89. Print.

Hyde, Christopher. "The Inconceivable Universe: The Borgesian Neobaroque in Charlie Kaufman's *Being John Malkovich*." *Barroco* 3.3 (2009): n. pag. Web. 13 June 2016.

Landy, Joshua. "Still Life in a Narrative Age: Charlie Kaufman's *Adaptation*." *Critical Inquiry* 37.3 (2011): 497-514. Print.

LaRocca, David. Introduction. *The Philosophy of Charlie Kaufman*. Ed. David LaRocca. Lexington: UP of Kentucky, 2011. 1-20. Print.

Lawrenson, Edward. "Gone in 60 Years." *Sight and Sound* 19.6 (2009): 26-29. Print.

"Made in America." *The Sopranos*. HBO. 10 June 2007. Television.

Miller, Arthur. *Death of a Salesman*. In *Twenty-Three Plays: An Introductory Anthology*. Ed. Otto Reinert and Peter Arnott. New York: Little Brown, 1978. 916-80. Print.

O'Shea, Colm. "Out of His Head: Metaphysical Escape Attempts in the Screenplays of Charlie Kaufman." *Bright Lights Film Journal* 63 (31 Jan. 2009): n. pag. Web. 13 June 2016.

Pirandello, Luigi. *Six Characters in Search of an Author*. Trans. Edward Storer. *Twenty-Three Plays: An Introductory Anthology*. Ed. Otto Reinert and Peter Arnott. New York: Little Brown, 1978. 738-73. Print.

The Purple Rose of Cairo. Dir. Woody Allen. Screenplay by Woody Allen. Perf. Mia Farrow and Jeff Daniels. Orion, 1985. Film.

Shakespeare, William. *As You Like It*. In *The Riverside Shakespeare*. Ed. G. Blakemore Evans. Boston: Houghton Mifflin, 1974. 369-402. Print.

Simerka, Barbara, and Christopher B. Weimer. "Duplicitous Diegesis: *Don Quijote* and Charlie Kaufman's *Adaptation*." *Hispania* 88.1 (2005): 91-100. Print.

Smith, David L. "Synecdoche, in Part." *The Philosophy of Charlie Kaufman*. Ed. David LaRocca. Lexington: UP of Kentucky, 2011. 239-53. Print.

Stranger Than Fiction. Dir. Marc Forster. Screenplay by Zach Helm. Perf. Will Farrell, Dustin Hoffman, and Emma Thompson. Columbia, 2006. Film.

Synecdoche, New York. Dir. Charlie Kaufman. Screenplay by Charlie Kaufman. Perf. Philip Seymour Hoffman, Samantha Morton, Michelle

Williams, Catherine Keener, Emily Watson, Dianne Wiest, Jennifer Jason Leigh, Hope Davis, and Tom Noonan. Sony, 2008. Film.

Tomasulo, Frank P. "*Adaptation* as Adaptation: From Susan Orlean's *The Orchid Thief* to Charlie (and 'Donald') Kaufman's Screenplay to Spike Jonze's Film." *Authorship in Film Adaptation*. Ed. Jack Boozer. Austin: U of Texas P, 2008. 161-78. Print.

The Truman Show. Dir. Peter Weir. Screenplay by Andrew Niccol. Perf. Jim Carey. Paramount, 1998. Film.

Uyl, Douglas J. Den. "Me and You: Identity, Love, and Friendship in the Films of Charlie Kaufman." *The Philosophy of Charlie Kaufman*. Ed. David LaRocca. Lexington: UP of Kentucky, 2011. 111-31. Print.

Von der Ruhr, Mario. "The Divided Self: Kaufman, Kafka, Wittgenstein, and *Human Nature*." *The Philosophy of Charlie Kaufman*. Ed. David LaRocca. Lexington: UP of Kentucky, 2011. 66-88. Print.

Banished from Parnassus:
Cervantes in the Shadow of Success

Frederick A. de Armas
University of Chicago

This essay is about how Miguel de Cervantes positions himself as author of *Don Quixote*. It is about his need to defend his stance as outsider; and about why and how he must move away from the realms of courtly literature and aristocratic concerns. I will argue that being in the shadow of those considered to be the great writers of his time, he uses a specific strategy to overcome his perceived lack, thus becoming a critic of his own work, and even suggesting how it should be read. In order to understand this strategy we will analyze in detail the Prologue to the 1605 novel. After all, as Howard Mancing reminds us, prologues are where "the reader expects to find generic and thematic orientation for the text that follows." Indeed, he goes on to argue that "of all Spanish Prologue writers, Miguel de Cervantes was the undisputed master of the genre" (*The Cervantes* 2.587).

Numerous critics and contemporary thinkers have accepted the intentionality expressed in the Prologue to the 1605 *Don Quixote*.[1] Towards the end, a friend reassures the fictive author: "... llevad la mira puesta a derribar

---

1 Howard Mancing asserts: "No one, to my knowledge, doubts that the *yo* of the prologue who relates himself to the character and text by claiming to be not the "padre" ("father," that is, the original author) but the "padrastro" ("stepfather," that is, the editor), and who tells the story of being visited by a friend while pondering the problem of writing a prologue for his book is anyone other than the person referred to on the title page where it says "compuesto por ... Miguel de Cervantes Saavedra" (*The Chivalric* 191-92). To this important statement, I would add that we should look at how an author fashions himself and what is the role of this very curious friend that comes to visit him.

la máquina mal fundada de estos caballerescos libros, aborrecidos de tantos y alabados de muchos más" ["carry your aim steady to overthrow the ill-compiled machine of books of chivalry, abhorred by many, but applauded by more"] (58, 20).[2] While the first readers of the novel often considered it as a funny book, its pages used to fashion carnival figures, and its worth, mere entertainment;[3] eighteenth-century critics came to the conclusion that the work was worth elevating and admiring since it stamped out the monstrous tomes of the chivalric. England was the first country where *Don Quixote* was canonized. A luxury edition in four volumes was conceived by Lord John Carteret, Earl of Granville.[4] He would publish it as a present to Queen Caroline—the reason: She had a room or museum, often described as a cave, dedicated to Merlin the magician in Richmond Park.[5] And since the famed Arthurian magus makes an appearance in *Don Quixote*, it was thought a worthy addition to her room. Carteret commissioned John Vanderbank to do an illustration for the frontispiece of this edition, which appeared in 1738.[6] Here, Cervantes himself has been transformed into a classical hero or demigod.[7] I

---

2   All citations are from Luis Andrés Murillo's edition of *Don Quijote*. In this essay, all English translations of Cervantes's novel are by Charles Jarvis's version in the Oxford World's Classics.

3   In spite of the immense popularity of the book from its inception—six editions the year it was published; translated into English and French during Cervantes's lifetime (Thomas Shelton 1612, Cesar Oudin 1614), then in 1622 into Italian and 1648 into German—it was never considered as a serious book, and its images were replicated in carnival parades.

4   It is curious that Lord Carteret turned to Cervantes since he was one of the main figures in the Opposition at the time and was advocating war with Spain. He stood against Robert Walpole who was close to the Queen. Indeed, he was part of the group that ridiculed the Queen's "cave" where her "wizard" Walpole must abide. At the same time, the Opposition and Carteret were in favor of reviving England's mythical past (Colton 12-16).

5   Amanda S. Meixell explains: "the architectural structure was not really a cave at all but rather a thatched Gothic cottage that consisted of a circular room with openings on three sides that contained collections of English books" (62).

6   Vanderbank (1694-1739) also included a portrait of Cervantes in the Carteret volume. He was known not just for his book illustrations, but also as a portrait painter. He painted a portrait of Sir Isaac Newton and also included his portrait as frontispiece in his *Principia* (1729). For Vanderbank's work, see Cervantes, *Vida y hechos*.

7   Some believe he is Hercules Musagetes. A temple of Hercules and the Muses was erected in the Circus Flaminius in Rome after his capture of Ambracia in 189 BC. This round temple used to exhibit Hercules with a lyre and the Muses. Rachel Schmidt believes that the Cervantes in the illustration is above all a Hercu-

would argue that he appears as both Hercules and Apollo, holding a club, the favored weapon of the former, and the lyre, the traditional instrument of the latter. As this god-like Cervantes goes to do battle, nine women stand by him with both fear and hope. They are the Muses who have been displaced from their home by monsters. To battle them, Cervantes is granted a new weapon by a Satyr (satire)—a mask of Don Quixote and thus he sets out to destroy the monstrous books of chivalry that have taken over Mount Parnassus. To further increase its authority and canonicity, the preface calls it a comic epic.

It is not my purpose here to discuss how this classicizing interpretation spread to Spain, leading to the publication of an annotated edition by the Real Academia. In 1780, the novel was then canonized as an imitation of the classics—Virgil, Homer; being an epic in a lighter tone. Nor is it my purpose here to discuss how this vision was replaced with what has been called a Romantic Approach to the novel, elevating it and its main characters as reflections of the soul of Spain and transforming satire into symbol.[8] I would rather return to the *Prólogo* and place it side by side with Vanderbank's illustration in order to question the intentionality trumpeted not so much by the author, but by the author's friend and revived in the *frontis*.[9]

The Prologue contains an evocation of the perfect countryside, which brings the muses from Parnassus: "El sosiego, el lugar apacible, la amenidad de los campos, la serenidad de los cielos, el murmurar de las fuentes, la quietud del espíritu son grande parte para que las musas más estériles se muestren fecundas y ofrezcan partos al mundo que le colmen de maravilla y de contento" ["Whereas repose of body, a desirable situation, unclouded skies, and above all, a mind at ease, can make the most barren Muses fruitful and produce such

---

les Musagetes (49). After all, there was a Gallic Hercules, represented as extremely old and said to signify eloquence better than Mercury. Some give him chains in his tongue and ears to show that his eloquence was more powerful than the strength of his body. Although Hercules is usually represented with a club, he is at times shown with the lyre with which he killed Linus, a friend of Orpheus, who criticized Hercules's playing (Keilen 182).

8   This romantic approach, according to Anthony Close includes: "(a) the idealization of the hero and the denial of the novel's satiric purpose; (b) the belief that the novel is symbolical and that through this symbolism it expresses ideas about the human spirit's relation to reality and about the nature of Spain's history; (c) the interpretation of its symbolism, and more generally, of its whole spirit and style, in a way which reflects the ideology, aesthetics and sensibility of the modern era" (1).

9   Meixell has shown that a second illustration "reveals the sense that the *Quijote* does not destroy romance, but rather celebrates chivalric fiction, achieving its status as a classic at least in part through its association with the Arthurian tradition" (78).

offsprings to the world, as fill it with wonder and content"] (50; 15). This inspiration will allow him to compose such works as to deserve a place in Parnassus, the home of the Muses and a site that was very much in vogue. Images of the great bards abiding on this exalted mountain were by now a common staple of poets, painters and academicians, going back to Raphael's famous painting at the Vatican.[10] At first glance, it seems to make sense that Vanderbank draws on this image as well as the image of a writer who will satirize chivalry so as to return to a more classical manner that will allow for his canonization.

However, the authorial voice tells us that the book as child was born "en una cárcel, donde toda incomodidad tiene su asiento y donde todo triste ruido hace su habitación" ["in a prison where every inconvenience keeps its residence, and every dismal sound has its habitation"] (50; 15).[11] Thus his work will become not a beautiful creature of the mind but "avellanado, antojadizo y lleno de pensamientos varios" ["meagre, adust, and whimsical, full of various wild imaginations"] (50; 15). The question then arises. Is the novel a satire against the fanciful romances of chivalry, a work that is meant to save Parnassus from such monstrous beings, or is it itself a fanciful monster, albeit a new kind of creature?

The Prologue, I would argue, constructs an author who is far from Apollo and his Muses, who takes shelter in the prison in which his book was born. If this were the only time that Cervantes turns away from Parnassus, perhaps we could argue for another interpretation. But such is not the case. In 1614, the year before his death, the Spanish author writes a lengthy poem entitled *Viaje del Parnaso* [Voyage to Parnassus]. Although arriving safely at this august grove, he fails to find a suitable place in which to rest his weary body. He thus begins a complaint to Apollo, listing his curriculum, attempting to impress the god with his literary career. Not particularly interested in his

---

10   Quevedo's *El Parnaso español* (1648) brings together hundreds of his poems under the tutelage of the muses. His *Las tres musas últimas castellanas* (1670) was published long after his death with the three remaining Muses: Euterpe as muse of amorous poetry, Caliope of satiric poetry and Urania of religious verse.

11   It is generally accepted that Cervantes is alluding here to his incarceration in 1597. Jean Canavaggio explains that his imprisonment comes as a result of his job as commissary agent entrusted to collect 2.5 million in back taxes in the Granada region. An unfair judge in Seville, Gaspar Vallejo decides to "incarcerate him on the spot instead of sending him to Madrid" (171). He writes to king Philip II who orders the judge to release him and send him to Madrid to deal with these matters, but apparently Vallejo keeps him in the famous jail of Seville, with some two thousand other inmates, from September all the way to April (176).

plight, the god tells him that since there are no spots left under the trees, if he wishes to stay, he should just fold his cape and sit on it. However, Cervantes (as Apollo may be well aware) has no such cape and must remain standing and thus not a part of the society of poets (4.95-96). This is not the only cape incident in Cervantes's works. Turning to a second such moment one critic asserts: "It is certainly true that the author of the original *Don Quixote* failed in all his attempts to participate in aristocratic practices, even in their most marginalized forms. In other words, Cervantes possessed no cape, that synecdochic sign of noble status" (Mariscal 154).

Returning to the poem, we could even imagine Apollo as a royal figure, as Philip III of Spain, as the Count of Lemos, Viceroy of Naples, or perhaps as one of the great lords of the realm known for their patronage.[12] Thus Cervantes could be fashioning himself as one of those not welcomed to the inner circle at Court.[13] He must use his own wits to defend his work, showing it to

---

12   When in 1608 the Count of Lemos was offered the Viceroyalty of Naples, Lupercio Leonardo de Argensola was chosen as the count's secretary. According to Geoffrey Stagg, this poet-secretary "contrived to isolate the Count from those writers who might be considered possible rivals for the Grandee's favor" (24-25) and which included Góngora and Cervantes. Neither was invited to be part of this new and brilliant court. Lemos departed for Naples in 1610.

13   I borrow the term "self-fashioning" while accepting the caveats proposed by Antonio Sánchez-Jiménez:

En primer lugar, la traslación directa de las teorías de Greenblatt resulta arriesgada, pues este estudioso llegó a ellas tras un análisis detallado de la literatura de la Inglaterra isabelina, y no de la producción de la España de los siglos XVI y XVII. Por ejemplo, Greenblatt sostiene que el 'self-fashioning' siempre se lleva a cabo en oposición a algo ... . Lope no necesita explícitamente oponerse a nada para crear una imagen determinada, sino que más bien le basta asociarse a una tradición ya formada. (10)

In the first place, the direct utilization of Greenblatt's theories may be risky since he developed his ideas through a detailed analysis of Elizabethan English literature and not from the literary production from Spain in the sixteenth and seventeenth centuries. For example, Greenblatt asserts that 'self-fashioning' always occurs in opposition to something ... . Lope does not need to oppose anything to create a particular image, but can simply associate himself to an already existing tradition. (my own translation)

I would say the same is true of Cervantes. While he moves away from a prevailing mode of auto-representation, he does not seek to oppose a "threatening Other"

be as good, albeit in a totally different manner. At the same time, the poem is a clear indication of the writer's anxieties. His defense of his work is rather whimsical at times.[14] I would argue, however, that the poem is far from being a failure. It is intended to represent failure and as such it is a success. It reflects Cervantes's own biography, an exercise in countless failures. Having been part of the battle of Lepanto in his youth, his exploits are soon forgotten and the rest of his life is ambulant, peripatetic, in the shadow of others. I think that it is the shadow that marks Cervantes as a writer. And I am not speaking of the pleasant shadow of the trees in Parnassus, but of another darker self that he seeks to embrace. Indeed, at the end of the poem, he finds himself back home, in his own bed—as if the whole voyage never took place, as if it had been a dream, perhaps a somber fantasy. By placing himself outside of Parnassus, outside the realms of the sun-god and in contrast to the famed figures of his time, Cervantes embraces his shadowy presence and marks his work as different, as other.[15]

When Cervantes published the first part of *Don Quixote*, he was already in his 50's and he was still a fairly unknown writer who some may have remembered for his early plays, now overshadowed by Lope de Vega's popularity, or by a pastoral romance that never became that successful. Cervantes quite carefully exploits not being part of the inner circles of literati, of those who thought themselves as members of Parnassus.

The Prologue includes a number of elements that point to this shadowed vision and one that makes Cervantes into a critic not just of his novel but also of the works of his time. Let us begin with a crucial moment, the portrait of the author. The fictive author depicts himself at the moment when he despairs of writing the Prologue and adorning it and his book with the much coveted biblical, poetic and philosophical authorities of antiquity: "Muchas veces tomé la pluma para escribille, y muchas la dejé, por no saber lo que escribiría; y estando una suspenso, con el papel delante, la pluma en la oreja, el codo en el bufete y la mano en la mejilla, pensando lo que diría ..." ["I often

---

(Greenblatt 10). Rather, he finds a new way to represent himself, but one based on a lesser tradition that goes back to Marsilio Ficino's vision.

14   Cervantes claims in the *Voyage to Parnassus* that his *novelas* show "con propiedad un desatino" [a foolish act with propriety]. In other words, he shows a foolish act or a blunder in a proper fashion. While he praises some of his ballads, he calls others "malditos" [damned] (103).

15   Ellen Lokos explains: "Cervantes knew that he could not expect the kind of rewards he was entitled to in the society he was living in ... the poet had renounced the possibility of satisfaction in the earthly realm, or even on Parnassus" (24).

took the pen in hand, and as often laid it down, not knowing what to say: and once upon a time, being in deep suspense, with the paper before me, the pen behind my ear, my elbow on the table, and my cheek in my hand, thinking what I should say ..."] (51-52; 15-16). The text draws upon the traditional pose of the thinker, most often considered as a melancholy figure. We need only remember the pensive image at the very center of Raphael's fresco, *The School of Athens*. He also has his hand on his cheek and has paper in front of him. Raphael's fresco depicts a double image, that of the philosopher Heraclitus and that of Michelangelo, both known for their melancholy. As we know, "from the sixteenth century onwards, there are frequent references to the melancholic disposition of artists in relation to their exceptional talents" (Van den Doel 108).[16] Michelangelo in both his artistic and poetic endeavors depicts himself thusly, while his biographers pick up on his qualities of solitude, whimsy and inspired genius, which derive from his temperament.[17] It is thus not surprising to find that the Cervantes of the Prologue is alone in his musings and has produced "un hijo seco, avellanado, antojadizo y lleno de pensamientos varios" ["a child meagre, adust, and whimsical, full of various

---

16   Javier Portús prefers to take this image of the melancholy artist (and poet) back to the fifteenth century:

A partir del siglo XV se produjo un intenso proceso de ... reivindicación de la aportación específica del individuo en los procesos culturales. Como consecuencia de todo ello, se enriqueció notablemente la casuística relacionada con la caracterología del poeta, el pintor, etc., a los que se asignaban una serie de características relacionadas con sus temperamentos, humores, o con los rasgos de su personalidad. (136)

Starting with the fifteenth century there was an intense process of ... revindication of individual contributions in the cultural processes. As a consequence, the causes related to the character of the poet, the painter, etc., to whom were assigned a series of characteristics related to their temperaments, their humors, or their personality traits. (my own translation)

17   Giorgio Vasari asserts: "Michelangelo took pleasure in solitude, as a man deeply enamoured of his art, which wants a man to be alone and pensive for his own purposes" (472). Francisco de Holanda, in his *Roman Dialogues* (1548) has Michelangelo speak of talented artists who "are unsociable not from pride but because they deem only very few spirits worthy of their art; ... and in order not to debase the elevated imagination that keeps their mind in perpetual ecstasy" (qtd. in Van den Doel 108).

wild imaginations"] (50; 15). His child or book is dry because the melancholy humor shares two qualities, dryness and coldness. This quality and temperament not only echoes those of the author but also those of his main character. From the very start of the novel, we discover that Don Quixote's brain has dried up from too much reading. The knight's emaciated body is also a reflection of his dryness.

Melancholy figures were known to suffer from visions, be they celestial or demonic, providing ecstasy or severe distress. And thus Cervantes shows his child or book as filled with "extravagant fancies," which at times seem closer to the demonic than to the celestial.[18] Invoking Cornelius Agrippa, Robert Burton claims that "melancholy persons are most subject to diabolic temptations and illusions and most apt to entertain them" (175). While the melancholy author writes of his fancies, his child is equally eccentric, a knight-errant that is almost mad. Paradoxically, it is a madness that makes us laugh. Towards the end of the Prologue we encounter one more advice from the elusive friend: "Procurad también que, leyendo vuestra historia, el melancólico se mueva a risa, el risueño la acreciente" ["Endeavor also, that, by reading your history, the melancholy may be provoked to laugh, the gay humour be heightened"] (58; 20). Thus, melancholy madness can trigger laughter. By juxtaposing the melancholy with the jovial, the friend provides yet one more clue as to the author's condition. Jupiter as the most benefic of Ptolemaic planets in ancient and Renaissance astrology was countered by Saturn, the most malefic.

We know from the extensive labors of Klibansky, Panofsky and Saxl that the conflictive nature of melancholy actually derives from Saturn, a planet which was said to rule melancholy, but that was also considered the most malefic of celestial bodies. Indeed, in the Prologue, Cervantes tells us that his book was born in a prison (11), and imprisonment is one of the more often cited consequences of a saturnine influence.

The Renaissance's depiction of the visionary artist, poet and scholar owes many of its iterations to Marsilio Ficino. The Renaissance philosopher and translator of Plato was most concerned with Saturn, a planet that featured prominently in his horoscope. In a letter to Giovanni Cavalcanti he writes: "You command me, my Giovanni, to sing a hymn of recantation to Saturn about whom I have recently complained a great deal .... Saturn seems

---

18   Robert Burton affirms "that the Devil, being a slender and incomprehensible spirit, can easily insinuate and wind himself into human bodies, and cunningly couched in our bowels, vitiate our healths, terrify our souls with fearful dreams" (174).

to have impressed the seal of melancholy on me from the beginning; set, as it is, almost in the midst of my ascendant Aquarius, it is influenced by Mars, also in Aquarius" (*The Letters* 33; Seznec 61). Saturn was not only on the ascendant, the most important place in a horoscope, but was also in Aquarius. Ruth Clydesdale, who has studied the astrological component of Ficino's letters, explains that Aquarius, being one of two of Saturn's houses, "is therefore able to express itself in a particularly powerful way" (123). I would add that it is the nocturnal house of the seventh planet, thus further increasing its shadowy presence. In this letter we find a clue as to Ficino's future path: "I shall, in agreement with Aristotle, say that this nature itself is a unique and divine gift" (34). Thus, to counterbalance this planetary influence Ficino wrote *Three Books on Life*, publishing it in 1489. It was a bestseller, an immensely popular work, with nearly thirty editions published through 1547. The book included many ways to remedy the excesses of melancholy and the baneful influence of Saturn. But it was also meant to reinstate the positive aspects of the seventh planet. As the highest of planets in the Ptolemaic cosmos, Saturn would, of necessity provide the highest gifts to the human being, although such rewards would be balanced with suffering. In *De vita* the philosopher affirms that the child of Saturn is: "an individual set apart from others, divine or brutish, blessed or bowed down with the extreme of misery" (*Three Books* 251). Clydesdale asserts that for Ficino: "the solitary man given to deep thought is ideally placed to contemplate the divine and hence Saturn can elevate his chosen ones 'to the heights above their physical strength and the customs of mortals'" (125).[19] Needless to say, Don Quixote, is most certainly someone lacking the physical strength needed to carry out his chivalric visions. And there are instances in the novel where he is indeed helped by Saturn (Fajardo; De Armas, *Don Quixote* 162-80). Through Ficino, the seventh planet became for some not only a destructive force but a symbol of the new artist or writer who suffered Saturn's melancholy in order to receive its most precious gift, wisdom, which was to be wrenched out of madness, one of the planet's worst effects.

As someone outside the literary centers of his time, Cervantes consciously crafts a new persona for himself. He may be rejected by Apollo in Parnassus; he may not be under the influence of a solar ruler and his court. He need not be part of the great masses of poets that cluster around the Sun. Instead, he is a solitary figure that writes under Saturn. It was said that this planet was the old Sun that had dried up (Bouché-Leclerq 93). His arch-rival,

---

    19   Clydesdale quotes here from the *Three Books of Life* (213).

and the most popular writer of the times, Lope de Vega, often complained of the malefic effects of Saturn in his horoscope, but he always embraced the powers of Venus and Sol (De Armas, "The Saturn"). Cervantes counters by embracing Saturn. He may not be the most acclaimed writer in his own time, and he may not hold favor at court, but as an individual apart, he can write of the "extravagant fancies" of a would-be knight.

The appearance of a mendacious and crafty friend in this aloneness may seem startling. But the Prologue may be inviting us to view it as another one of the author's whimsical fancies. There may be no such friend. Like the *Voyage to Parnassus*, the appearance of this individual in the midst of the writer's musings, can be but a dream, another fanciful moment. It is then that we realize that the Cervantes of the Prologue never declares that his book is an indictment against chivalric romances. It is the mendacious and clever friend who says so. The Cervantes of the Prologue actually ends his prefatory remarks by praising Don Quixote and Sancho. Is there a gentle irony here? -- Of course. Although no intentions are stated, a reading of the book shows that it is an inventive, inspired and whimsical way to write not just about chivalry but also about so many other genres such as pastoral, sentimental, *novelle* and even epic.[20] And even, as Thomas Pavel states, to include subspecies such as farce, situation comedy, comedy of characters and comedy of manners (112). The fact remains that the Cervantes of the Prologue never acknowledges the satirical intent which Vanderbank uses to canonize Cervantes. And the figure of the Prologue certainly never wants to be in the company of Apollo or appear as an antique hero as in the 1738 frontis.

The Prologue, then, sets up the way in which Cervantes wants to be viewed, as a solitary artist, as one who had to endure untold sufferings, including incarceration, so as to reach a new inspired wisdom, one that may be presented in a dry and whimsical manner, but one that has a dark and shadowed power that can eclipse the writers of Parnassus.[21]

---

20 On the clash of genres in the work, see De Armas's *Don Quixote among Saracens* (80).

21 The question remains as to Cervantes as critic of the chivalric. It has been argued that Cervantes, in his *Galatea* declared that he was going to follow a Virgilian career, moving from the low style of pastoral to the high style of epic. His last work, the *Persiles*, is his epic (De Armas, "Cervantes" 268-85). Is his *Quixote* an apprenticeship to epic or something totally different? For Pavel, the *Persiles*, as an imitation of the *Ethiopian Story*, is a Greek novel. Cervantes must first debunk chivalry in the *Quixote* in order to create a new kind of fiction, very different from the first: "The choice goes to the very core of the human condition. Can we fight ceaselessly to im-

Works Cited

Bouché-Leclerq, Auguste. *L'astrologie grecque*. 1899. Chicago: Bolchazy-Carducci, 1979. Print.

Burton, Robert. *The Anatomy of Melancholy*. Ed. Floyd Dell and Paul Jordan-Smith. New York: Tudor, 1938. Print.

Canavaggio, Jean. *Cervantes*. Trans. J. R. Jones. New York: Norton, 1990. Print.

Cervantes, Miguel de. *Don Quixote*. Trans. Charles Jarvis. Ed. E. C. Riley. Oxford: Oxford UP, 1998. Print. Oxford World's Classics.

———. *El ingenioso hidalgo Don Quijote de la Mancha*. Ed. Luis Murillo. Vol. 1. Madrid: Castalia, 1978. Print.

———. *Viaje del Parnaso*. Ed. Vicente Gaos. Madrid: Castalia, 1984. Print.

———. *Vida y hechos del ingenioso hidalgo don Quijote de la Mancha*. 4 vols. London: J. y R. Tonson, 1738. *UCM Biblioteca Complutense*. Web. 1 Nov. 2016.

Close, Anthony. *The Romantic Approach to* Don Quixote. Cambridge: Cambridge UP, 1978. Print.

Clydesdale, Ruth. "'Jupiter Tames Saturn:' Astrology in Ficino's *Epistolae*." *Laus Platonici Philosophi: Marsilio Ficino and his Influence*. Ed. Stephen Clucas, Peter J. Forshaw, and Valery Rees. Leiden: Brill, 2011. 117-32. Print.

Colton, Judith. "Merlin's Cave and Queen Caroline: Garden Art as Political Propaganda." *Eighteenth Century Studies* 10 (1976): 1-20. Print.

De Armas, Frederick A. "Cervantes and the Virgilian Wheel: The Portrayal of a Literary Career." *European Literary Careers: The Author from Antiquity to the Renaissance*. Ed. Patrick Cheney and Frederick A. de Armas. Toronto: U of Toronto P, 2002. 268-85. Print.

---

pose our law on the world, or should we simply fortify ourselves against the world's relentless adversity?" (109). And yet, as the novel progresses, Cervantes seems to sympathize with his madman as laughter gives way to reflection. And, there was no need to debunk chivalry since it no longer existed in the real world of the times. It was simply a bookish pastime. Thus, debunking might be just an excuse to re-invent the genre. It is true that within the novel, most books of chivalry are sent to the fire by the priest and the barber who attempt to curb in this manner Don Quixote's madness. However, they are comic figures and need not represent Cervantes's views. Towards the end of the 1605 novel, a Canon from Toledo and Don Quixote have a long conversation on chivalry and on the plays of the period. Once again, we have an ambiguous presentation.

———. *Don Quixote among the Saracens: A Clash of Civilizations and Literary Genres*. Toronto: U of Toronto P, 2011. Print.

———. "The Saturn Factor: Examples of Astrological Imagery in Lope de Vega's Works." *Studies in Honor of Everett W. Hesse*. Ed. William C. McCrary and José A. Madrigal. Omaha: Society for Spanish and Spanish-American Studies, 1981. 63-80. Print.

Fajardo, Salvador J. "The Enchanted Return: On the Conclusion of *Don Quijote* I." *Journal of Modern and Renaissance Studies* 16 (1986): 233-51. Print.

Ficino, Marsilio. *The Letters of Marsilio Ficino*. Preface by Oskar Kristeller. Vol. 2. London: Shepeard-Walwyn, 1975. Print.

———. *Three Books on Life*. Trans. and ed. Carol V. Kaske and John R. Clark. Binghamton: Medieval and Renaissance Texts and Studies, 1989. Print.

Greenblatt, Stephen. *Renaissance Self-Fashioning*. Chicago: U of Chicago P, 1980. Print.

Keilen, Sean. *Vulgar Eloquence: On the Renaissance Invention of English Literature*. New Haven: Yale UP, 2006. Print.

Klibansky, Raymond, Erwin Panofsky, and Fritz Saxl. *Saturn and Melancholy: Studies in the History of Natural Philosophy, Religion and Art*. London: Thomas Nelson, 1964. Print.

Lokos, Ellen D. *The Solitary Journey: Cervantes's* Voyage to Parnassus. New York: Peter Lang, 1991. Print.

Mancing, Howard. *The Cervantes Encyclopedia*. 2 vols. Westport: Greenwood P, 2004. Print.

———. *The Chivalric World of* Don Quijote: *Style, Structure, and Narrative Technique*. Columbia: U of Missouri P, 1982. Print.

Mariscal, George. *Contradictory Subjects: Quevedo, Cervantes, and Seventeenth-Century Spanish Culture*. Ithaca and London: Cornell UP, 1991. Print.

Meixell, Amanda S. "Queen Caroline's Merlin Grotto and the 1738 Lord Carteret Edition of *Don Quijote*: The Matter of Britain and Spain's Arthuric Tradition." *Cervantes: Bulletin of the Cervantes Society of America* 25.3 (2005): 59-82. Print.

Pavel, Thomas G. *The Lives of the Novel: A History*. Princeton: Princeton UP, 2013. Print.

Portús, Javier. "Envidia y conciencia creativa en el Siglo de Oro." *Anales de Historia del Arte* volumen extraordinario (2008): 135-49. Print.

Sánchez-Jiménez, Antonio. *Lope pintado por sí mismo: Mito e imagen del autor en la poesía de Lope de Vega*. Woodbridge: Tamesis Books, 2006. Print.

Schmidt, Rachel. *The Canonization of Don Quixote through Illustrated Editions of the Eighteenth Century*. Montreal: McGill-Queen's UP, 1999. Print.

Seznec, Jean. *The Survival of the Pagan Gods*. Trans. Barbara F. Sessions. Princeton: Princeton UP, 1972. Print.

Stagg, Geoffrey. "Propaganda and Poetics on Parnassus: Cervantes's *Viaje del Parnaso*." *Cervantes: Bulletin of the Cervantes Society of America* 8.1 (1988): 23-38. Print.

Van den Doel, Marieke. "Ficino, Diacceto and Michelangelo's Presentation Drawings." *The Making of the Humanities. I: Early Modern Europe*. Ed. Rens Bond, Jaat Maap, and Thijs Weststeijn. Amsterdam: Amsterdam UP, 2010. 107-32. Print.

Vasari, Giorgio. *The Lives of the Artists*. Trans. Julia Conoway Bondanella and Peter Bondanella. Oxford: Oxford UP, 1998. Print.

The Mind's "I" in *Don Quijote*[1]

Edward H. Friedman
Vanderbilt University

> —[Camila] transforms herself from passive object to active agent; she takes control of her life and her story and in the process relegates to secondary status the men who quibble over abstract concepts.
> - Mancing, "Camila's Story" 16

MIGUEL DE CERVANTES'S *DON QUIJOTE* (1605, 1615) is replete with characters with inquiring minds. The most obvious, perhaps, is Anselmo, the title figure of *El curioso impertinente* [The Man Who Was Recklessly Curious], an intercalated novella in Part 1, chapters 33-35. Using his reluctant friend Lotario as accomplice, Anselmo—he who cannot control an impertinent curiosity—devises a plan to test the fidelity of his wife Camila. The plot backfires, as Camila and Lotario become lovers and the initial doubts are recast as a self-fulfilling prophecy. At the end, Anselmo recognizes his culpability, pardons his wife and friend, and dies of grief. He has not let well enough alone. He has not respected the protocols, if such protocols exist, of temptation. And, alas, he has not recognized that women are delicate and ultimately inconstant vessels. The exemplary tale is notable for a number of reasons. It reflects topics introduced in the full narrative, such as madness and obsession, rivalry, the play of history and fiction, metatheater, and variations on the theme of love. It follows a debate in Juan Palomeque's inn on the merits of true stories versus fabricated ones. It also

---

[1] Howard Mancing has been one of my most trusted guides to *Don Quijote*. For this and for his friendship over many years, I am honored to be part of this recognition of his work.

makes its way into the account, early in Part 2, by the university graduate Sansón Carrasco, of the response to the publication of the Arab historian Cide Hamete Benengeli's chronicle (which concurs with the publication of Cervantes's Part 1). Carrasco informs Don Quijote that readers have criticized *El curioso impertinente*, not for its lack of literary merit but for its digressive quality, its irrelevance with regard to the primary plot. This is hardly a clear-cut contention, but the comment keeps questions of structure front and center.

The thesis of Howard Mancing's "Camila's Story" (2005) is key to this essay, in that Mancing maintains that narrative trumps abstract reasoning in *El curioso impertinente*. He differentiates between the first half of the presentation, in which Anselmo and Lotario discuss the testing of Camila in rather dry theoretical terms, and the second half, in which Camila and her maid Leonela devise means of hiding their indiscretions. The women replace discourse with action, theory with praxis, and Camila—once she succumbs to the charms of Lotario—is converted into the dominant agent of the novella. There is an underlying ideology here, but it cedes to the plot and, significantly, to the metaplots of the female characters.[2] A similar phenomenon transpires in *Don Quijote* as a whole, wherein the narrative argument yields, to a great extent, to metanarrative. When one looks at the comprehensive structure of *Don Quijote*, what seem to stand out are references to the inner workings of the artistic process. Superimposed on the tale of the anachronistic knight errant is the story of the composition of the text, buoyed by a series of narrators who comment on the technique, rigors, and ruptures of writing: the accumulation of data, the organization of material, the dialectics of tradition and innovation, theory, criticism, and reception. The invention of the printing press has brought books to the forefront, into the world at large, and Cervantes celebrates the act of writing and the act of reading in *Don Quijote* by emphasizing storytelling, interpretation, and analysis. He doubles the plot through running commentary on fact-gathering, accuracy, and polysemy. He uses the occasion to explore two exceptionally intricate subjects: history and truth, both depicted as relative rather than absolute. The art object relates to social, philosophical, and ideological issues, but also to itself and to all aspects of intertextuality. The narrative is anything but seamless and anything but straightforward, and these elements mark its difference, its uniqueness, and an irony that can only be described as baroque.

---

2   David Arbesú Fernández argues that the novella evokes the medieval debate, in which Lotario symbolizes authority and Anselmo symbolizes experience. Mancing complements the vision by pointing out the decisive role of Camila.

Cervantes introduces, from the outset, an inquiry into authority. *Don Quijote* never forgets its debt to the past while contesting the weight of precedent. The literary analogue has intimate ties to the notions of perception and perspective, focal points throughout the text. The figure of the author, in its various manifestations, is simultaneously in control and—most conspicuously, it must be noted—at the mercy of others, who take liberties with details and with the big picture. The sense of ongoing, and shifting, narration is a symbolic statement, a means by which to access the speculative nature of the story and its metanarrative import, less a supplement than an indivisible component of the self-fashioned chronicle. The examination of madness, justice, and the imagination encompasses the plot and its broader implications. Cervantes knows how to keep things light and profound, to take his comedy seriously (see Russell); he is a master of connecting, interweaving, and pushing individual factors to do double- or triple-duty. The core of the narrative may be the errant knight's misadventures, but literary and historical revisionism—and a deconstructive agenda—seem to be on his mind at every twist and turn. Mancing sees in *El curioso impertinente* a movement from thought to action, from deliberation to rhetorical strategies, that is, from theory to praxis. The complete *Don Quijote* builds on a similar progression, but adds a dimension, which could be labeled *theory in praxis* and, which, by uniting the two and accentuating their inseparability, takes the form of metanarrative. It is Don Quijote's metafictionality—his point of origin, his modus operandi, his most salient feature, his overriding trait, as it were—that gives the character and the narrative a special texture. *El curioso impertinente* shows that Camila's victory over Anselmo, albeit one that leads to a tragic ending, is a reworking of her husband's model. She outdoes the would-be metadramatist and his apt pupil Lotario, and, as inscribed in the structure of *Don Quijote*, their sad story makes the reader, or listener, conscious of plot mechanisms, of the relation of fiction to reality, of the practice of illusion, and of the art of deception. At the moment that the priest Pero Pérez finishes his reading aloud of the novella, he cannot restrain from offering a critical opinion. Here Cervantes critiques himself. The tale does not exist in a vacuum. It is audience-oriented and surrounded by other fictions, by what purports to be a true history, and by reviews of several kinds. Messages in this case are mixed messages.

If *El curioso impertinente* transposes abstraction into direct action, *Don Quijote* extends the procedure to blur the distinction. Cervantes *activates* abstract concepts. He makes the trials, tribulations, joys, and openness of writing and reading plot-worthy. He piques the reader's curiosity by interrogating the stages and the results—always tentative, always unstable—of word processing. He elevates literature by investigating and dissecting its components and by linking literature to other disciplines and to life. I would classify his undertaking as audacious rather than impertinent, for he is confronting narrative paradigms and, one has to acknowledge, much more. Some fifty years before Diego Velázquez paints himself into the frame of *Las Meninas*, Cervantes becomes, jointly, what Wayne Booth calls an *implied author* and what Miguel de Unamuno calls an *ente de ficción*. *Don Quijote* provides a stream of signals from the author to the reader and thus attaches the communicative system to the encoding and the decoding—the creation and the "consumption"—of the text. The reader is involved in and detached from the plot, which blends realism and metafiction while paying its respects to and satirizing idealism. The field of references and of associations in *Don Quijote* is staggering, and the reader can hardly be idle. As Sansón Carrasco notifies Don Quijote and Sancho Panza at the beginning of Part 2, the chronicle by Cide Hamete Benengeli has pleased its readers, but for an array of reasons; the narrative lends itself to diverse reactions, and every reader establishes a set of preferences and priorities. Part 2 of *Don Quijote* subsumes and alters Part 1, and the spurious sequel by the pseudonymous Alonso Fernández de Avellaneda—intrusive and ultimately indispensable—is situated between the two "legitimate" parts in a striking manner. Narrative realism from the eighteenth century to the present relies on a type of figurative disappearance: of the narrator as persona and of the tools of the writer's trade. *Don Quijote* follows precisely the opposite path.

On one level, Cervantes operates as a puppeteer, concealing himself in the background while exposing the strings of his performance. On another, he highlights the experimental facets of his narrative. Whether consciously or unconsciously, he gives the text and its narration a tentative bent, a circumstance parallel to the character in search of a manuscript. He exaggerates the motif of *process* that brings together the disparate threads and aleatory thrust of the narrative. *Don Quijote* is monumentally self-referential, but Cervantes likewise is concerned with the interdependence of text and society, of word and world. *Don Quijote* justifiably may be deemed a theory of the novel, but it serves, as well, as a treatise on perceiving and comprehending exterior realms and on assessing history, or histories. Paradoxically, *Don Quijote* is a didactic enterprise, a resounding example of the dichotomy *dulce et utile*. The narrative is so often humorous and entertaining that the reader may have to look closely for the lessons, but they are most certainly there, and they are infinite. The value of the subtext is at the heart of the narrative, and, expressed in poststructuralist parlance, the subtext—fictional, critical, theoretical—of *Don Quijote* displaces, or decenters, the linear argument, the plot per se. All that is *meta-* dominates all that is not, vis-à-vis quantity and quality. Metafiction and realism coexist and complement each other, but not in equal doses. The author is instructing the reader about the beauties of literature—art for art's sake—while demonstrating that literature is an instrument for delving into the most substantial and profound existential (and metaphysical) areas and, to be sure, for studying its own properties, formulas, and aims. *Don Quijote*—perchance viewed quixotically—is an expansive conduit, a text that stays with its readers, a "never-ending adventure" ("aventura inacabable" [1:1]). My thesis is that the metaliterary trappings of *Don Quijote* bridge the gap between past and future, and that the design of the narrative proves that art can theorize and can make theory a welcome diversion, in the double sense. The metatheoretical underpinnings of *Don Quijote* are neither coincidental nor removed from the principal story. Cervantes guides the reader through a story that is more than a story, more than a feigned history, and more than a parody; *Don Quijote* is, above all, a paean to the intricacies and conundrums of literature.

The first words of the prologue to the 1605 *Quijote*—*desocupado lector* [idle reader]—immediately forge a bond between the author and the reader, and this reciprocal relation will endure throughout the narrative. The prologue about the writing of a prologue—ergo, a metaprologue—sets a tone and gives the text a subversive edge, most appreciably when the "friend" suggests that "Cervantes" ignore time-honored conventions. It is the friend who defines the purpose of the book: to condemn and destroy chivalric romance. It is Cervantes, however, who places ironic signs and rejoinders in almost every line (and between lines). The prologue is not quite "a map of misreading," but it manifests, to allude to another coinage of Harold Bloom, "the anxiety of influence." Cervantes initiates a pattern of using the past to indicate change and to make reading a contemplative and interactive (and proactive) venture. I would submit that the opening chapter of Part 1 encapsulates the scheme and the spirit—the quintessence—of *Don Quijote*: its foregrounding of literature, its stress on multiperspectivism, its negation of the objectivity of history, its judgments on truth and perception, its special treatment of madness, its pairing of art and life, and its focus on the power of the imagination. The prominence of intertextuality—of fiction and of social codes, of past and present—is demarcated from the start. As the narrator seeks facts, the reader is made privy to the ups and downs of the search. And, within the microcosm, the man who renames himself Don Quijote becomes a metadramatist in the theater of the world, real and invented. The knight recalls and improvises, and he is aware of his historical role in a chronicle yet to be written. Others participate, sometimes inexplicably, in his fantasies. In chapter 5, Don Quijote claims to know who he is, and that statement captures the enigma of his identity and the soul of Cervantes's vision.

The scrutiny of Don Quijote's library (1:6) exemplifies the dual force of the narrative. The exercise in literary criticism, which includes a verbal portrait of Cervantes as "more versed in misfortunes than in verses," is also an allegory of the Inquisition (and a camouflaged denunciation of the policies of Church and State). Books are positioned in a center that increases in size in order to accommodate, and to mask, matters of gravity. The incorporation of book reviews into the narrative is rare, and in this instance the sentences are aligned to indictment of Christians whose faith is under suspicion. One end of the spectrum is comic, whereas the other could not be more sobering, and Cervantes fits the critique into the mock-heroic record. That record becomes problematic when the narrator announces at the end of chapter 8 that he has no more information to impart; he has run out of data. The lacunae are resolved, at least to the conclusion of Part 1, when the authorial figure discovers, in a marketplace in Toledo, the manuscript of the Arab historian Cide Hamete Benengeli, which he has translated by a *morisco* (1:9). That something will be lost in translation is a given, but much will be gained through this ingenious device, which merges historiography with politics and the quest for truth. The interruption of the narrative occurs in the chapter in which Don Quijote has set out anew with a squire, Sancho Panza: foil, comic relief, representative of oral culture and of "reality," and, most particularly, because it embraces the other items, as a dialogue partner. The chivalric plot is text and pretext, as metafiction becomes the macrocosm. Cervantes anticipates poststructuralist decentering and, with it, the presuppositions of deconstruction, which do not lead away from the strength of words to convey meaning but admonish us to probe how meanings are produced and, as a corollary, how histories are made (see, e.g., Culler; Leitch). The interpretation of texts and of life, *Don Quijote* seems to confirm, is not an exact science, yet approximations are valid and necessary. Creativity and mental stimulation go hand in hand; the artist and the consumer share inquiring minds.

Cervantes pays homage to the literary past, but, in the main, not reverentially. He uses allusions to chivalric, pastoral, picaresque, and other genres as motivation for rewriting. The shepherdess Marcela, for example, places pastoral romance in a new register, with a woman who wants freedom and independence rather than a husband, and who resists objectification. At the inn of Juan Palomeque and in the Sierra Morena range, Don Quijote and Sancho find themselves—and their narrative—among competing narratives and narrative voices, as story yields to discourse, or, it could be said, discourse becomes the story. Cardenio and Dorotea tell interweaving tales, and the characters in their plotline finally come together. Dorotea acts in a drama elaborated by the priest and the barber from Don Quijote's unnamed village of La Mancha. Don Quijote retells the story of Maritornes and the muleteer—of things that go bump in the night, so to speak—in the mode of high chivalry. The reading of a fictional text—*El curioso impertinente*—is juxtaposed with the oral history narrated by the captive, which reveals that fact can be stranger, and more far-fetched, than fiction. Prior to the two lengthy interpolations, Cervantes inserts the defense of fiction (seen as fact) by the innkeeper (1:32). By the second half of Part 1, chivalric and mock-chivalric feats have receded into the background, and narrators have become protagonists. Another poststructuralist term, *deferral*, applies to the method of storytelling in these chapters, from the entry into the Sierra Morena to Don Quijote's departure from the inn in a cage. On the journey homeward, Don Quijote meets a canon from Toledo, a man with a Tridentine mindset and revulsion toward the books of chivalry. Cervantes matches the canon with Pero Pérez in a discussion of chivalric romance and then of the current state of the theater (1:47-48). The targets of the vituperation are, respectively, Don Quijote and Lope de Vega. The attack on chivalric fiction underscores its lack of redeeming qualities and its commitment to pure entertainment at the expense of education. Through the canon, *Don Quijote* pays lip service, and possibly more, to the Counter Reformation. The assault on the *comedia nueva* relates only negligibly to Church and State. The unsuccessful and frustrated Cervantes uses the two clerics as his representatives—his mouthpieces—to berate the triumphs, popular and critical, of Lope and even to call for more stringent censorship. Cervantes transfers his wrath; he vents within the borders of fiction. The derogatory gesture will have consequences. In the concluding chapter of Part 1, the narrator promises to endeavor to supply the rest of the history. He has made a start, but many open spaces remain.

Don Quijote, Part 1, then, appears to adhere to a preconceived plan that draws attention to self-referentiality, with an experimental counterpart in which spontaneity and surprise amplify the template. Within this dialectical arrangement, Cervantes deals with transcendent themes—truth, justice, perception, honor, the impact of history, and so forth—through the lens of reading and writing. The author and the reader are the sine qua non of the task. Cervantes integrates a corps of narrators to spotlight the authorial dimension: the making of the text and a realization of the significance of the reader. The fictionalized Cervantes sets the narrative in motion, while Don Quijote, fixated on his readings, wants to turn his readings into life experiences. And he is not the only character with this goal. *Don Quijote* is about mergers, about attempted syntheses, some of which bear results and others of which do not. Books unify and unite authors and readers, but they are capable of disrupting the boundaries between the real and the imaginary. The romances of chivalry have been pronounced as too light, and in his modification Cervantes positively adds heft. He deepens content without sacrificing a concentration on form. He proves himself to be adept at innovation and, unconditionally, to be a master of irony. The field of referents that he negotiates is enormous, and the phrase "the human comedy" (later employed by Honoré de Balzac and William Saroyan) indeed can be applied to *Don Quijote*. In Part 1, the world comes into the book. In Part 2, the book comes into the world.

Literature, criticism, poetics, theory, society, and authority enter Part 1 of *Don Quijote*. In the second part, Cervantes seizes the opportunity to broaden and to narrow his bases. The focal object becomes Part 1 itself—Cide Hamete Benengeli's chronicle and Cervantes's book—as the manuscript that has been published, read, and critiqued. Self-reference gains in complexity, and books in the abstract and all-purpose sense switch to *the book* about Don Quijote's exploits and about the composition of the self-proclaimed history. In Part 2, Don Quijote and the reader learn of the reception to Part 1. Don Quijote must accept his celebrity status, and the reader must adjust criteria for evaluation according to altered equations posed by the text. The major intertext is no longer chivalric romance but Part 1 itself. Metafiction is on the rise. When one addresses the topic of a plan for Part 2, it is crucial to note that two stories converge. As Cervantes is completing his sequel, another second part, credited to the mysterious Avellaneda, is published in the fall of 1614. The "false" continuation enters Cervantes's Part 2 in chapter 59 and mediates the remaining chapters, but that is not all. Cervantes chooses to respond to Avellaneda in the 1615 prologue: defending himself against cruel accusations, halfheartedly praising Lope de Vega, and declaring that he will leave Don Quijote "dead and buried" at the end of Part 2, so that there can be no more unauthorized sequels. By replying to Avellaneda's charges and mentioning his invasive tome, Cervantes gives credence to the competition, and the prologue flavors a reading of the text. His original plan occupies chapters 1 through 58, but it is offset by statements in the prologue, which seem to be penned by Cervantes rather than "Cervantes." From what we can surmise of the "original plan," the author upgrades and personalizes reader-response. The chronicle is criticized, and prominent characters in Part 2—among them, Sansón Carrasco and the duke and duchess—are readers of Part 1. To a degree, Don Quijote falls victim to his fame. He becomes more passive, which allows Sancho Panza to become more active, more aggressive. The publication of Cide Hamete's chronicle has wrought changes in characterization, direction, and focus. The ten years between the two volumes become one month in the narrative, and the narrator gives short shrift to the closing words of chapter 52 of Part 1. Don Quijote has not been cured of his peculiar brand of madness, and Sansón Carrasco—with a private agenda—encourages him to embark on a third sally. The knight is a historical personage, spurred to enhance his reputation. Cervantes himself has won fame at the advanced age of fifty-eight. He also is prompted and tested by success, which he would have hoped to re-create. Don Quijote's fame is a blessing and a curse. The false sequel is a curse and a blessing.

The prologue to the 1615 *Quijote* is a decisive afterthought. Part 1 has removed Cervantes from obscurity. Avellaneda has reminded him of failure and the breadth of Lope's conquests and the strength of his advocates. The continuation officially begins in chapter 1, in which concern over Don Quijote's state of health gets the narrative under way. Sansón Carrasco is an informant about the recent and, by and large, well-received chronicle. Chapter 52 of Part 1 comments on the trip of Don Quijote and Sancho to Zaragoza, where jousting tournaments will be taking place, and that city will be their destination. In a conversation with his wife Teresa (2:5), Sancho shows signs of assertiveness (and authority) that will become more evident in his decision to "enchant" Dulcinea (2:10) as a means of avoiding a meeting with Aldonza Lorenzo. There is now an addendum to the mission: to "disenchant" Dulcinea. Sansón Carrasco concocts a metaplot in which he will follow Don Quijote in disguise (as the Knight of the Wood or of the Mirrors) and vanquish him. He is confident that he will be able to send Don Quijote home in defeat. When he loses the battle, his magnanimity turns to a desire for vengeance, and he must listen to a scolding by his makeshift squire, Sancho's neighbor Tomé Cecial, who asks rhetorically which of the "knights" is madder. Cervantes illuminates Don Quijote's eccentricities by contrasting him to the "normal" Don Diego de Miranda, a family man with no books of chivalry in his library, and by having him—in the middle of his encounter with Don Diego—challenge a (fortunately lethargic) lion (2:17). In subsequent chapters, Don Quijote is more apt to comment on poetry (with Don Lorenzo, son of Don Diego) or partake of wedding activities (in which Basilio is the metadramatist) than engage in combat. A turn in the road and a change of direction on Cervantes's part take Don Quijote into the Cave of Montesinos, where the author's pre-Freudian imaginary reaches depths of subconsciousness, and where the knight's obsession with chivalric romance and with Dulcinea are bound (2:23). The episode explores the mind and the question of truth, with a divining monkey and later an enchanted head in supporting roles. Don Quijote's next skirmish is with the puppets of Maese Pedro, aka Ginés de Pasamonte, the released galley slave of Part 1 (2:26). The remedy here, as with the enchanted boat, is payment of damages.

Corresponding to the Sierra Morena sequence in Part 1, Don Quijote's stay with the duke and duchess in Part 2 is overflowing in characters and competing story lines. The aristocrats, like royalty in need of jesters, use their unlimited resources and their reading of the chronicle to entertain themselves, in their palace and on the island of Barataria governed by Sancho Panza. The knight and the squire are actors—not fully prepped—in the ducal metatheater. The duke and duchess reach the epitome of reader-response, and Cervantes achieves a new variation of metafiction. Sancho's meeting with the *morisco* Ricote (2:54) reminds the reader that fiction and history continue to intermingle. The story of Ricote's daughter Ana Félix (2:63) does the same. When Barcelona replaces Zaragoza as the destination, metafiction meets urban reality (and urban fictions). Ricote, who is first seen near the island of Barataria, appears in Barcelona along with Ana Félix, whose tale summons Byzantine romance. Don Quijote visits the home of the lofty citizen Don Antonio Moreno (owner of the enchanted head), canters on the streets, visits a printing establishment with the Avellaneda sequel in stock, and makes a trip to the docks. It is in Barcelona that Don Quijote is defeated by his nemesis Sansón Carrasco, renamed the Knight of the White Moon, and the protagonist must return to his village, where he also *must* die. The death is a function of the story line and of Cervantes's decision to bring closure to the narrative.

The impertinent Avellaneda is a nightmare and a dream. The interloper insults and humiliates Cervantes as he transgresses previously staked authorial territory. Cervantes is understandably enraged, although he handles the offensive behavior with admirable restraint, given the situation and the virulence of Avellaneda's allegations. One might say, however, that Cervantes cannot seem to get Avellaneda out of his head. He makes the inauthentic text a centerpiece of *Don Quijote*, Part 2, thereby tying it to his own Part 1. Cervantes's conception of a rivalry between Parts 1 and 2 is intensified by the publication of the Avellaneda sequel, which takes competition to a new plane. From chapter 59 forward, the genuine Part 2 keeps its adversary in sight: at the inn where Don Jerónimo and Don Juan have a copy of the troublesome tome, in Altisidora's near-death experience where devils use Avellaneda books rather than balls in a game of tennis (2:70), in Don Álvaro Tarfe's declaration that "our" Don Quijote and Sancho Panza are the bona fide characters (2:72), and in Alonso Quijano the Good's apology (in his will) to Avellaneda for giving him material for the ghastly sequel (2:74). Could the literary genius Miguel de Cervantes have thought of a more impressive way to represent baroque rivalry than to inject another book, with another Don Quijote, another Sancho Panza, and a mortifying appraisal of the opposing author? Avellaneda animates Cervantes and Don Quijote, and the "spurious" sequel builds upon the unpredictability, the random feel, and especially the irony of the narrative. Avellaneda complicates and validates the work of Cervantes, and the thorn in the side, *con perdón*, comes out smelling like a rose. Cervantes could have erased Avellaneda for future generations, but he was probably too proud to suffer in silence. The winners of the competition are the "real" second part and its readers, and the metafictional mode. And as theory advances, *Don Quijote* never loses its immediacy, its relevance.[3]

Curiosity in Part 1 relates to response to Don Quijote's strange affect. His oddness produces awe—*admiratio*—in those with whom he comes into contact. When he is known—and illustrious—he does not surprise his interlocutors, although he still baffles them. Cervantes must bear this in mind as he blends reactions within the text to the "real" readers' foreknowledge and their curiosity regarding what will happen next. And, wonderfully, no one—not even the "lawful" author—knows what will happen next.

One of the seemingly limitless ironies of *Don Quijote* is that it is Alonso Quijano who is dead and buried at the end. Don Quijote the character and *Don Quijote* the text live on in the arts and in the ways in which we view the world. Cervantes redefines the relation between theory and praxis, and he performs a precocious deconstruction of the literary past, with reconstruction in tow. *Don Quijote* could be titled *Paradox Regained*, for the interpre-

---

3   See Friedman, *Cervantes*; Friedman, "Don Quixote." I have tried to convert my reading of *Don Quijote* to dramatic and poetic form in *Crossing the Line* and *Quixotic Haiku*, which may lack sophistication but not appreciation for their source. I would mention that when I teach seminars on theory, I have to apologize to students for using *Don Quijote* as an example far too often.

tive options are incalculable.[4] Not only Alonso Quijano but the idle reader is laid to rest as the sanctioned second part concludes. As the text gets "curiouser and curiouser," in the phrase of Lewis Carroll, the reader may be likely to become ever more curious while moving through the multifaceted and mutable narrative. The trip can last a lifetime, but the customers usually have no complaints.

Works Cited

Arbesú Fernández, David. "*Auctoritas* y experiencia en *El curioso impertinente.*" *Cervantes: Bulletin of the Cervantes Society of America* 25.1 (2005): 23-43. Print.

Bloom, Harold. *The Anxiety of Influence: A Theory of Poetry*. 2nd ed. New York: Oxford UP, 1997. Print.

———. *A Map of Misreading*. 2nd ed. New York: Oxford UP, 2003. Print.

Cervantes Saavedra, Miguel de. *Don Quijote*. Ed. Tom Lathrop. Legacy ed. Newark, DE: Juan de la Cuesta, 2012. Print.

Culler, Jonathan. *On Deconstruction: Theory and Criticism after Structuralism*. Ithaca: Cornell UP, 1982. Print.

Friedman, Edward H. *Cervantes in the Middle: Realism and Reality in the Spanish Novel*. Newark, DE: Juan de la Cuesta, 2006. Print.

———. *Crossing the Line: A Quixotic Adventure in Two Parts*. Newark, DE: Juan de la Cuesta, 2012. Print.

———. "Don Quixote: Staying Alive." *In Memoriam: L. Teresa Valdivieso. Ensayos y remembranzas*. Ed. Enrique Ruiz-Fornells Silverde. Erie: Enlaces Culturales, 2014. 25-40. Print.

———. *Quixotic Haiku: Poems and Notes*. Newark, DE: Juan de la Cuesta, 2015. Print.

Leitch, Vincent B. *Deconstructive Criticism: An Advanced Introduction*. New York: Columbia UP, 1982. Print.

Mancing, Howard. "Camila's Story." *Cervantes: Bulletin of the Cervantes Society of America* 25.1 (2005): 9-22. Print.

Presberg, Charles D. *Adventures in Paradox:* Don Quixote *and the Western Tradition*. University Park: Pennsylvania State UP, 2000. Print.

Russell, P. E. "*Don Quixote* as a Funny Book." *Modern Language Review* 64.2 (1969): 312-26. Print.

---

4   Charles Presberg uses *Adventures in Paradox* as the title of his study of *Don Quijote*.

Don Quixote and the Knight of the White Moon

JOHN JAY ALLEN
University of Kentucky (emeritus)

THE FIRST READERS OF Miguel de Cervantes's masterpiece saw only a parody of the books of chivalry, and that must have been the case with virtually all of the readers during the first decade after 1605, when Part II did not exist. This attitude still prevails among many readers today as they begin the second volume. But long before the well-known quite different reception of the novel by the 19th-century Romantics, some readers of the Second Part began to identify with the knight. Motteux felt, in 1700, that "all men have some beloved Dulcinea in their thoughts, who propels them toward foolish adventures" (qtd. in Knowles 280-81). In 1750, Samuel Johnson, the celebrated lexicographer, asserted that "very few readers, amid the laughter or the pity, can deny having experienced visions of the same kind, and when we laugh, our hearts inform us that he is no more ridiculous than we, except that he says what we have only thought" (qtd. in Knowles 281). Around the same time, there were other commentaries that revealed the beginnings of the idealization of the knight. Alexander Pope said of a friend, in 1739, that he was "such a child in the true simplicity of his heart, that I love him, as he loves Don Quixote, for being the most moral and rational madman in the world" (qtd. in Tave 154). Sarah Fielding, sister of the famous English novelist, said in 1754 that

> to travel through an entire book just to laugh at our principal traveling companion is an insupportable burden. And we imagine that the reading of Cervantes's incomparable comedy must provide little pleasure to those who receive from it no more entertainment or advantage than that of

laughing at the dreams of Don Quixote and sharing the malicious jubilation of his antagonists … . Such a powerful and beautiful representation of his madness with respect to one single thing, and of his extraordinarily good judgment with respect to everything else, is truly wasted in the case of those readers who only consider him an object of laughter. (III.120)

These notes of commiseration and esteem already reveal the seeds of the Romantic interpretation of the novel that would dominate nineteenth-century criticism.

The divergence of reactions among the readers of the novel that continues to manifest itself today arises from the complexity of the Second Part that Cervantes published in 1615, ten years after the appearance of Part I. It is not difficult to see the participation of readers of Part II like Henri Hurault, Count of Cheverny, and his wife, Françoise Chabot de Charny, in the uncomplicated laughter of the readers of Part I. In 1625 the count and countess began a ten-year reconstruction of their chateau in the Loire valley that still conserved some vestiges of the feudal castle that preceded it. They contracted its embellishment to several local artists of the town of Blois, among them Jean Mosnier, the painter whose impressions of Don Quixote adorn the dining room and an anteroom.

The association established by the Count and Countess of Cheverny between the dining room of their new castle and the castle of the duke and duchess who hosted Don Quixote in a novel recently translated at the time into French, establishes an indelible parallel between this noble couple and that of Cervantes, and it represents the reaction that might have been expected of those early readers, heavily conditioned by their reading of Part I as a creation independent of Part II. Identification with the duke and duchess must have been normal, perhaps the most common reaction among readers of that generation.

The image of the protagonist as a madman, eloquent and well-intentioned, but crazy, and unconscious of the tricks and ridicule of those around him, persists in the reader who begins Part II. This image surely remained fixed, above all in those first readers who only began to read the continuation of the story years after having read Part I. For readers from 1615 onward to appreciate the essential changes that he introduced in his protagonist, Cervantes needed to indicate the way forward very clearly and proceed little by little in the transformation of the knight.

At the insistence of Don Quixote in the first chapter of the continuation that a single knight could finish off the Turkish threat—a clear revelation of the persistence of his madness—the barber tells the story of the madman of Seville, whom the chaplain wanted to set free, believing him sane. In contrast to his reaction to the transparent parody of the ridiculous chivalric activity sketched out by the innkeeper during the first sally of Part I, Don Quixote now realizes immediately the intention of the barber in telling his story: "'Pues ¿éste es el cuento, señor barbero,' dijo don Quijote, 'que por venir aquí como de molde, no podía dejar de contarle? ¡Ah, señor rapista, señor rapista, y cuán ciego es aquel que no vee por tela de cedazo!'" ["So, that's your story, señor barber? said don Quixote. This is the one that was so much to the point that you just had to tell it? Ah, señor shaver, señor shaver, how blind can anyone be who can't see through cheesecloth!"] (II.1.41; 518).[1]

Following that, the barber continues playing him, asking Don Quixote: "¿Qué tan grande le parece a vuestra merced, mi señor don Quijote, ... debía de ser el gigante Morgante?" ["How tall does your grace, my señor don Quixote, think the giant Morgante was?"] (II.1.51; 521). The reply, addressed to the priest and the barber, is impressive: "hay diferentes opiniones, si los ha habido o no en el mundo; pero la Santa Escritura, que no puede faltar un átomo en la verdad, nos muestra que los hubo, contándonos la historia de aquel filisteazo de Golías, que tenía siete codos y medio de altura, que es una desmesurada grandeza" ["there are different opinions as to whether or not they existed in the world. But Holy Scripture, which cannot stray an atom from the truth, tells us the story of that big Philistine Goliath, who was seven and a half cubits tall, which is an inordinate size"] (II.1.51; 521). Not only does he counter the barber's joke—and invalidate the objection of the priest—with a quote from the Bible, when we could have expected a citation from a novel of chivalry, but he cites an anthropological authorization, the recent discovery of human bones in Sicily, that seems to ratify the existence of some outsized humans.

This departure from the previously credulous behavior of Don Quixote throughout Part I clearly reveals that the protagonist has changed during his month of convalescence. And Cervantes has considered the possible changes over ten years. In the course of the initial chapters of Part II we follow the progression of Don Quixote from his initial state of innocent credulity toward ironic skepticism. Think of his reply to the intention of his niece to dissuade him from further chivalrics—the elegant distinction between courtier knights and knights-errant that replaces his previous incapacity to distin-

---

1   All Spanish citations from *Don Quijote* are from my edition and refer to part, chapter, and page. All citations in English are from Tom Lathrop's translation, citing page only.

guish between fictional knights and historical ones, or the contrast among lineages that crushes her resistance: "¡Ay, desdichada de mí! ... ¡Todo lo sabe, todo lo alcanza!" ["Ay, woe is me .... My uncle ... knows everything; he understands everything"] (II.6.80; 554).

As I have pointed out before, the continuation of this process of transformation of the protagonist surfaces again in a confrontation with Sancho with respect to his salary.[2] In Chapter 7, Sancho struggles with Teresa's insistence that he ask Don Quijote for a fixed salary, embarrassed by the crass materialism of the matter:

> —Señor, ya yo tengo relucida a mi mujer a que me deje ir con vuestra merced a donde quisiere llevarme.
> —*Reducida* has de decir, Sancho—dijo don Quijote—; que no *relucida*.
> —Una o dos veces—respondió Sancho—, si mal no me acuerdo, he suplicado a vuestra merced que no me enmiende los vocablos, si es que entiende lo que quiero decir en ellos, y que cuando no los entienda, diga: "Sancho, o diablo, no te entiendo;" y si yo no me declarare, entonces podrá enmendarme; que yo soy tan fócil ... .
> —No te entiendo, Sancho—dijo luego don Quijote—, pues no sé qué quiere decir *soy tan fócil*.
> —*Tan fócil* quiere decir—respondió Sancho—*soy tan así*.
> —Menos te entiendo agora—replicó don Quijote.
> —Pues si no me puede entender—respondió Sancho—, no sé cómo lo diga; no sé más, y Dios sea conmigo.
> —Ya, ya caigo—respondió don Quijote—en ello. Tú quieres decir que eres *tan dócil*, blando y mañero, que tomarás lo que yo te dijere, y pasarás por lo que te enseñare.
> —Apostaré yo—dijo Sancho—que desde el emprincipio me caló y me entendió, sino que quiso turbarme, por oirme decir otras doscientas patochadas.
> —Podrá ser—replicó don Quijote—. Y en efecto, ¿qué dice Teresa?
> —Teresa dice—dijo Sancho—que ate bien mi dedo con vuestra merced, y que hablen cartas y callen barbas, porque quien destaja no baraja, pues más vale un toma que dos te daré. Y yo digo que el consejo de la mujer es poco, y el que no le toma es loco.

---

2   In what follows I summarize the thrust of the essay, "The Importance of Being an Ironist," essential for fully understanding the crucial encounter under discussion here (Allen).

—Y yo lo digo también—respondió don Quijote—. Decid, Sancho amigo; pasá adelante, que *habláis hoy de perlas*. (II.7.82-83; my emphasis)

> "Señor, I've dissuaded my wife to let me go with your grace wherever you want to lead me."
>
> "*Per*suaded, you should say, Sancho," said don Quixote, "and not *dis*suaded."
>
> "Once or twice," responded Sancho, "if I remember correctly, I've asked your grace not to fix my words if you understand what I mean, but when you don't understand, just say, 'Sancho, I don't understand you,' and if I'm not yet clear, I'm fossil enough to let you correct me."
>
> "I don't understand you, Sancho," said don Quixote, "since I don't know what 'fossil enough' means."
>
> "*Fossil enough* means," responded Sancho, "I'm *sufficiently that way*."
>
> "I understand *that* even less," replied don Quixote.
>
> "Well, if your grace doesn't understand me," responded Sancho, "I don't know how else to say it. I don't know anything else, and may God be with me."
>
> "Now I catch on," responded don Quixote. "You mean that you're so docile—accommodating and meek—that you will go along with what I tell you to do, and you'll do what I instruct you to do."
>
> "I bet," said Sancho, "that since I began, your grace understood me, but you just wanted to hear me say another two hundred stupid things."
>
> "That may be," replied don Quixote, "but indeed, tell me—what does Teresa say?"
>
> "Teresa says," said Sancho, "that I should 'tie a string on my finger with your grace,' and that 'documents speak, not beards,' because 'he who cuts doesn't shuffle' and 'a bird in the hand is worth two in the bush.' And I say that 'the advice of a woman is not worth very much and he who doesn't heed it is crazy.'"
>
> "I agree too," responded don Quixote. "Tell me, Sancho, move along, because you're saying real gems." (556-57)

The reader understands perfectly that "podrá ser" [that may be] is ironic, that here it means "por supuesto" [of course]. 'Habláis hoy de perlas" [You're saying real gems], says Don Quixote, recognizing and savoring with pleasure the discomfort of his squire. This scene is followed directly by a discussion with Sansón Carrasco about Part I in which Sansón "exaggerates the linguistic parody," as Edward Riley points out, provoking Don Quixote's use of what

Riley characterizes as "*a tone of burlesque irony quite difficult to imagine in the Quixote of the first Part*" (*Introducción* 112; emphasis mine). Don Quixote speaks of the phenomenal bachelor Sansón Carrasco, perpetual joker and merrymaker of the patios of the schools of Salamanca, sound of body, fleet of foot, endurer of both heat and cold, and hunger and thirst, with all the requisite qualities to be a squire of a knight-errant (II.7; 559).

This entire sequence constitutes essential preparation for the reader to appreciate the conversation between Don Quixote and Sancho in Chapter 11, when they face the galley slaves:

> Don Quijote [...] detuvo las riendas a Rocinante y púsose a pensar de qué modo los acometería con menos peligro a su persona. En esto que se detuvo, llegó Sancho, y viéndole en talle de acometer al bien formado escuadrón, le dijo:
>
> —Asaz de locura sería intentar tal empresa: considere vuesa merced, señor mío, que para sopa de arroyo y tente bonete, no hay arma defensiva en el mundo, si no es embutirse y encerrarse en una campana de bronce; y también se ha de considerar que es más temeridad que valentía acometer un hombre solo a un ejército donde está la Muerte, y pelean en persona emperadores, y a quien ayudan los buenos y los malos ángeles; y si esta consideración no le mueve a estarse quedo, muévale saber de cierto que entre todos los que allí están, aunque parecen reyes, príncipes y emperadores, no hay ningún caballero andante.
>
> —Ahora sí—dijo don Quijote—has dado, Sancho, en el punto que puede y debe mudarme de mi ya determinado intento. Yo no puedo ni debo sacar la espada, como otras veces muchas te he dicho, contra quien no fuere armado caballero. A ti, Sancho, toca, si quieres tomar la venganza del agravio que a tu rucio se le ha hecho, que yo desde aquí te ayudaré con voces y advertimientos saludables.
>
> —No hay para qué, señor—respondió Sancho—, tomar venganza de nadie, pues no es de buenos cristianos tomarla de los agravios; cuanto más que yo acabaré con mi asno que ponga su ofensa en las manos de mi voluntad, la cual es de vivir pacíficamente los días que los cielos me dieren de vida.
>
> —Pues ésa es tu determinación—replicó don Quijote—, Sancho bueno, Sancho discreto, Sancho cristiano y Sancho sincero, dejemos estas fantasmas y volvamos a buscar mejores y más calificadas aventuras. (II.11.120)

Don Quijote [...] pulled back on Rocinante's reins, and began to consider how he could attack with the least danger to himself. Sancho arrived, and seeing him ready to attack the well-formed squadron, said: "It would be foolhardy to try to take on such a venture, because there's no defensive armor in the world to keep your hat on amidst flying stones, unless you hide under a bronze bell. You also have to consider that it's more recklessness than bravery for a single man to attack an army led by Death, where emperors fight in person, and where good and bad angels lend assistance. And if this consideration doesn't make you pause, you should realize that among all those there you see, kings, princes, and emperors, but there's no knight-errant."

"Now," said Don Quixote, "you've hit upon the point that can and should make me change my mind. I can't nor should I unsheathe my sword, as I've told you many times, against anyone who has not been dubbed a knight. It's up to you, Sancho, to avenge the offense they did to your donkey, and I'll lend support from here with shouts to offer sound advice."

"There's no need, *señor*," responded Sancho, "to take vengeance on anyone, since good Christians shouldn't avenge offenses. Furthermore I'll arrange with my donkey to submit his offense to my own will, which is to live peacefully all the days of life that heaven has allocated me."

"If that's your decision," replied Don Quixote, "good Sancho, discreet Sancho, Christian Sancho, sincere Sancho, let's abandon these phantoms and seek better and worthier adventures. (587-88)

I have singled out this categorical renunciation by Sancho before as an important element in the consideration of the uses and effects of irony in Cervantes's masterpiece: "good Sancho, discreet Sancho, Christian Sancho and sincere Sancho." Don Quixote cannot be serious. A straight reading, without irony, would be "Sancho, what you just said reveals how good you are, how discreet and how Christian, how sincere you are." Why would he choose precisely those specific words to praise him: *good, discreet, Christian, sincere*?

"Good" and "Christian" are the hypocritical terms with which Sancho has just characterized himself moments before. "Discreet" is a jarring contrast with both of them, and "sincere" is the ironic climax that stresses the quality most absent from Sancho's renunciation. What Don Quixote has said is inexplicable without an ironic intention. The comment simply cannot be read as if it were meant seriously, innocently, as one more sign of Don

Quixote's incapacity to perceive Sancho's hypocrisy. Understood ironically, his words have a clear sense. Without irony, they are incoherent. To qualify what Sancho has said as sincere, underlining and praising the sincerity of his expression makes no sense. There is no way to explain the emphasis on sincerity. If Cervantes has insisted on having Don Quixote describe Sancho at that moment with four emphatic adjectives, words that he, or we in his place, could well have picked to use ironically with Sancho, he knew perfectly well what he was doing. Selected to integrate an ironic reply, each word contributes effectively to the desired effect.

"Good Sancho:" Don Quixote introduces his reply with the adjective used by Sancho moments before to describe himself, counting himself among those "good Christians" who do not seek revenge upon those who have offended them. "Discreet Sancho" clashes with that same ingenuous 'goodness,' because it is impossible to square it with the 'discretion' with which he evades a confrontation with an adversary much stronger than he. The final stroke, "Christian Sancho," closes with sarcasm this commentary on the attempt by Sancho to include himself among those 'good Christians' who renounce vengeance.

The ironic procedure introduced here with those two adjectives is the one that Cervantes used in Don Quixote's first encounter with a person in need, at the outset of his chivalric career. "[Y]o soy el valeroso don Quijote de la Mancha, el desfacedor de agravios y sinrazones" ["I'm the valiant don Quixote de la Mancha, the redresser of wrongs and injustices"] (I.4.139; 41), Don Quixote had said to Juan Haldudo, in his encounter with the man and his servant Andrés. This episode ends with the beating of Andrés, followed by the ironic comment of the narrator: "Y desta manera deshizo el agravio el valeroso don Quijote" ["And in this way the brave[3] don Quixote redressed that wrong"] (I.4.140; 42).

In this episode it is clear that the affirmation does not constitute an expression of the paradoxical irony of the unfortunate results that a naive intervention sometimes produces. The adjective *valiant* counts too heavily against Don Quixote, because it cannot be a characterization suggested by his actions; it can only be a sarcastic echo of his description of himself moments before, when he introduced himself to Juan Haldudo. Riley, one of the most perceptive and careful readers of *Don Quixote*, missed this irony:

---

3   Lathrop translates *valiente* here as *brave*, and loses Cervantes's irony.

> As [Don Quixote] searches for chivalric analogies in his everyday life, so does the sympathetic narrator. And so do we. Once, at least, the perspective is fractured by a tremendous irony. After the adventure with the ill-used Andrés, we read: "and thus did the valorous Don Quixote repair the injury" (I.4; i. 98). He has, in fact, made it much worse, but the narrator's comment mirrors the Knight's inordinate self-satisfaction. (*Don Quixote* 156-57)

But the truth is that the irony here is Cervantes's own. The narrator's perspective is not fractured; the narrator does not sympathize with Don Quixote. He is *citing* Don Quixote, and with sarcasm; he is not imitating him. He is mocking Don Quixote when he repeats the adjective from his own previous self-characterization.

The procedure is exactly the same as in the case of "good Sancho" and "Christian Sancho," adjectives that Sancho used when he included himself among the "good Christians," separating in the repetition the two terms to insist even more vehemently, in repeating the "Sancho." And what is more, the separation of "good" from "Christian" permits the insertion of "discreet." "Sincere" Sancho brings the coup de grace—totally inexplicable unless it is ironic, unless it functions to underline precisely the quality lacking in Sancho's response.

And why not "good, discreet, Christian, sincere Sancho?" Why repeat "Sancho" again and again? The effect is to bring in four individual Sanchos for demolition. It demands the consideration of each characteristic independently; it presents each term for pairing with or in opposition to the rest. And the series progresses to a triumphal climax. Cervantes closes the ironic praise by underlining the most notorious element in Sancho's defense, the very insincerity of it.

If I have pressed on with the analysis here, insisting on what seems obvious, it is because Anthony Close and Ruth El Saffar, two of the most brilliant *cervantistas* of their generation, did not see irony in the affirmation by Don Quixote (Close 355; El Saffar 254). How could these scholars be convinced that Don Quixote had been impressed by the goodness and discretion—and above all, by the Christian sincerity—of Sancho at that moment? Because the Don Quixote that Cervantes had presented in Part I of the novel was perfectly capable of that sort of blindness; in fact, that ingenuousness characterized him.

If we were not dealing with a character who has convinced us in the course of Part I of his total incapacity for irony, we would all have seen immediately the ironic attitude of Don Quixote in that dialogue with Sancho. To avoid as much as possible this mistaken reaction, Cervantes insisted at the outset of Part II on showing that his protagonist had recovered and changed fundamentally, despite maintaining an unshakeable faith in the idea of knight errantry.

Don Quixote's masterful command of the Spanish language and his domination of Sancho Panza are displayed at the beginning of Part II when Cervantes presents us with a series of reversals in which all of the tricksters end up tricked in the adventures of the third sally: first Sancho, reduced to tears when Sansón offers to serve as Don Quixote's squire, and then obliged to whip himself to achieve the disenchantment of Dulcinea; then Sansón, defeated and humiliated in his role as the Knight of the White Moon in the joust that he forces on Don Quixote; then Altisidora, disdained; the duke, frustrated by the lovelorn Tosilos; and the duchess, her intimate discomfort made public in the conversations of Don Quixote with Rodríguez. The tables are turned on each of the characters one by one.

This process of the reorientation of the readers' perspective with respect to the encounters of Don Quixote in Part II is essential for the interpretation of the text. But the fact that Cervantes had established Don Quixote's ingenuousness and his insensitivity to the irony of his jokesters so firmly since the beginning of his chivalric career takes many readers, and many *cervantistas*, too, on a path radically different from the one that I am proposing, precisely in this critical moment of the 1615 Part II. There are readers who do not see these changes in the protagonist, who simply do not credit the possibility of an ironic or skeptical Don Quixote, despite the careful preparation with which Cervantes reveals this new subtlety in the development of his character. And this lack of perception brings serious consequences for the resolution of the central enigma of the continuation of the plot.

Let's explore a bit the trajectory of this evolution of the ingenious gentleman from La Mancha. Accustomed now to seeing the ease with which Don Quixote transforms reality throughout and distracted by the series of fascinating episodes of the continuation, it is easy to overlook the fact that in this Second Part he does so only rarely. And on the few occasions when it happens there are always special circumstances, such as the artistic conformation of an episode, in the case of the destruction of Maese Pedro's puppets, or the ingenious falsification of reality involved in others' deliberate fakery. But in this Part II inns are never castles, nor windmills giants.

The first adventure of this third sally is the search for Dulcinea, when despite the assurances of Sancho that the woman whom he sees before him is his lady, he sees only the rustic farm worker. The next encounter is with the actors of *The Parliament of Death*, in which Don Quixote responds to the decision not to fight with these outlandish figures with the irony that first provoked this examination of the newly prominent lucidity of the protagonist. Immediately after this episode comes the encounter with Sansón Carrasco, disguised as the Knight of the Mirrors.

Chapter 16 brings the encounter with the Caballero del Verde Gabán, and the next, the challenge of the lions, which I will deal with shortly, followed by the development of the relations between Basilio and Quiteria and the dream of the Cave of Montesinos. Incited by the fiction of Master Peter's puppet show, he destroys the puppets, the first clear sign of madness in Part II. The episode of the braying aldermen does not provoke any distortion of reality and the empty boat is an invitation impossible for the fertile imagination of Don Quixote to refuse. At that point the reader arrives at the series of episodes with the duke and duchess (Chapter 30), in whose castle or pleasure house, a distinction which escapes our author, all of the adventures are manufactured, except the adventure of Clavileño (Chapter 37), a deception that produces the outlandish invention of Sancho, while Don Quixote experiences nothing but the reality of the experience.

The adventures of the sojourn with the duke and duchess offer enough indications of this new stage in the development of the protagonist to have provoked in Mark Van Doren the impression that Don Quixote now only fakes the madness of believing himself a knight errant.

At times the adventures of Part II recall the deception of the encounter with the fulling mills of Part I. When he heard the mysterious sound of the mill hammers at night in the forest, in Chapter 20 of Part I, he thought briefly that the experience was a real adventure, and he was surprised and embarrassed when he realized the truth. Sancho made fun of him, and Don Quixote became furious, insisting upon the seriousness of his valor when faced with the danger that he thought threatened. In that moment of frustration, he asked for a serious encounter with which to prove himself.

Given that in Part II Don Quixote does not transform reality with the same facility as before, in order to precipitate the crisis with which Cervantes intends to close the chivalric career of his protagonist, the novelist must present him with a threat that transcends the possibility of any skepticism on Don Quixote's part. He must face a mortal threat, in a totally credible encounter.

Anxious to prove himself in this phase of his career, Don Quixote (Chapter 17) faces a real lion. He demonstrates at that moment that he has the valor to meet a true threat. We are now in the last sequence of this extensive preparation for the final encounter with Sansón Carrasco, who approaches him now disguised as the Knight of the White Moon. Don Quixote has finally conjured up in this encounter the proof that will establish definitively the unshakeable strength of his spirit.

Before presenting the crucial encounter, Cervantes takes care to prepare Sansón Carrasco psychologically as well, with the humiliating defeat that he suffers in the duel with Don Quixote. The reader will remember his reaction to that event at the close of Chapter 15:

> pensar que yo he de volver a la mía [casa] hasta haber molido a palos a don Quijote es pensar en lo escusado; y no me llevará ahora a buscarle el deseo de que cobre su juicio, sino el de la venganza, que el dolor grande de mis costillas no me deja hacer más piadosos discursos. (II.15.160)

> if you think I'll go home before I've thrashed don Quixote you're very wrong. And it's not my vow anymore to try to find him so he'll recover his sanity, but rather for revenge. The great pain in my ribs won't allow me to have a more charitable thought. (613)

The moment for the climactic confrontation that will end the chivalric career of the protagonist has arrived. Cervantes's preparation for that scene is masterful. He inserts the encounter into the extensive exotic episode of Ana Félix and the freeing of Don Gregorio from his captivity in Barbary, and the beginning could scarcely be introduced more abruptly. As Riley pointed out years ago, the principal chivalric encounters of Don Quixote are frequently introduced with an epic or lyric description of the dawn of the crucial day (*Introducción* 112). The previous duel with Sansón was introduced as follows:

> En esto, ya comenzaban a gorjear en los árboles mil suertes de pintados pajarillos, y en sus diversos y alegres cantos parecía que daban la norabuena y saludaban a la fresca aurora, que ya por las puertas y balcones del Oriente iba descubriendo la hermosura de su rostro, sacudiendo de sus cabellos un número infinito de líquidas perlas, en cuyo suave licor bañándose las yerbas, parecía asimesmo [que] ellas brotaban y llovían blanco y menudo aljófar; los sauces destilaban maná sabroso, reíanse las fuentes, murmuraban los arroyos, alegrábanse las selvas y enriquecíanse los prados con su venida. (II.14.151)

Just then a thousand kinds of multicolored birds began to chirp in the trees and through their various happy songs it seemed as if they were welcoming and greeting the fresh Aurora, who was beginning to show her beautiful face through the doors of the Orient, shaking from her hair an infinite number of liquid pearls. Grass was bathed in this gentle liquor and from it rained tiny pearls. Willows distilled delicious manna, fountains laughed, streams murmured, the forest rejoiced, and the meadows gloried in her coming. (606-07)

The contrast with this abrupt encounter could not be sharper: "Y una mañana, saliendo don Quijote a pasearse por la playa armado con todas sus armas, porque, como muchas veces decía, ellas eran sus arreos, y su descanso el pelear" ["One morning when don Quixote went out for a ride along the shore, in full armor (because, as he'd say many times, 'his armor was his only adornment and fighting his only rest' ...)"] (II.64.579; 977).

And with this distant echo of the ballad recited by Don Quixote as he set out on his very first sally, in the second chapter of the book, Cervantes has established the serious tone required for the episode that follows. The arrogance of the vengeful Sansón leaves Don Quixote—and the reader— "suspenso y atónito" ["dumbfounded and awestruck"] (II.64.935; 977) and the equanimity and dignity with which our protagonist replies, quite sure of himself, is notable, and in harmony with the seriousness required by the encounter. It is worthwhile to recall here the entire reply:

—Caballero de la Blanca Luna, cuyas hazañas hasta agora no han llegado a mi noticia, yo osaré jurar que jamás habéis visto a la ilustre Dulcinea, que si visto la hubiérades, yo sé que procuráredes no poneros en esta demanda, porque su vista os desengañara de que no ha habido ni puede haber belleza que con la suya comparar se pueda. Y así, no diciéndoos que mentís, sino que no acertáis en lo propuesto, con las condiciones que habéis referido acepto vuestro desafío, y luego, porque no se pase el día que traéis determinado; y sólo excepto de las condiciones la de que se pase a mí la fama de vuestras hazañas, porque no sé cuáles ni qué tales sean: con las mías me contento, tales cuales ellas son. Tomad, pues, la parte del campo que quisiéredes; que yo haré lo mesmo, y a quien Dios se la diere, San Pedro se la bendiga. (II.64.580)

Knight of the White Moon, news of whose deeds has not reached me until now, I'll dare to swear you've never seen the illustrious Dulcinea, for if you had seen her, I know you wouldn't have begun this crusade; because if you saw her, you would be convinced that there has never been, nor can there be, a beauty to compare with hers. So, not saying that you are lying, but rather you're misinformed in what you've said—with the conditions that you've stated, I accept your challenge, and immediately, so the day you've reserved for this business will not pass by. I'll only exclude the provision that the fame of your deeds would become mine, because I don't know what they are and what they consist of. I'm happy with my own, such as they are. Take the side of the field you want and I'll do the same, and 'whom God shall prosper, let St. Peter bless.' (977-78)

I cannot imagine myself in such a situation, never having encountered circumstances that threatening. But Cervantes had been there. It is important to note that this trajectory parallels the military career of Cervantes, above all at the moment when that Spanish soldier insisted—despite his illness—on participating in the Battle of Lepanto, a moment that continued to animate him decades later, as he shows in the Prologue to Part II: "si ahora me propusieran y facilitaran un imposible, quisiera antes haberme hallado en aquella facción prodigiosa que sano ahora de mis heridas sin haberme hallado en ella" ["if the impossible were offered to me right now—that I could be free from my wounds by not having participated in that battle—I would refuse"] (II.Prol.35-36; 508). The reader should recall at this point the title of Astrana Marín's biography: *Vida ejemplar y heroica de Miguel de Cervantes Saavedra* [The exemplary and heroic life of Miguel de Cervantes Saavedra]. Cervantes's useless left hand is the "red badge of courage" of Stephen Crane's story, written centuries later about one of those critical moments of a soldier under fire.

I have realized in recent years that the trajectory of Don Quixote through this ethical phase is much more indirect and drawn out than it had seemed to me to be initially. It begins with the first chapters of the third sally, at the beginning of Part II. But it follows a troubled path on which he stumbles and falls back repeatedly before going forward again. That is what led José Manuel Martín Morán to the conclusion that there is no coherent development in the character or Don Quixote (17). In the initial, ethical, phase our protagonist ignores the content of his actions, focusing on the form, the esthetics, as I have pointed out before in connection with his blindness with respect to the innkeeper's parody. He enters only very slowly into the ethical phase of his trajectory. In that first stage, as Søren Kierkegaard describes the course of human life, when Don Quixote begins to participate in "the great struggle between good and evil, accepting the burden of a finite being who submits to an infinite requirement ... the individual realizes more and more his own incapacity, as well as that of others, in comparison to the infinite requirement's demands" (199). Consciousness of one's own failure and of the failure of everyone else to achieve the ideal leads to the second phase.

When Don Quixote comes upon the images of the saints in Chapter 58 of Part II, he reflects on his situation: "Yo hasta agora no sé lo que conquisto a fuerza de mis trabajos; pero si mi Dulcinea del Toboso saliese de los que padece, mejorándose mi ventura y adobándoseme el juicio, podría ser que encaminase mis pasos por mejor camino del que llevo" ["I don't know what I'm conquering by dint of my labors. But if my Dulcinea del Toboso is able to be released from her own travails, both my luck and my mind will get better, and it may be that my steps will lead me to a better road than the one I'm on"] (II.68.508; 924). Soon after, in the encounter with the Catalan bandits, Roque Guinart advises him: "no os despechéis ni tengáis a siniestra fortuna esta en que os halláis, que podía ser que en estos tropiezos vuestra torcida suerte se enderezase; que el cielo, por estraños y nunca visto rodeos (de los hombres no imaginados), suele levantar los caídos y enriquecer los pobres" ["don't despair, nor consider your situation to be a catastrophe of Fortune, because it may be that through these stumblings your luck will turn around. Heaven, through strange and roundabout ways, undreamed-of by men, tends to lift up the fallen and enrich the poor"] (II.60.540; 944).

In this phase, according to Kierkegaard, "the individual acquires a deeper sense of having failed, of his weakness and anguish, and a desire for repentance" (200). "[C]ada uno es artífice de su ventura" ["Every man is the architect of his own destiny"], Don Quixote says. "Yo lo he sido de la mía, pero no con la prudencia necesaria, y así, me han salido al gallarín mis presunciones" ["I have been of mine, but not with the necessary prudence, and so my pride has cast me down"] (II.66.581; 985). At the close of this second phase, says Kierkegaard,

> the individual recognizes his culpability ... . The ethical phase culminates in repentance. Anxiety arises in us for something beyond all this that will lead us outside the world of our natural existence. This anxiety at not finding what we sought takes us to a transition to a third level, the religious, with its consciousness of an eternal power that permeates existence. (200)

"[V]uelva en sí, y déjese de cuentos" ["Collect your senses and stop this foolishness"], Sansón Carrasco says to Don Quixote on his deathbed. "Los de hasta aquí" ["What has happened up to now"], replies Don Quixote, "que han sido verdaderos en mi daño, los ha de volver mi muerte, con ayuda del cielo, en mi provecho" ["has truly been to my detriment, but my death, with the help of heaven, will set things right"] (II.74.634; 1030).

The trajectory that Don Quixote has followed, in a process that so impressed Flaubert and Dostoyevsky, is not, as Martín Morán would have it, a collection of undifferentiated elements arranged in no particular order to constitute a whole, but a narrative that anticipates in the components of Don Quixote's career the sequence of stages of the passage of human life formulated by Kierkegaard.

It is extremely difficult to replicate this process in a work of fiction, and the representation of the conversion experience is particularly fraught. At that moment, the transformation is internal, and the objections of many critics witness to the difficulty of representing this crucial experience properly. James Wood, among others, was disconcerted by the deathbed conversion of Don Quixote. Note, in comparison, the delicacy of Leon Tolstoy's portrayal of the conversion of the protagonist of "The Death of Ivan Ilych" in these circumstances. He delivers it to us from the inside, following each moment of the psychological struggle with death, a process that completely escapes the family that surrounds him at that times.

Tolstoy finds an ideal metaphor to represent that critical moment. "Suddenly," he says, speaking of Ivan on his deathbed, "some force struck him in the chest and side, making it still harder to breathe, and he fell through the hole, and there at the bottom was a light. What happened to him," said Tolstoy, "was like the sensation one sometimes experiences in a railway carriage when one thinks one is going backwards while one is really going forward and suddenly becomes aware of the real direction" (57). Cervantes succeeds in presenting that revolution in perspective without the resources of nineteenth-century realistic fiction.

The realization on Don Quixote's part of the limitations of his perspective is the critical point of his conversion—the radical change of attitude—that comes at the end of his life, allowing him to transcend the limitations of a comic character in order to develop into a much more complex figure. "The comic element," Mary McCarthy once noted, "is the incorrigible element in all human beings: the capacity to learn, from experience or instruction, is what is forbidden to all comic creations, and to what you and I have that is comic. The capacity to learn is the prerogative of the hero or the heroine" (289).

James Wood has stressed the importance of the difference between what he calls "the comedy of correction" and "the comedy of forgiveness" (25). The first of these two categories is a way of laughing *at* someone. The comedy of forgiveness is a way of laughing *with* someone. "Secular or modern comedy," he says, "seems to me to be almost entirely a creation of the modern novel" (25). And *Don Quixote* is, he says, at another point,

> the foundation of secular comedy. The trick of the unreliable narrator only functions if we think initially that we know more about a character than he knows about himself—and thus we believe that it is a matter of the comedy of correction, to realize, finally—that we know less about that character than we thought at the beginning, and thus we find ourselves seduced by the comedy of forgiveness. (25)

As I have insisted in other studies of Cervantes's masterpiece, the reader comfortably shares the initial perspective toward the protagonist and enjoys the ridicule with which the narrator presents him. But Don Quixote begins to realize in the course of his adventures that he has been mistaken. He changes from his focus on style to the substance of language, from the esthetic to the ethical; he learns and he changes. He confesses his error in the encounter with the images of the saints, though he continues to be unwilling to accept the consequences of this recognition. And as this process continues, we readers feel less sure of our own interpretations of what happens, which have been opposed to those of Don Quixote. We draw nearer to the protagonist as he follows the trajectory that I have indicated, one that leads him to transcend the irony of his own situation.

Reinhold Niebuhr once pointed out that,

> an ironic situation is distinguished from a pathetic situation by the fact that the person in question at that moment has some responsibility. It is distinguished from a tragic situation by the fact that that responsibility does not result from a conscious decision, but rather from an unconscious weakness. If the religious sentiment of a final judgement of our actions were to create a consciousness of those pretensions of ours to knowledge, virtue or power that had helped forge the ironic incongruity,

the irony would dissolve in the experience of contrition and the dissolution of the pretensions that caused the irony. (169)

Niebuhr's analysis—the theologian is speaking here theoretically—characterizes exactly the experience of Don Quixote at the close of this marvelous novel.

Poetry, Marianne Moore once said, presents us with "imaginary gardens with real toads in them" (qtd. in Pinsky). In the scene that we have discussed, Don Quixote, lying on the beach in Barcelona, has no idea who it is that threatens him with a lance at his helmet.

"Vencido sois, caballero, y aun muerto, si no confesáis las condiciones de nuestro desafío" ["You're vanquished, knight—and dead, if you don't confess the conditions of our dispute"] (II.64.897; 979). Don Quixote, thoroughly thrashed and dazed, without raising his visor and speaking as if from a tomb, said in a weak voice, "Dulcinea del Toboso es la más hermosa mujer del mundo, y yo el más desdichado caballero de la tierra, y no es bien que mi flaqueza defraude esta verdad. Aprieta, caballero, la lanza, y quítame la vida" ["Dulcinea del Toboso is the most beautiful woman in the world, and I the most unfortunate knight on earth. It's not right that my weakness should forfeit this truth. Plunge your lance home, knight, and take my life, since you've taken my honor"] (II.64.897; 979).

Works Cited

Allen, John Jay. "Quijote: The Importance of Being an Ironist." *eHumanista/Cervantes* 1 (2012): 437-47. U of California Santa Barbara. Web. 16 Nov. 2016.

Cervantes Saavedra, Miguel de. *El ingenioso hidalgo Don Quijote de la Mancha*. Ed. John Jay Allen. 32nd ed. Madrid: Castalia, 2014. Print.

———. *Don Quixote: Fourth-centenary Translation*. Trans. and with notes by Thomas Lathrop. New York: Signet, 2011. Print.

Close, Anthony. "Sancho Panza: Wise Fool." *MLR* 68 (1973): 344-57. Print.

El Saffar, Ruth. "Concerning Change, Continuity, and Other Critical Matters: A Reading of John J. Allen's *Don Quixote: Hero or Fool* Part II." *Journal of Hispanic Philology* 4 (1980): 237-54. Print.

Fielding, Sarah. *The Cry: A New Dramatic Fable*. London: R. and J. Dodsley, 1754. Print.

Kierkegaard, Søren. *Concluding Unscientific Postscript to* Philosophical Fragments. Ed. and trans. Howard V. Hong and Edna H. Hong. Vol. 1. Princeton: Princeton UP, 1992. Print. *Kierkegaard's Writings XII.*

Knowles, Edwin. "Cervantes and English Literature." *Cervantes Across the Centuries.* Ed. Ángel Flores and M. J. Benardete. New York: Dryden P, 1947. 267-93. Print.

Martín Morán, José Manuel. *El* Quijote *en ciernes: Los descuidos de Cervantes y las fases de elaboración textual.* Torino: Edizioni dell'Orso, 1990. Print.

McCarthy, Mary. *On the Contrary: Articles of Belief, 1946-1961.* New York: Farrar, 1961. Print.

Niebuhr, Reinhold. *The Irony of American History.* Chicago: U of Chicago P, 1952. Print.

Pinsky, Robert. "Marianne Moore's Poetry: Why Does She Keep Revising It?" *Poem: A Weekly Poem Read by the Author.* Slate, 30 Jun 2009. Web. 21 June 2016.

Riley, Edward C. *Don Quixote.* London: Allen & Unwin, 1986. Print.

———. *Introducción al* Quijote. Barcelona: Crítica, 1990. Print.

Tave, Stuart. *The Amiable Humorist.* Chicago: U of Chicago P, 1967. Print.

Tolstoy, Leon [Lev Nikolayevich]. *The Death of Ivan Ilych.* 1886. Trans. Louise and Aylmer Maude. *Wvnet.edu.* n.d. Web. 13 Sept. 2016. The Electronic Series Publication. Ed. Jim Manis.

Van Doren, Mark. *Don Quijote's Profession.* New York: Columbia UP, 1948. Print.

Wood, James. "The History of Laughter." *The New Republic* 225.25 (22 Dec. 2003): 25-30. Print.

Chiaroscuro in Cervantes's *Persiles* (1617)

MARSHA S. COLLINS
The University of North Carolina at Chapel Hill

MIGUEL DE CERVANTES'S *ENARGEIA* or pictorial vividness, his cultivation of ekphrasis and painterly techniques, increasingly draw more critical attention. In 1975, Helena Percas de Ponseti noted the increase in pictorial and sculptural techniques in Part 2 of *Don Quijote*, observing that these elements intensify the visual presence of the symbolic in Cervantes's 1615 continuation of the novel (2.305). More recently, critical focus on the author's painterliness has intensified, and widened to embrace other works by Cervantes, including his visual treasure trove, the *Persiles*.[1] These analyses increase understanding of the role of the visual in Cervantes's works, and provide new insight into this important dimension of the great writer's creative praxis. My essay continues along these lines of inquiry, examining Cervantes's deployment of *chiaroscuro*, the interplay or juxtaposition of light and dark, at the macro- and micro-levels of his posthumously published romance. This particular aspect of the *Persiles*' painterly qualities seems especially revealing in regards to the author's preoccupation with merging episteme with techne, a lifelong concern leading to his masterful imbrication of moral philosophy with matters of style and craft in creating fictional worlds.

In the West, the origins of *chiaroscuro* and painting are one, at least according to the *Natural History* (c. 77-79) of Pliny the Elder, who identifies the birth of painting with an act of skiagraphia or skiagraphy, shadow-drawing, by a lovesick maiden in the Peloponnese. According to Pliny's myth, which

---

[1] To mention just a few of the more recent contributions to this growing body of criticism, see Laguna; and De Armas's edited volumes *Writing* and *Ekphrasis,* as well as his books *Cervantes* and *Quixotic*. On the *Persiles* in particular, see Bearden 100-27; Alcalá Galán, "La representación;" Alcalá Galán, *Escritura* 75-112; Egido.

circulated widely in early modern Europe, the daughter of Butades of Sicyon fell in love with a young man from Corinth, and to keep his image ready to mind, traced the outline of his shadow on the city wall. Her compassionate father then used that outline to fashion a clay mask of her beloved, or in some versions of the tale, he actually made a clay sculpture of the youth from head to toe based on his daughter's drawing.[2] The conceptual implications of this artistic leap from sketching to fabricating a mask, a three-dimensional, ceramic rendering of his face with features in relief, or a more volumetric, life-like rendering of his head and body, have resonated down the centuries, and play an active part in the way in which writers and artists view *chiaroscuro* in the age of Cervantes. According to René Verbraeken, while Leonardo da Vinci may not have coined the term, his articulation of the artistic purposes of *chiaro e scuro*, light and shade, or clear and shadowed light, lent impetus to use and discussion of the concept during the epoch of a burgeoning print industry, and increasingly after 1550 the linking "e" disappeared. In his *Treatise on Painting* (1489-1518), Leonardo ascribes two primary functions to *chiaro e scuro*, in which readers can detect both the artist's direct knowledge of painting techniques and echoes of the Butades myth. The first pertains to modeling, in which the play of light and dark endows a body or object with volume, something that casts shadows when illuminated. The second pertains to composition, the distribution of light and dark in general over a surface to create an area of tonal relief that enables the painter to generate the illusion of space and evoke objects in space (Verbraeken 13-20). The latter function would also give rise later to another primary use of *chiaroscuro*, to set a mood or emotional tone, with the prints of Rembrandt coming to mind as splendid examples of *chiaroscuro* at work in this way.

 Leonardo's views on *chiaroscuro* quickly began to surface in other texts. For instance, in Baldesar Castiglione's *Courtier* (1518), Count Ludovico da Canossa states the following regarding the traditional *paragone*, which compares painting and sculpture: "[S]tatues lack many things which paintings do not lack, and especially light and shade (*chiaro e scuro*) (for the color of flesh is one thing and that of marble another). And this the painter imitates in a natural manner, with light and dark, less or more, according to the need—

---

2 The story of Butades of Sicyon and his daughter Kora or Callirhoe can be found in Book 35 of Pliny the Elder's *Natural History*. More information on this myth and its implications for Western Art History can be found in Victor Stoichita, *Short History* 11-41; and the catalogue of Stoichita, von Arburg, et al., produced for the 2009 exhibition "La Sombra" at the Thyssen-Bornemisza Museum in Madrid. This marvelous exhibit inspired this essay in part.

which the sculptor in marble cannot do" (Bk. 1: 59). Note that here Count Ludovico attributes to the technique of *chiaroscuro* an illusion of greater naturalism in contouring human flesh and making its painted representation more life-like. About one hundred years later, Cervantes credits nature's own composition painted with the *chiaroscuro* of twilight's semi-darkness with setting the tone or mood for the duke and duchess' grotesque masque of Merlin and the ordered disenchantment of Dulcinea in *Don Quijote*, Pt. 2, chapter 34: "[U]n cierto claroescuro ... ayudó mucho a la intención de los duques, ... [y] a deshora pareció que todo el bosque por todas cuatro partes se ardía, y luego se oyeron ..." ["(A) certain chiaroscuro ... furthered the plans of the duke and duchess, ... (and) it suddenly seemed that the entire forest on all four sides was ablaze, and then ... were heard ..."] (793; 687).[3] Nightfall's *chiaroscuro* generates the eerie atmosphere and deep shadows perfect for the conjuration of demons, wizards, and bearded ladies, and elicits the desired spectator's response of fear and wonder. Leonardo's views on *chiaroscuro* unsurprisingly appeared as well in some form in a wide range of treatises on painting of the epoch, including those of Giorgio Vasari (1550), Ludovico Dolce (1557), Giovanni Lomazzo (1584, 1590), Vicente Carducho (1633), and Francisco Pacheco (1649).[4]

In the opening scene of the *Persiles*, readers experience Cervantes's mobilization of various aspects of *chiaroscuro* to dramatic effect, gripping them imaginatively and drawing them into the twilight, Northern World of his romance pilgrimage. Here, essentially the author executes a type of monochromatic painting known as *grisaille*, which generally consists of colored paper to which the artist applies ink or paint of two colors, one darker than the paper and the other a white gouache used to create bright highlights. Such paintings, also transferred to the print media at the time, often functioned as studies or designs for sculpture or sculptural relief.[5] Onto the gloomy shadowland of his dimly lit Northern World (the gray paper) Cervantes first paints an even darker, more lugubrious, subterranean dungeon, "una profunda mazmorra, antes sepultura que prisión de muchos cuerpos vivos que en ella estaban sepultados" ["a deep dungeon which seemed more a tomb than a prison for the many living bodies buried there"] (127; 21), in which the initial emphasis is on the paradox of a deep, pitch-black sepulcher filled with live

---

3   This citation is from the Riquer edition of *Don Quijote* and the translation from Grossman.

4   For more on Leonardo's influence in Spain, see Villaseñor Black.

5   For more on *chiaroscuro* and print techniques, see Landau and Parshall 179-202, 273-81.

bodies.[6] Readers cannot see anything clearly at this instant, but they can hear, if only the voices of the barbarian guardian Corsicurvo and the response of Sigismunda's poor, old nurse Cloelia. Cervantes then adds brilliant light to the picture, and along with it the contours of volumetric form in space, when he hauls the cross-dressed Persiles into the light of day—such as it is. The hero's unfurled golden curls and cleaned, luminous face seem to provide a supplemental light source to the painting, "le sacudieron los cabellos, que, como infinitos anillos de puro oro, la cabeza le cubrían" ["they shook out his hair, which covered his head with countless rings of pure gold"] (128; 21), like an actor brought onto stage through a trapdoor who then basks in an intense spotlight. Persiles, whose beauty and glorious halo of reflected light leave his captors dumbfounded, then brings the now three-dimensional scene to life by looking up to heaven and addressing his divine maker, symbolically embodied in the sun: "'Gracias os hago, ¡oh inmensos y piadosos cielos!, de que me habéis traído a morir adonde vuestra luz vea mi muerte, y no adonde estos escuros calabozos, de donde agora salgo, de sombras caliginosas la cubran'" ["I give thanks to you, oh immense and merciful Heavens, for you've brought me out here to die where your light may shine upon me and you didn't leave me in those dark cells where my death would have been shrouded in black shadows"] (129; 21).

Cervantes's deployment of *chiaroscuro* not only brings the scene and indeed the entire narrative to life, but also establishes a pattern of formal strategies, and a basic system of values that will serve as the foundational episteme for the romance, and that will be repeated with modifications throughout. As a number of treatises on painting argued in the era, although the issue was highly contested, a monochromatic sketch should precede painting in color, functioning as a sort of visual counterpart to the *diseño interno* (the concept in the mind's eye) for the final, completed artwork. In Spain, a debate actually unfolded during the first half of the seventeenth century over which was more important and challenging for the artist, line or color, that is, the Roman/Florentine emphasis on draftsmanship as exemplified by Raphael and Michelangelo, or the Venetian emphasis on color as modeled by Titian and Giorgione. As Giorgio Vasari had argued half a century earlier, the *diseño interno* constitutes a divinely inspired sketch in the mind that the architect, sculptor, or painter then transfers to line drawing or *dibujo* (in Spanish). Francisco Pacheco, following Vasari, states that *diseño* precedes *dibujo*—line

---

6 All citations from *Los trabajos de Persiles y Sigismunda* are from the Romero Muñoz edition. All English translations of the Spanish citations are from the translated edition of the *Persiles* by Colahan and Weller.

drawing—which in turn precedes *bosquejo*—the first application of colors, in generally a vague and unclear, or impressionistic way (Vitagliano 915-23). I suggest that this opening sequence of the *Persiles* functions in similar fashion, as the sort of thematic and structural *diseño interno* of the work as a whole rendered as a rather elaborate monochromatic *dibujo*. The final scene of the romance gives some idea of the persistence and consistency of these visual and epistemic patterns in the text. As readers may recall, Sigismunda tells Persiles that she plans to become a nun, which drives the sobbing hero out of Rome and into the night's darkness, where pastoral surroundings and the moonlight, "la clara luz de la noche" ["the clear light of the night"] (697; 345), and, of course, by this point, the moon and other luminous, celestial bodies have become synonymous with the divine, Marian aura identified with his beloved. In fact, the cool breeze and the calming sound of a gently flowing brook soothe the protagonist's troubled spirits, and "llevábale la imaginación Auristela y la esperanza de tener remedio de sus males" ["He was carried away with thoughts of Auristela, while the wind promised hope of finding a solution for his problems"] (698; 346). Precisely at this moment Persiles's dire situation begins to turn around, for under the moonlit night sky he hears the voices of his tutor Serafido and Rutilio, the penitent, Italian dancemaster who stayed behind on The Hermitages Island. The rest of the dramatic conclusion unfolds at daybreak close to St. Paul Outside-the-Walls, where in the new morning light the multiple, vexed relationships are disentangled and the conflicts resolved and the marriage of Persiles and Sigismunda celebrated, albeit atop the bodies of the evil Pirro and the ailing Prince Maximino.

In between the opening and closing scenes, on the macro-level, most of the episodes in Books 1 and 2, which correspond to the trials and adventures in the Northern World, resemble monochromatic painting, ranging in black-and-white from the shades of *grisaille* to the juxtaposition of extreme, deepest black and blinding light found in tenebrist painting. For instance, Cervantes uses the violent contrasts of tenebrism to mirror the violent bloodbath in the chaotic melee that breaks out among the barbarians over the possession of Sigismunda, and to heighten the sense of moral and spatial confusion. As the arrows start to fly, one barbarian decides to express his anger by setting fire to the woods: "Comenzaron a arder los árboles y a favorecer la ira el viento, que aumentando las llamas y el humo, todos temieron ser ciegos y abrasados. Llegábase la noche, que, aunque fuera clara, se escureciera, cuanto más siendo escura y tenebrosa" ["The trees began to burn, the wind fanned the wrath of the blaze, adding to the flames and smoke, and everyone was afraid of being blinded and burned. Evening was coming on and even if it had been a clear night, it would have been quite dark; but as it happened, it was overcast and gloomy, and the darkness promised to be complete"] (156; 34). The former captives are rescued by young Antonio, but momentarily conditioned to identify the hot, hellish flames with death and destruction, terror strikes them anew as shortly afterwards they see a single, airborne flame racing towards them in the total darkness: "En esto vieron que hacia ellos venía corriendo una gran luz, bien así como cometa, o, por mejor decir, exhalación que por el aire camina" ["Then they saw a great light coming quickly toward them almost like a comet, or perhaps like a shooting star racing through the air"] (158; 35). But Cervantes relieves their fears, and the readers', with a quick reversal of polarities as their young savior tells them that his father has arrived, carrying a torch to lead them to safety. Threatening flames dissolve into a flame of hope that will dispel the literal and metaphorical darkness that engulfs them. Cervantes then presents a variation of this animated tenebrist painting in Book 2 when Policarpo, in an act that reflects the self-destructive nature of his own unhealthy passion, sets fire to his own palace to divert attention from his attempted kidnapping of Sigismunda, who has escaped earlier along with Persiles and the rest of their company under cover of night.

Yet, when all is said and done, the predominant mood and tone of the Northern World is one of almost unrelenting gloom, low light, dark seas, fog and storm clouds, black, forbidding cliffs, harsh ice and snow, voices in the dark, and limited vision, a threatening world that reflects the lawless, uncivilized nature of most of the inhabitants and the absence or flawed presence of the Catholic Christian faith and practice. As has often been noted, the *Persiles* is saturated with Christian religious symbols and symbolism, and the work as a whole displays a distinctly Pauline cast. The Bible's use of the interplay of light and dark for moral and didactic purposes is, of course, a commonplace, and Cervantes likely had specific verses of the Bible in mind in wedding *chiaroscuro* to spiritual exemplarity, ranging from the Old Testament's Genesis chapter 1, in which the earth "was a formless void and darkness covered the face of the deep" (*New Oxford Annotated Bible*, Gen. 1.2), and God created light, saw that it was good and separated the light from the darkness, to passages from the New Testament such as Paul's First Letter to the Thessalonians, chapter 5, in which the apostle reminds his audience that they are "all children of light and children of the day" (1 Thess. 5.5) and exhorts them since they "belong to the day" (1 Thess. 5.8) and are "not of the night or darkness" (1 Thess. 5.5), to "put on the breastplate of faith and love, and for a helmet the hope of salvation" (1 Thess. 5.8).

As overarching textual strategy, however, a very different cultural reference might come to mind for today's readers. Famously, in *The Wizard of Oz*, the initial black-and-white scenes in Kansas give way to the dazzling display of Technicolor when Dorothy awakens in Oz after the tornado. Cervantes treats readers to a similar contrast when monochrome is replaced with colorful images, landscapes, and animated paintings when the protagonists arrive in Lisbon and proceed on their pilgrimage to Rome in Books 3 and 4. Such a contrast conforms to the predominant view at the time about the history of painting, which according to Pliny, and subsequently according to many early modern treatises, was monochromatic for a time and then gradually evolved into the more contemporary painting in color. The contrast also supports the view of the Northern World as a more primitive place, markedly less advanced in a variety of ways than Christian Europe. Indeed, Cervantes may have chosen to paint his Northern World in more simple, often dark, monochromatic shades with low visibility, and the *diseño interno* of the moral compass introduced there appears relatively clear, with certain exceptions (the story of the Portuguese Manuel de Sosa is a case in point). Nevertheless, as Michael Armstrong-Roche has demonstrated, while the author may paint the seemingly more civilized and sophisticated world of Catholic Christian Europe in brighter and more alluring colors, the episodes of violence that erupt there, and the moral dilemmas that arise, are often more complex and disturbing in their own ways, and frequently lacking in clarity (33-110).[7]

On the micro-level, within the romance's hemispheres of dark and light respectively, Cervantes embeds contrasting episodes for specific purposes. For instance, Persiles's patently fragmented, digressive story, which he begins to narrate on Policarpo's island, displays his heroic use and mastery of epideictic oratory and rhetorical ornamentation with sensual, sensory overload and an abundance of vibrant color and light effects—sparkling gems, the seductive, colorful clothing of beautiful women, even details like the shiny white breastplate of Sulpicia's armor. Persiles paints this exotic world of refulgent surfaces and many colors within the framework of the monochromatic Northern palette, playing for time as Policarpo's designs on Sigismunda, and

---

[7] In addition to Armstrong-Roche, other recent studies that engage with darker or more ironic elements in the *Persiles* include Sacchetti; Childers 83-159. On the complex matter of time, space, and narrative organization in the *Persiles*, see Williamsen; Lozano Renieblas. I certainly find ironic, complex, and ambiguous elements in abundance in the *Persiles*, but I still find the romance a fundamentally idealizing and moralizing work. In this respect, my overall critical perspective of the text remains close to that of Joaquín Casalduero and Alban Forcione.

the lengths to which the ruler is willing to go to make her remain on the island grow stronger and more apparent. Conversely, in colorful, Christian Europe, readers encounter the episode of the widow Ruperta, whose desire for vengeance, and perhaps listening too much to the old Rolling Stones song, "Paint it Black," lead her to repaint her world in *chiaroscuro*, draping every possible surface around her with black cloths. Here, Cervantes reverses polarities again in dramatic fashion, for a potential climax of black, vengeful death is magically transformed into a happy, radiant wedding ceremony, in which Ruperta the would-be murderess whose long, white wimple makes her stand out in the dark like a relief sculpture, or, for Croriano, makes her appear initially to be a ghost, metamorphoses into the new wife of her intended victim as she is conveniently already dressed in white, a color traditionally associated with spiritual purity. Notice the reversal of fields and values here. In the dark, his beauty stays her hand, "como hace el sol a la niebla, ahuyentaba las sombras de la muerte que darle quería" ["just as the sun does to the fog, chased away the shadows of the death she was planning to inflict on him"] (594; 286); while bathed in the lights the servants bring, Croriano sees her "como quien vee a la resplandeciente luna de nubes blancas rodeada" ["as one sees the shining moon surrounded by white clouds"] (595; 287). Ruperta abandons her murderous death wish, and chooses life and love as embodied in the handsome, young man before her.

Cervantes's mobilization of *chiaroscuro* to function symbolically throughout the romance to advance a moralizing episteme—which aligns with the Tridentine imperative for art "to set the images before the eyes of the faithful," whether this was or was not the deliberate intention of the author—should by now be apparent. The point is not that Cervantes seeks to voice or support actively Catholic Reformation ideology, but rather that his use of *chiaroscuro* in the *Persiles* reflects stylistic characteristics frequently identified with Baroque art, which is in turn often associated with that ideology of the time, but stylistically extends beyond the limited confines of expressing one view, religious or otherwise. For Sigismunda's matchless, luminous beauty is, in fact, more than a match for the haloed, wonder-inducing Persiles, and the celestial imagery that surrounds her identifies the princess as a Marian figure, emphasized perhaps most memorably in her resemblance to those pictures of the Inmaculada in Rome that seem to proliferate of their own volition, which depict the Apocalyptic Woman of Revelations, standing on the moon.[8] Numerous incidents reinforce this Marian association. In

---

8   For different interpretations of the depiction of Sigismunda, including her portrait in Rome, see Alcalá Galán, "La representación;" Graf; López Alemany. On

Book 1, for example, Prince Arnaldo kneels before Sigismunda and addresses her as "¡ ... norte por donde se guían mis honestos pensamientos y estrella fija que me lleva al puerto donde han de tener reposo mis buenos deseos!" ["unchanging star of the North that guides my honorable thoughts and leads me to the port where all my good intentions will find their resting place"] (229; 75). The exclamation will hold true, but just not quite in the way he envisions. Like Constanza, who becomes that symbol of unwavering faith and charity who constantly accompanies the heroic, virtuous twosome on their pilgrimage, Persiles and Sigismunda embody a miraculous message of hope that arises from their steadfast love and faith in each other and God that enables them to withstand all trials and overcome all obstacles. Those precious attributes they carry with them always, the pair of perfect, lustrous pearls (like them, and like Mary, the pearl without price), and the brilliant, diamond-encrusted cross that dazzles the eyes even as it remains firm in the face of the wicked Hipólita who would like to co-opt it for her own perverse purposes, are shining reminders that the young couple and their friends model that Jobian motto of hope conveyed through the rhetoric of *chiaroscuro*, and engraved in the Juan de la Cuesta emblem, "post tenebras spero lucem"—"after darkness, I hope for light."

As Howard Mancing has recently pointed out, we are just beginning to study and understand how the human imagination, which constitutes "a kind of mental simulation," is primed by "the creation of mental images that are not based on actual perception" ("Embodied" 50).[9] Mancing also reminds us that Cervantes's *Don Quijote* has been a major influence and source of inspiration for the development of the study of "theory of mind" in relation to literature ("Embodied" 27-29).[10] In the *Persiles*, Cervantes demonstrates that in the creation of mental images, and in the stimulation of the human imagination, he is true to himself until the very end of his own pilgrimage on earth. Notably, in his final literary work, *chiaroscuro* plays a key role in generating a consistently moralizing episteme from the opening to the final scenes. And so it seems fitting that his narrator gets carried away in Book 3 of the *Persiles*,

---

the merging of Immaculist and Apocalyptic Woman iconography in sixteenth-century Spanish art, see Stratton 35-66.

9   In this regard, see Domínguez' "Janus Hypothesis" on the integral relationship between memory, images, and the imagination in general, and the close relationship between memory and imagination in Cervantes's *Don Quixote*.

10   For examples of how Cervantes's characters and fiction model and enact theory of mind, see Jaén; Mancing, "Sancho;" Barroso Castro; Reed; Simerka 197-226; Simon.

and employs the same discourse of *chiaroscuro*, and of Marian lore, to exalt poetry itself:

> [L]a excelencia de la poesía es tan limpia como el agua clara, que a todo lo no limpio aprovecha; es como el sol, que pasa por todas las cosas inmundas sin que se le pegue nada; es habilidad que tanto vale cuanto se estima; es un rayo que suele salir de donde está encerrado, no abrasando, sino alumbrando; es instrumento acordado que dulcemente alegra los sentidos y, al paso del deleite, lleva consigo la honestidad y el provecho. (442)

> [E]xcellence in poetry is as clean as clear water, which improves everything unclean. It's like sunlight, which touches everything dirty without any dirt sticking to it; it's a skill as valuable as it is esteemed; it's a lightning bolt that leaps out from its hiding place, not to burn but to illuminate; it's a well-tuned instrument sweetly cheering the senses, bringing with it not only delight but purity and usefulness as well. (204)[11]

Without a doubt, Cervantes sought to achieve just such illumination in his masterpiece of *chiaroscuro*, the *Persiles*.

Works Cited

Alcalá Galán, Mercedes. *Escritura desatada: Poéticas de la representación en Cervantes*. Alcalá de Henares: Centro de Estudios Cervantinos, 2009. Print.

———. "La representación de lo femenino en Cervantes: La doble identidad de Dulcinea y Sigismunda." *Cervantes: Bulletin of the Cervantes Society of America* 19.2 (1999): 125-39. Print.

Armstrong-Roche, Michael. *Cervantes' Epic Novel: Empire, Religion, and the Dream Life of Heroes in* Persiles. Toronto: U of Toronto P, 2009. Print.

Barroso Castro, José. "Theory of Mind and the Conscience in *El casamiento engañoso*." *Theory of Mind and Literature*. Ed. Paula Leverage, Howard Mancing, Richard Schweickert, and Jennifer Marston William. West Lafayette: Purdue UP, 2011. 289-303. Print.

---

    11   Similar celebrations of poetry can be found in other works by Cervantes, for instance, in *Novelas ejemplares*, *La gitanilla* 60; *Novelas ejemplares*, *El licenciado vidriera* 282-85.

Bearden, Elizabeth B. *The Emblematics of the Self: Ekphrasis and Identity in Renaissance Imitations of Greek Romance*. Toronto: U of Toronto P, 2012. Print.
Casalduero, Joaquín. *Sentido y forma de* Los trabajos de Persiles y Sigismunda. 1945. Madrid: Gredos, 1975. Print.
Castiglione, Baldesar. *The Book of the Courtier*. Trans. Charles S. Singleton. Ed. Daniel Javitch. New York: Norton, 2002. Print.
Cervantes, Miguel de. *Don Quijote de la Mancha*. Ed. Martín de Riquer. Barcelona: Juventud, 2000. Print.
———. *Don Quixote*. Trans. Edith Grossman, New York: Ecco, 2005. Print.
———. *Novelas ejemplares*. Ed. Jorge García López. Barcelona: Crítica, 2001. Print.
———. *Los trabajos de Persiles y Sigismunda*. Ed. Carlos Romero Muñoz. 2nd ed. Madrid: Cátedra, 2002. Print.
———. *The Trials of Persiles and Sigismunda: A Northern Story*. Trans. Clark A. Colahan and Celia Richmond Weller. 1989. Indianapolis: Hackett, 2009. Print.
Childers, William. *Transnational Cervantes*. Toronto: U of Toronto P, 2006. Print.
De Armas, Frederick A. *Cervantes, Raphael and the Classics*. Cambridge: Cambridge UP, 1998. Print.
———. *Ekphrasis in the Age of Cervantes*. Lewisburg: Bucknell UP, 2005. Print.
———, ed. *Quixotic Frescoes: Cervantes and Italian Renaissance Art*. Toronto: U of Toronto P, 2007. Print.
———, ed. *Writing for the Eyes in the Spanish Golden Age*. Lewisburg: Bucknell UP, 2004. Print.
Domínguez, Julia. "The Janus Hypothesis in *Don Quixote*: Memory and Imagination in Cervantes." *Cognitive Approaches to Early Modern Spanish Literature*. Ed. Isabel Jaén and Julien Jacques Simon. New York: Oxford UP, 2016. 74-90. Print.
Egido, Aurora. "La memoria y el arte narrativo del *Persiles*." *Nueva Revista de Filología Hispánica* 38.2 (1990): 621-41. Print.
Forcione, Alban K. *Cervantes' Christian Romance: A Study of* Persiles y Sigismunda. Princeton: Princeton UP, 1972. Print.
Graf, Eric C. "Heliodorus, Cervantes, and La Fayette: Ekphrasis and the Feminist Origins of the Modern Novel." *Ekphrasis in the Age of Cervantes*. Ed. Frederick A. De Armas. Lewisburg: Bucknell UP, 2005. 175-201. Print.

Jaén (Jaén-Portillo), Isabel. "Literary Consciousness: Fictional Minds, *Real Implications.*" *Selected Papers from the 22nd International Literature and Psychology Conference*, June 29 - July 4, 2005. Ed. Norman Holland. IPSA. Web. 20 May 2016.

Laguna, Ana María G. *Cervantes and the Pictorial Imagination: A Study in the Power of Images and the Images of Power in Works by Cervantes*. Lewisburg: Bucknell UP, 2009. Print.

Landau, David, and Peter Parshall. *The Renaissance Print: Ca. 1470-1550*. New Haven: Yale UP, 1994. Print.

López Alemany, Ignacio. "A Portrait of a Lady: Representations of Sigismunda/Auristela in Cervantes' *Persiles*." *Ekphrasis in the Age of Cervantes*. Ed. Frederick A. De Armas. Lewisburg: Bucknell UP, 2005. 202-16. Print.

Lozano Renieblas, Isabel. *Cervantes y el mundo de Persiles*. Alcalá de Henares: Centro de Estudios Cervantinos, 1998. Print.

Mancing, Howard. "Embodied Cognitive Science and the Study of Literature." *Cognitive Cervantes*. Ed. Julien J. Simon, Barbara Simerka, and Howard Mancing. Spec. cluster of essays of *Cervantes: Bulletin of the Cervantes Society of America* 32.1 (2012): 25-69. Print.

———. "Sancho Panza's Theory of Mind." *Theory of Mind and Literature*. Ed. Paula Leverage, Howard Mancing, Richard Schweickert, and Jennifer Marston William. West Lafayette: Purdue UP, 2011. 123-32. Print.

The New Oxford Annotated Bible. Ed. Michael D. Coogan, Marc Z. Brettler, Carol A. Newsom, Pheme Perkins. 3rd ed. Oxford and New York: Oxford UP, 2001. Print.

Percas de Ponseti, Helena. "Ideologías: El lenguaje como pintura." *Cervantes y su concepto del arte: Estudio crítico de algunos aspectos y episodios del Quijote*. 2 vols. Madrid: Gredos, 1975. Print.

Reed, Cory A. "'¿Qué rumor es ése?': Embodied Agency and Representational Hunger in *Don Quijote* I.20." *Cognitive Cervantes*. Ed. Julien J. Simon, Barbara Simerka, and Howard Mancing. Spec. cluster of essays of *Cervantes: Bulletin of the Cervantes Society of America* 32.1 (2012): 99-124. Print.

Sacchetti, María Alberta. *Cervantes' Los trabajos de Persiles y Sigismunda: A Study of Genre*. London: Tamesis, 2001. Print.

Simerka, Barbara. *Knowing Subjects: Cognitive Cultural Studies and Early Modern Spanish Literature*. West Lafayette: Purdue UP, 2013. Print.

Simon, Julien J. "Contextualizing Cognitive Approaches to Early Modern Spanish Literature." *Cognitive Approaches to Early Modern Spanish Lit-

erature. Ed. Isabel Jaén and Julien Jacques Simon. New York: Oxford UP, 2016. 13-33. Print.

Stoichita, Victor I. *A Short History of the Shadow*. London: Reaktion Books, 1997. Print.

Stoichita, Victor, Hans-Georg von Arburg, et al. *La Sombra: Exhibition Catalogue*. Madrid: Fundación Caja Madrid, 2009. Print.

Stratton, Suzanne L. *The Immaculate Conception in Spanish Art*. Cambridge: Cambridge UP, 1994. Print.

Verbraeken, René. *Clair-Obscur,- histoire d'un mot*. Nogent-le-Roi: Librairie des Arts et Métiers, 1979. Print.

Villaseñor Black, Charlene. "Pacheco, Velázquez, and the Legacy of Leonardo in Spain." *Re-Reading Leonardo: The Treatise on Painting across Europe, 1550-1900*. Ed. Claire Farrago. Farnham, Surrey: Ashgate, 2009. 349-74. Print.

Vitagliano, Maria A. "Painting and Poetry in Early Modern Spain: The Primacy of Venetian *Colore* in Góngora's *Polyphemus* and *The Solitudes*." *Renaissance Quarterly* 66 (2013): 904-36. Print.

Williamsen, Amy R. *Co(s)mic Chaos: Exploring* Los trabajos de Persiles y Sigismunda. Newark, DE: Juan de la Cuesta, 1994. Print.

About the Authors

JOHN JAY ALLEN is Professor of Spanish, Emeritus at the University of Kentucky. His work focuses on Cervantes and the *corrales* of *comedias*. His recent publications include *La piedra de Rosetta del teatro comercial europeo* (Escena Clásica, 2015), *Don Quijote en el arte y pensamiento de Occidente*, by Allen and Patricia Finch (Cátedra published a revised and updated edition in 2015). Allen is also the editor of the Cátedra *Don Quijote*. The thirty-first edition of the Second Part appeared in 2014, revised and updated with an extensive expansion of the Introduction. Cátedra published a Commemorative Edition of Allen's text of the *Quijote* in 2015. It is illustrated with the earliest images of episodes from the two Parts, painted by Jean Mosnier, c. 1630.

BRUCE R. BURNINGHAM is Professor of Hispanic Studies and Theatre at Illinois State University, where he serves as Chair of the Department of Languages, Literatures, and Culture. He specializes in medieval and early modern Spanish and Latin American literature, Hispanic theater, and performance theory. He is the author of *Radical Theatricality: Jongleuresque Performance on the Early Spanish Stage* (2007) and *Tilting Cervantes: Baroque Reflections on Postmodern Culture* (2008). He is Editor of *Cervantes: Bulletin of the Cervantes Society of America*.

CATHERINE CONNOR (-Swietlicki) is Professor of Spanish at the University of Vermont. She is author of the book *Spanish Christian Cabala* and numerous essays on early modern culture and the arts, published in *Cervantes, Bulletin of the Comediantes*, as well as other major journals and books. Since 2001, she has explored the bio-cultural and neuro-scientific processes that make possible our complex personal and social creativity in life and art. Her current book project explores the *Quixote*'s complex humanistic and scientific contributions to interdisciplinary studies.

FREDERICK A. DE ARMAS is Andrew W. Mellon Distinguished Service Professor in Romance Languages and Comparative Literature at the University of Chicago. He has served as President of the Cervantes Society of America and is now President of AISO (Asociación Internacional Siglo de Oro). He has been awarded several NEH Fellowships and has directed several NEH Seminars. He is the author of approximately 200 essays. His more recent books and collections include *Ekphrasis in the Age of Cervantes* (2005); *Quixotic Frescoes: Cervantes and Italian Renaissance Art* (2006); *Objects of Culture in the Literature of Imperial Spain* (2013); *Nuevas sonoras aves: Catorce ensayos sobre Calderón de la Barca* (2015). His book *Don Quixote among the Saracens: Clashes of Civilizations and Literary Genres* (2011) was recognized with honorable mention for the PROSE Award in Literature 2011.

MARSHA S. COLLINS is Caroline H. and Thomas S. Royster Distinguished Professor for Graduate Education at the University of North Carolina at Chapel Hill. Her research interests include Idealizing Forms of Fiction, Literature and the Visual Arts, Early Modern Court Culture, and Modern Spanish Literature in the Context of European Culture and History. Recent publications include *Imagining Arcadia in Renaissance Romance* (Routledge, 2016), as well as articles on Cervantes, Góngora, Lope de Vega, and romance.

EDWARD H. FRIEDMAN (PhD, Johns Hopkins University) is Gertrude Conaway Vanderbilt Professor of Spanish, Professor of Comparative Literature, and director of the Robert Penn Warren Center for the Humanities at Vanderbilt University. His primary field of research is early modern Spanish literature, with emphasis on the picaresque, Cervantes, and the *comedia*. His creative works include adaptations of Cervantes's *Don Quijote* and *El laberinto de amor*. He is a past president of the Cervantes Society of America.

CHARLES VICTOR GANELIN is Professor of Spanish at Miami University (Ohio). He has published on various aspects of the *comedia* as well as on the *Quijote* and the *Novelas ejemplares*. His current work focuses on the "sensual turn" in literary studies, an ongoing project that incorporates Cervantes, the *comedia*, and, most recently, women poets of the early modern period. He has been invited to re-edit his first book, a critical edition of Andrés de Claramonte's *La infelice Dorotea*.

MASSIMILIANO ADELMO GIORGINI earned his doctorate in Peninsular Golden Age Literature at Purdue University with Howard Mancing as his advisor. Giorgini has presented in 19 international conferences on topics ranging from Coded Language to Theory of Mind, and has given a TEDX Talk on *Don Quixote*. Among his publications are studies in psychology journals, book chapters on literature and cinema, and articles on Cervantes's works. Giorgini currently works for the federal government as a linguistic intelligence analyst.

Isabel Jaén holds PhDs from Purdue University and the University of Madrid and is Associate Professor of Spanish at Portland State University. She is a former executive member of the MLA Cognitive Approaches to Literature Division (Chair in 2011) and co-founder and former co-director of the Literary Theory, Cognition, and the Brain working group at the Whitney Humanities Center at Yale University (2005-15). She is co-editor of *Cognitive Literary Studies* (U of Texas P, 2012) and *Cognitive Approaches to Early Modern Spanish Literature* (Oxford UP, 2016) and has published numerous journal articles on topics such as Cervantes and human development, cognitive approaches to teaching *Don Quixote*, and empathy and gender activism in Zayas' *Amorous and Exemplary Novels*.

Carolyn A. Nadeau (PhD, Pennsylvania State University) is the Byron S. Tucci Professor of Spanish at Illinois Wesleyan University. Her research focuses on early modern Spanish literature particularly Cervantes, the picaresque, and food and health manuals. Her award-winning monograph, *Food Matters: Alonso Quijano's Diet and the Discourse of Food in Early Modern Spain* (U of Toronto P, 2016), contextualizes the shifts in Spain's gastronomic history. She is currently working on a critical edition and translation of Francisco Martínez Montiño's 1611 cookbook, *Arte de cocina, pastelería, vizcochería y conservería*.

Rachel Schmidt (PhD, Princeton) is a Professor in the Department of Classics and Religion at the University of Calgary. Her publications include *Critical Images: The Canonization of Don Quixote through Illustrated Editions of the Eighteenth Century* (McGill-Queen's University P, 1999) and *Forms of Modernity:* Don Quixote *and Modern Theories of the Novel* (U of Toronto P, 2011). She is writing a book on the *Persiles* and is participating in a research team studying the visual culture of the *Celestina*.

Barbara Simerka is Professor Spanish and Comparative Literature at Queens College/CUNY. She is author of *Knowing Subjects: Cognitive Cul-*

tural Studies and Early Modern Spanish Literature (2013) and *Discourses of Empire* (2003) and co-editor of *Cognitive Cervantes* (*Cervantes: Bulletin of the Cervantes Society of America*, Spring 2012). She has written numerous studies of mirror neuron functions (social intelligence, empathy) in early modern Spanish texts and contemporary feminist science fiction. Her current project explores empathy for and identification with villains in narrative, ranging from Roman histories to Neo-Senecan tragedy to *House of Cards*.

JULIEN JACQUES SIMON is Associate Professor of Spanish and French at Indiana University East. His research focuses on early modern studies, cinema and literature, and cognitive literary studies. He is co-founder of the Literary Theory, Cognition, and the Brain working group at the Whitney Humanities Center in Yale University (2005) and former member of the executive committee for the MLA Division on Cognitive Approaches to Literature (chair in 2013). He is co-editor of *Cognitive Literary Studies* (U of Texas P, 2012), *Cognitive Cervantes* (*Bulletin of the Cervantes Society of America*, spring 2012), and *Cognitive Approaches to Early Modern Spanish Literature* (Oxford UP, 2016).

STEVEN WAGSCHAL (PhD, Columbia) is Associate Professor of Spanish and Affiliated Faculty Member of Cognitive Science and Renaissance Studies at Indiana University, Bloomington. His research focuses on early modern Spanish discursive texts as these intersect with cognitive studies, philosophy and art history. He is the author of *The Literature of Jealousy in the Age of Cervantes* (Missouri UP, 2006), editor of *Peribáñez y el Comendador de Ocaña* by Lope de Vega (Cervantes & Co., 2004) and co-editor (with Ryan Giles) of the forthcoming *Beyond Sight: Engaging the Senses in Iberian Literatures and Cultures, 1200-1750* (U of Toronto P, 2017). He is currently finishing a monograph on animal cognition in medieval and early modern Spain and Spanish America, tentatively entitled *Minding Animals in the Old and New Worlds*.

JENNIFER MARSTON WILLIAM is Professor of German at Purdue University. She publishes and teaches in the areas of 20th- and 21st-century literature, film studies, and cognitive studies. She has written two monographs: *Killing Time: Waiting Hierarchies in the Twentieth-Century Novel* (Bucknell UP, 2010) and *Cognitive Approaches to German Historical Film: Seeing is Not Believing* (Palgrave Macmillan, 2016). She is also a co-editor of the volume *Theory of Mind and Literature* (Purdue UP, 2011).

AMY R. WILLIAMSEN is Professor of Spanish at the University of North Carolina-Greensboro where she serves as Head of the Department of Languages, Literatures and Cultures. Her specializations include Early Modern Spanish literature, Hispanic Women Writers, Theater and Performance, Contemporary Literary Theory, and Cognitive Science. She is the cofounder of *GEMELA*, the author of *Co(s)mic Chaos: Exploring Los trabajos de Persiles y Sigismunda*, and the co-editor of *Critical Reflections: Essays on Spanish Golden Age Literature in Honor of James A. Parr*; *Engendering the Early Modern Stage: Women Playwrights in the Spanish Empire*; *Ingeniosa Invención: Studies in Honor of Professor Geoffrey Stagg*; and *María de Zayas: The Dynamics of Discourse*. One of her recent articles appeared in the *Bulletin of the Cervantes Society of America*.

Tabula Gratulatoria

John Jay Allen
Ellen Anderson
Frederick A. de Armas
Shifra Armon
Emilie L. Bergmann
Jessica Ribble Boll
David Boruchoff
Bruce R. Burningham
Joan Cammarata
Jean Canavaggio
Tony Cárdenas
William H. Clamurro
Marsha S. Collins
Catherine Connor-Swietlicki
Julia Domínguez
Robert Felkel
Dominick Finello
Dian Fox
Edward H. Friedman
Charles Victor Ganelin
María Antonia Garcés
Martha Garcia

continued...

Chad Gasta
Juan Pablo Gil-Oslé
Massimiliano Adelmo Giorgini
Sarah Gretter
Tatevik Gyulamiryan
Isabel Jaén
Patricia Kenworthy
John T. Kirby
Francisco Layna Ranz
Paula Leverage
Ignacio López Alemany
Isabel Lozano-Renieblas
Patricia W. Manning
Theresa McBreen
Michael J. McGrath
Edward Mullen
Carolyn A. Nadeau
James and Patricia Parr
Stephen Pierson
Walter L. Reed
Elizabeth Rhodes
Rachel Schmidt
Ryan Schmitz
Jorge A. Silveira
Barbara Simerka
Julien Jacques Simon
Sherry Velasco
Steven Wagschal
Jack Weiner
Jennifer Marston William
The Williamsen family